and the monkey lets go

scott hunter

www.mascotbooks.com

And the Monkey Lets Go: Memoirs Through Illusion and Doubt

For more information, please contact:
Mascot Books
620 Herndon Parkway, Suite 320
Herndon, VA 20170
info@mascotbooks.com

Library of Congress Control Number: 2019914435

CPSIA Code: PRV1219A
ISBN-13: 978-1-64543-121-3

Printed in the United States

To Henry, and others who've struggled
with difficult situations.

and the monkey lets go

memoirs through illusion and doubt

scott hunter

Bonnie
Love Amherst
Basketball
#32

Scott

When the monkey lets go of the branch
and falls into the pool of water,
the whole world will shine with dazzling brilliance.

-Zen Koan

chapter 1

I laughed, though I was frightened. Walking up the granite steps between Corinthian columns, I entered the Amherst College library. To me, it was a cathedral to knowledge, unlike the Presbyterian church in New Kensington where I'd been fed all the Christian bullshit growing up.

The central room of the library was huge. Shelves of books, step ladders to reach the high ones. I pulled a large tome from the shelves and placed it on one of the long mahogany tables that graced the room. Sitting down on a velvet-cushioned high-backed chair, I opened the dictionary to the letter S—s-y-p-h-i-l-i-s. It was caused by sexual intercourse, nothing about excessive masturbation. Relief flooded through my being.

Secure that I had no symptoms and that my penis wouldn't be falling off any time soon, I dove into course work. Freshman year was a struggle; math and physics classes were easy, but German and economics were impossible. Both were foreign languages, and I couldn't wrap my mind around either. Three three-to-five-page essays a week in English composition for eleven weeks taught me how to write. History of Western Civilization class was the challenge. The 400 pages of weekly reading from Edward Gibbon's six volume *The History of the Decline and Fall of the Roman Empire* were nasty, but Gibbon's *History* became my bible. Gibbon was rational, and the library became hallowed ground, my church.

Though smart enough to be enrolled in Amherst in 1963, I was clueless. My final essay on the French Revolution in second semester Western Civilization was a prime example. When the professor returned our essays, I noticed my classmates' essays had letter grades, A's and B's on their front page. Written across mine was 'Mr. Hunter, please make an appointment to see me in my office.'

At the appointed time, I poked my head into the professor's office, knocked on the door frame, and said, "Sir, Scott Hunter; we have an appointment."

He greeted me: "Mr. Hunter, please come in and sit down."

I sat.

"Your paper, Mr. Hunter." He paused and leaned back in his chair, taking off the glasses that usually perched on top of his head in his curly hair and biting on one of the temple pieces. His huge antique desk dwarfed him. Finally, he placed his glasses on the desk and folded his hands under his chin: "Do you realize there were two sides to the French Revolution?"

That was a revelation to me. He suggested I write a makeup essay on the Russian Revolution. I got a C+ on it. My freshman year D+ average was a gift from my professors, but I learned to study and write.

When I had to declare a major, I had no idea what I wanted to be. Mom and Dad had never helped me develop any of my ideas beyond "study hard." I had the feeling that Dad didn't like his job at Alcoa, so I didn't want to be a scientist. My experience with a botched hernia operation had turned me against doctors. I didn't have the confidence or self-esteem to be a professor like Grandpa Hunter. With no goals besides graduating from Amherst, I learned that geology, dramatic arts, and psychology were the easy majors. I wasn't into rocks, so I chose psychology as my major and dramatic arts as my minor. With no real grasp of psychology and too shy to get on stage, all I learned to do was to complete projects and get things done.

Amherst College taught me to think and drink and I became a functional alcoholic. I played freshman football, so I was sober those first eight weeks, but after the last game of the season, I drank a case of beer and passed out. The beautiful Mt. Holyoke coed who was my date disappeared with someone else. I was drunk every weekend for the next three and a half years, and each weekend became progressively longer. By senior year, the weekend ended on Sunday night and began Monday night.

My grades improved, though I graduated in the bottom quarter of my class with a cumulative C+ average. Socially, I was the life of the party and even had girlfriends. I was able to have sexual relationships with some of them; as long as I was drunk.

The first time I took a drink, I was sixteen and home alone on a Saturday evening. Relaxing on the couch, I surveyed the living room and took a deep breath. *So, this is what it feels like to be independent and in control.*

Before I could turn the TV on, the doorbell rang. It was Stewart, a friend of my sister, looking for her. Since Marilyn was out on a date and Stewart had a six-pack to share, he asked, "Wanna drink a beer?"

"Sure."

We drove to a cemetery close by and drank a couple. It tasted a bit odd, but I was hanging out with one of Marilyn's friends—very cool.

Stewart left me back at the house. Relaxing again on the couch, I had never felt better in my life. *So, this is how alcohol worked! What a simple answer.* I was free from guilt. I could have gone up to any girl anywhere and said anything I wanted to. She would know I was the man. Alcohol was power.

chapter 2

In 1967, after graduation from Amherst, I got a summer job at Camp Minniwanca, a Four-Fold (Spiritual, Social, Physical, and Intellectual) American Way camp in Stony Lake, Michigan. The camp's conservative approach to life did not provide the thrill I was seeking, but one of my camp friends was local; she had a connection who could get us some marijuana, which I had never smoked before.

I drove the camp nurse's VW into Muskegon and bought three joints, my first exhilarating experience scoring pot. That afternoon, four of us drove out to the edge of the camp and parked the VW in a quiet little glen on the forested side of the sand dunes near Lake Michigan. We rolled up the windows and smoked the joints. Nothing happened.

Hot, stuffy, and unable to breathe, we burst out of the car. The coolness was refreshing, but still, nothing happened. We looked at each other; we'd been scammed. Money wasted.

Since we had the afternoon off, we decided to enjoy the lake view on the other side of the sand dunes. Climbing over the dunes, we were engulfed by the view of the lake.

POW!!!

Oneness was everywhere—no you or I, just us. We under-stood the infinite nature of water, earth, and sky, the friendship and happiness we were all feeling intensely, together. So, this was what the Beatles, Grace Slick, and Jim Morrison were talking about. The next couple of hours were an intense glimpse into the eternal workings of all things profound.

Now totally and eternally brothers and sisters, the four of us returned to camp to resume our responsibilities. The world was no longer ordinary. We were aware of the sacred mysteries, the peace and love marijuana provided.

I could write hundreds of pages about thousands of unpleas-ant experiences seeking to replicate that first day, years wasted trying to find happiness through drugs.

When the summer wound down and camp was over, without any direction in my life, I mooched off of some friends who had a cabin nearby for the Labor Day weekend. I was enjoying the first cool Saturday morning of September when a phone call from my parents informed me of an Army draft notice requiring my service in the Vietnam War.

No, thank you. Life is precious. Death in Vietnam is not an option.

All the draft dodgers were going to Canada, a short 300-mile drive from the cabin.

Then what?

It dawned on me that if I became a Presbyterian minister, I could get a 4D draft classification. I called the Reverend Charlie

Idler, my adolescent friend and minister, now the dean of admissions at the Pittsburgh Theological Seminary. He said if I could get there by Tuesday morning for the start of fall classes, he would enroll me. Suddenly, I was a candidate for the ministry.

I'd skipped one of the hurdles for acceptance—an interview with three ministers on the admissions board—which I had to make up a month into my first semester. I walked into the well-furnished reception room in the administration building and introduced myself to three older, heavyset gentlemen in conservative suits. Dressed casually, my long blond hair in a ponytail and sporting a bright red beard, I was not your typical ministerial candidate. I was, however, a graduate of Amherst College. The suits didn't intimidate me.

I frankly explained that I had received my draft notice and had hastily applied to seminary because I did not want to fight in the war. I was working my way toward qualifying for conscientious objector status so I could do alternative service. I hadn't made up my mind if I wanted to be a minister, but I was enjoying my studies at the seminary.

Of everything the three ministers asked me, I remember only one pointed question: "Who is the person who influenced you the most in your life?"

Without hesitation, I answered, "Herman Hesse."

I'd read *Siddhartha, Steppenwolf, Demian, Narcissus and Goldmund*, and *Magister Ludi* my junior and senior years at Amherst, and their effect on me was profound. Hesse was telling it like it was, no bullshit. I think the expected answer was Jesus Christ, which never entered my mind.

Oh, to have been a fly on the wall as the ministers discussed my interview. Yet, by the grace of God and the compassion of those three men, I was saved from the horrors of war.

Seminary presented problems. I was skeptical—no, incredulous—about Christianity. I am sure I was the only person at the seminary who didn't believe that Jesus was the Son of God, my personal savior. Charismatic evangelicalism was not my cup of tea. To paraphrase Robert Frost, "Seminary was a refuge from hasty decisions." I swallowed my pride and became enthusiastic about theological studies. Without revealing my lack of faith, I attended classes.

One of my first classes was Christian history, the premise of which was that the Bible is the only historical source, the Word of God, our true history. One day around mid-semester, I was sitting on one of those inexpensive metal and wood desk-chairs among eighteen or so straitlaced evangelistic Christians, smelling a little like the pot I'd smoked just before class, when I decided I'd had it. How could all these students listen to this? How could the professor profess it?

I interrupted him with a rant I'd been holding in for weeks: "Sir, excuse me, I'm having trouble understanding how the Bible is the only historical source. The Jewish people weren't the only ones writing things down during the Old Testament period. The Christians weren't the only ones writing during the establishment of the Christian Church. The Greeks, the Egyptians, the Babylonians all had written languages. Nebuchadnezzar is mentioned in the Book of Daniel. Do any of the Babylonian writings mention Daniel? The Babylonian writings would give us an interesting perspective on who he was. Paul wrote a lot of letters to the Christian churches fifty years after Jesus' death and resurrection. Were any government officials writing letters about the development of Christian churches in their jurisdictions? It would be interesting to see what they had to say."

The professor leaned back on his desk, adjusted his tweed blazer over his blue and white striped shirt, and paused for a moment to consider my questions. I didn't think anyone had ever challenged the Word of God like this in his classroom.

"Mr. Hunter, we're talking about the Bible here. Testimony handed down through centuries describing God's covenant with His people. We cannot question God's word," he said, with a look of concern.

I shook my head. I was on a roll. "Sir, I'm just saying, at Amherst, I was taught that you need at least two primary sources to study history. You can compare the two sources, discover similarities and contradictions, assume the similarities are accurate and the contradictions are suspicious, then compare the results with other sources. Eventually, a theory of historical truth can be worked out. The Bible is one primary source. We need to find other primary sources for comparison."

The professor stood up, leaned forward with both hands on his desk, and sternly stated, "Matthew, Mark, Luke, and John are four primary sources. Extensive interpretation has been done on the four Gospels. We know the truth. The Bible is the Word of God."

I was getting more excited. "But what about the Old Testament? Aren't there non-Christian sources from the same time that look at these events from a different perspective?"

He stood straight and held up one hand, stopping me. "Mr.

Hunter, the Bible is the Word of God. Let's move on."

I did a little research on my own and found out that there were other primary sources, that during the first few centuries of Christian history, every Peter, Paul, and Mary proclaimed his or her own ideology. The debates, schisms, and all-out brawls weren't considered serious problems until Christianity grew in size and stature and attracted the attention of Saul. Saul, a lawyer, allegedly lost a wrestling match with an angel, started calling himself Paul, and created the foundation for a bureaucratic, regulated faith. His letters established Church doctrine. The Bible was just stories, genealogies, history, and church policy.

What faith I had left eroded further when I realized the importance of the First Council of Nicaea, convened by Emperor Constantine in 325 A.D. Constantine, who became a Christian on his death bed, recognized the impact Christianity was going to have on the Roman Empire and moved to gain control of the Church. First, the council decreed that only priests could read the Bible, the official, infallible Word of God. Anyone else would be put to death for reading it. Then the council created the Nicene Creed, a loyalty oath to eliminate divergent beliefs.

Sitting in my room at the seminary, I realized I was a heretic. Or maybe a prophet. Suddenly, I was someone. I envisioned myself a Martin Luther, maybe even Martin Luther King, Jr., a leader of people. I had no people to lead, but I had a small stash of marijuana that I smoked every night. It was the dawning of the Age of Aquarius: sympathy, trust, harmony, understanding, living dreams and crystal revelations. I was right on time, the prophet for a new age.

I saw my future in front of me. I would confront the oppressive hierarchy of the male priesthood about the subjugation of women and their inferior stature in the church. Veneration of the Virgin Mary? A virgin mother? I knew all about that lie. Jen, my babysitter, had taught me all about the power of women. They certainly had power over me. How could they be oppressed? I would challenge the church about life after death and the medieval practice of church indulgences, paying for the forgiveness of sins and a life everlasting in heaven. That sounded like a racket to me. Christian capitalism was an oxymoron. I saw myself as the light that would illuminate the world. "Terras Irradiant," enlighten the land, was the motto on the seal of Amherst College.

I found myself constantly challenging the professors. If I hadn't, classes would have been intolerable. I'm sure my professors and classmates saw me as a pain in the ass.

chapter 3

Besides classes in Greek, Christian history, systematic theology, and Biblical exegesis, each ministerial candidate was assigned a 'student pastoral.' All the plum and traditional ministerial positions had been taken by the time I enrolled. The only position left was with the Shadyside Presbyterian Church, in the upscale bar and restaurant district of Pittsburgh where the hippies were gathering. To minister to those who strayed from the formal church and were lost in the land of long hair, beads, and free love, Shadyside sponsored The Loaves and Fishes Coffeehouse.

One Saturday evening when I was in charge of closing the coffeehouse, Jamie, a hippie and a regular, hung around and helped. After I had locked the door and we turned up the street towards the main drag, he asked, "You ever do acid?"

I boasted, "Oh, yeah, I did a hit a while ago with an old friend. Listened to Ravi Shankar at Carnegie Hall. I sure got stoned."

My friend had given me something, but I didn't think it was acid, because it'd had no effect on me at all.

Jamie unfolded a piece of aluminum foil and showed me

some of the smallest orange things I had ever seen. He said, "Orange Sunshine," and popped one of the miniature tablets into my mouth.

I figured nothing that small could have much of an effect.

After meeting up with a few of his friends, we all got in my car and drove up to Mt. Washington, across the Monongahela River from downtown Pittsburgh. The view was incredible. The Monongahela and Allegheny Rivers met to form the Ohio River, and the lights of Pittsburgh's north side and downtown highlighted the dark ribbons of water.

I had never felt so happy or full of myself. I was with friends. There was no fear, only joy.

Eventually, my companions needed a ride home. As I drove back into Pittsburgh, they said they were very impressed that I could drive. There was nothing to it. I just kept the car traveling along the converging white lines, like I had done so many times between Amherst and Smith College, returning from dates on drunken Saturday nights.

I felt accepted when they invited me up to their apartment, but when they disappeared into a back room, I felt abandoned and unwelcome. As I wondered why they left me alone, I picked up the Rolling Stones *Second Satanic Mystery Tour* album and became distracted, immersed in the cover.

When they returned, they asked, "How are you doing, Scott? Are you okay?"

I was spellbound. "Wow, this album is really cool. I understand how the center picture changes when I rock the cover back and forth. There's two pictures and ribbed plastic over it. But the way the smoke trails on the border drift and swirl around, I don't know how they do that."

They laughed at me. "Scott, your brain on acid is making the smoke drift and swirl."

Suddenly, I was totally stoned. *Oh, God!* What used to be a stable world was in motion, impermanent. I began processing new and unusual information very quickly. My companions, thinking I was about to lose it and not wishing to be responsible, found a way to usher me out of the apartment and into my car. I reassured them I could drive and had a place to go. I thanked them very much and drove away.

Back home, I climbed up the stairs to my second-story apartment. In my living room, everything was pulsating, breathing, being. Amazed that I had never understood all this before, it was all me, right now, oneness. I was everything, the universe. *So, this is what they're talking about at the seminary! The one true God inside me.* I was in awe of the Christian believer. I was going to have to tell them about this stuff. I had found the answer. Sitting on the back of my couch, I marveled at eternity.

The smile on my face was huge when I returned to the seminary and walked into the dining hall to eat Sunday breakfast with my brethren. Everything was so filled with wonder: the glass of orange juice, the silverware, the table, and the faces of everyone staring at me. But something was wrong.

Someone asked, "Scott, are you okay?"

I whispered, "God is within me."

A professor nearby looked up, bemused. "What?"

I nodded like they should know I was one of them. "Like you, God is within me. You understand, right? God is within me." I smiled.

People began gathering around me: "Scott, are you okay?"

I couldn't answer. There were walls between us. They were

dead. I was wonderful, wonder-filled, amazed, magnificent. I knew what they knew. God is within. They talked about God within, but I knew if I told them that very small hit of LSD was the portal to a complete experiential understanding of God…if I told them, *I am God,* they would be…skeptical. So, I left.

Back at my apartment, I decided the only way I could finish the paper on Christian theological thought I'd been struggling with was to reveal my acid trip. Titled *God Is You, the Inward Search for Divinity*, the seminary administration didn't accept my paper with the acclaim I'd expected.

Called into the dean's office, I was presented the choice of leaving the seminary for a while or beginning counseling with the dean, a certified psychoanalyst. Therapy sounded terrifying. I certainly wasn't going to open up to a characterless, suit-and-tie authority figure. I chose to leave the seminary. Fortunately, I'd spent enough time there to qualify as a conscientious objector. I began looking for alternatives to military service.

chapter 4

As an official conscientious objector to the Vietnam War, I needed to fulfill my two-year obligation to serve my country in a peaceful manner, like an unpaid position as a nurse's aide in a poverty-stricken area or a teacher in the inner city.

I flew into JFK and took the Long Island train towards the national offices of the Presbyterian Church in New York City, where I'd been told I could get a job. The noises and smells of underground New York City were intoxicating. In the sea of commuters, one guy stood out, with long black hair, a short beard, and an elfin grin on his face. The ability of potheads to recognize other pot smokers in a crowd is remarkable. Our eyes met and we nodded in recognition.

I said, "Nice day."

With a deep breath of not-so-fresh air, he said, "Good to be alive."

Hoping for a connection, I said, "Hey, I'm from out of town. This train will take me to Columbia University, right?"

"Sure, that's my stop. Here's the train. You go to the U?"

A train pulled into the station; we got on and continued our conversation northbound.

"No, I just got my conscientious objector draft status. Looking for alternative service. Anti-war."

With his thumb and index finger pinched together, he rose his hand to his lips. "Smoke pot?"

I smiled. "Sure!"

He knew a secluded corner at the Columbia U station, and we smoked some killer pot. Stoned, I climbed out of the underground and found the Presbyterian offices at 475 Riverside Drive. In the lobby, next to the elevators, I read the office directory. National Missions was on the twentieth floor.

Somehow, I ended up on the twenty-second floor. Confronting the first person I saw, she pointed to the writing on the door, "This is International Missions. National Missions is on the twentieth floor."

Turning back towards the elevators, I heard a voice from behind a cubicle wall: "Would you like to go to Thailand and teach English?"

Lights went off in my head: *Thailand—the pot capital of the world.*

A young woman appeared. "There's one teaching position left. We couldn't find a teacher for Nan Christian School in the capital of Nan Province. You'll love it. Northern Thailand is so beautiful. We will provide airfare and pay you twenty-five dollars a month."

My response? "Sign me up!"

On August 16, 1969, the weekend of the Woodstock Music

Festival, I was on a plane to Thailand. Knowing I would not have immediate access to pot in Thailand, I risked taking an ounce of good Mexican weed with me. Crazy or naïve, maybe both, I panicked as I approached customs. Luckily, the head of the Christian missionary program pointed me out to a customs official, and I was whisked through.

In Bangkok, I met the six other teachers in the program, who were on semester break. They were headed to Thong Pha Phum, a Christian missionary encampment on the Burmese (now Myanmarese) border. I tagged along. I learned my first Thai word, *gancha* (marijuana). They also clued me in to Nan. It was at the end of the paved road, fifty kilometers from Laos. There were rumors that communists were infiltrating across the border and that Thai Royalist Forces were headed there to cut them off. The U.S. Army was never far behind. The appearance of the army, if they got as far as Nan, would be the beginning of the end.

Nan Christian School had a bad reputation. The principal was a young man, newly educated in America, and the old guard who ran the school didn't appreciate him. He had no experience as a leader, and the school was in turmoil.

After an exciting trip up the Kwai River to the missionary encampment, we returned to Bangkok and said our good-byes. Three of us boarded beautiful, early twentieth-century cars on the night train to Chiang Mai, the picturesque old northern capital of Thailand. Wide awake, I watched the shadows of palm trees against a moonlit sky. Around 3 a.m., I got off the train in Prae with Don, the teacher there. In front of an open-air market, there was a bus that looked like a multicolored dragon with windows.

Don said, "That's your bus. It'll take you around three hours to get to Nan. Good luck."

I was on my own. The bus climbed over a mountain range and entered the Nan Valley as the sun rose. The view was absolutely magnificent, and I felt like I was in Shangri-La for a moment. I stepped off the bus and surveyed the one-story, wooden, open-front stores. Chickens hung from hooks in restaurants, large barrels of rice sat in front of produce stores, and the wooden sidewalk stretched the length of the rickshaw-laden street. Men were dressed in black pajamas, women in colorful blouses and ankle-length sarongs. Asians of all ages were staring at me.

In my bewilderment, I managed to ask, "Nan Christian School?"

A skinny, almost nude man with a rickshaw replied in rapid-fire syllables as he pedaled over to me. "You go Nan C'istian School?"

I nodded. "You're going to take me and my luggage in that?"

He put my suitcases on the seat and motioned for me to climb in next to them. Unable to sit down, I hung on as we headed out of town along a tree-lined residential street, my driver pedaling and talking away. We passed a soccer field surrounded by a large two-story red brick building and open-air shelters that I later found out were classrooms.

Turning right onto a dirt road down a little hill, we picked up speed and flew by small wooden shacks. We came to another compound, surrounded by an eight-foot brick wall next to a whitewashed church with a tall steeple. The rickshaw careened into the compound and stopped in front of an old three-story red brick colonial building.

I was welcomed to Nan Christian School by a group of western-dressed men and women in sarongs speaking very fast in a language I didn't understand. Then, I realized Sangkrit, the head

English teacher, had introduced herself and was speaking to me in English. Chamut, the American-educated principal, was speaking English, too, but I couldn't understand either of them.

Suddenly I felt overwhelmed, near desperate, and homesick. Shangri-La had disappeared. Panic set in. Here I was, a tall, white American, alone, halfway around the world in a very foreign place for the next two years. I was unprepared for life in Nan; actually, unprepared for life anywhere. I was a teacher and an American, both prestigious positions in Thai society. Everyone deferred to me. They were all waiting for me to manage my situation, but I was clueless.

Finally, I understood a suggestion from Sangkrit: "Achon [teacher] Hunter, maybe you need to sleep. We will show you your room."

Needing to get away and think, I nodded vigorously.

I was led to the second floor of the dormitory and into a large room, empty except for a small desk on one wall and a single bamboo bed squarely in the middle. An eight-foot double-door opened onto a balcony. The ceiling was twelve-feet high. It was a large empty box.

I sat down on the bed, thinking, *How am I going to get out of this? I need to get back to America, fast. This is a mistake.*

After pacing the length of the room for a few minutes, I ran outside, leaned over the second-story porch railing, and yelled, "Help!!!!"

My near-hysteria distressed the people in the courtyard, who were probably talking about me. Sangkrit came to the rescue again. "*Achon* Hunter, maybe you need some food."

Led into the open-air dining pavilion and seated at one of the picnic tables, I was offered a breakfast of unrecognizable vegetables and sticky rice, the traditional northern Thai glue-like rice scooped out of a bowl with fingers and molded into a sticky ball. The sticky ball of rice was used to scoop the vegetables out of another bowl. The bitter vegetables and the glue-like rice made me choke.

Two years in Nan? I'm going to die before I see home again.

Chamut spoke up: "Would you like to go downtown to a restaurant and have an American breakfast of soft-boiled eggs and steamed rice?"

Anything American sounded good, and if I headed back into town, maybe escape was possible.

Chamut called for a taxi, a small Datsun pickup with a bench on either side of the pickup bed and a roof overhead.

I started to calm down. In town for the second time, I noticed an outdoor market area, a movie theater, a three-story hotel, cars, jeeps, bicycles, and motorcycles. I took a deep breath, telling myself to pretend it was a Thai movie and I was the hero.

We got out of the taxi and walked into a restaurant. There were folding chairs and tables along one wall. A glass case full of exotic foods sat on a counter. Behind it, a cook was juggling three woks over a charcoal fire. Smoke and the aroma of food filled the air. It was unlike anything I had ever imagined.

When I sat down and ordered breakfast, I noticed hundreds of large black flies landing on everything, including the food. On the verge of hysteria again, I was shocked by the sound of a jeep skidding to a stop in front of the restaurant. A young man jumped out, leapt up the steps, and introduced himself in fluent English.

"I'm Prakorn Thanasukowit, the local doctor, educated in Canada. You're the new teacher? Welcome to Nan."

I blurted out, "I need something to eat. Why did they bring

me here? There are so many flies. I want to go to a good restaurant. They must hate me to bring me here."

"This is the best restaurant in town. They all have flies. You'll get used to it. Nan's a great place. Gotta run. Look me up at the hospital if you get sick." He jumped back into his jeep and drove away.

The good doctor's attitude changed my mood. After my first serious bout of amoebic dysentery, I learned to head to the local hospital for transfusions of intravenous glucose solution whenever diarrhea dehydrated me completely.

I got used to the broken English of the teachers at the school and became friends with Songji, a cigarette-smoker and non-practicing Buddhist. He taught at the school to help children learn. I could always find him away from the crowd on his favorite bench, crouched forward with his elbows on his thighs, a cigarette hanging from his lips, staring out over the rice fields behind the school.

He would take his cigarette, knock the ashes from it and say, "In my next life, I think I'll be a water buffalo. They don't do much and they seem to be enjoying themselves."

Songji understood my predicament: I was unaware of the social customs and protocol of regimented Thai culture. I was a teacher who should know everything. How was I going to learn to act properly if everyone was too embarrassed to explain things? Songji began to clue me in.

"Scott, your hair is too long. Teachers wear button-down shirts and ties. Your multi-colored, bell-bottom trousers aren't what teachers wear."

I got my hair cut, found a tie, wore dress shirts, and stopped wearing my bell-bottoms. I borrowed a bicycle and pedaled around Nan, getting to know the neighborhood.

One evening, I came upon a Buddhist festival at a temple. A band was playing rock and roll music, so I stopped to listen. A few young men encouraged me to dance on stage. I climbed onto the stage, asked a young girl to dance, and showcased the latest American dance moves.

The next morning, Songji found me and, trying to stifle a laugh, warned me, "Scott, you're going to get the cold shoulder from everyone this morning. Pretend like nothing happened. Last night, the women you were dancing with at the temple celebration, they were local prostitutes. You've embarrassed the school and yourself."

Dismayed, I pleaded, "Songji, how was I to know they were prostitutes?"

"Don't worry, Scott. No one will say anything. It will just be a little chilly from the teachers for a while. Ignore the students when they tease you. You'll learn." With a hearty laugh and a smile, he said, "You'll learn the hard way."

Unable to communicate with the students in their language, teaching English as a second language was impossible. Halfway through my first day of classes, I realized I was screwed. After fumbling through the rest of the day's classes, I returned to my room, sat on my bed, and stared at the geckos, fluorescent lizards, crawling up the wall.

Okay, I'm not a teacher. I understand nothing the students say to me. What do I do? I'm going to be with these kids for two years, I might as well get to know them.

The next morning, I walked into my first class and began, "Hello, my name is Achon Scott. What is your name?"

They answered, "Hello, my name is *Achon* Scott, what is your name?"

I went around the room, pointing to each student. "What is your name?"

After a full circuit, I said, "I remember some of your names. Your name is Paitoom."

A big smile appeared on Paitoom's face and spurred me on.

"I know you. You're Kamnan. And you're Boribun." My pronunciation created some laughter.

I turned it back to them. "Do you remember my name?"

In unison, the students yelled, "You are Achon Scott." More laughter. We were having fun.

I held up a pencil. "What is a pencil in Thai?"

"This is a pencil."

"In your language, in Thai, what do you call a pencil?"

One girl understood. "A pencil is *dinsaaw* in Thai language."

I held up a notebook. "And what is this?"

In unison, the class responded. "This is a *samoot*."

For the next month, every class, every meal, every evening was my language class. Once I could explain the English textbook's daily lesson in my very broken Thai, I began to teach English. Each day, I would hold conversations with the students, learning who understood me and who didn't. I got the students who spoke well to help the students who didn't.

There were days I just sat on my desk and talked about America; the students who understood my English would translate for the others. I would listen to the translations and pick up new Thai words and phrases. We learned the English and Thai names of the birds that flew through the classroom. When I taught them the words for bird shit and they taught me *nohk khee*, the laughter broke down the last barriers between us. At the end of the year, I prepared the students to pass the national exams. Everyone did well enough to move up to the next grade.

The school year ended with the approach of the rainy season (the end of April through July). I spent the three-month vacation in Bangkok and traveling with the other Christian teachers. I missed my students.

When I returned to Nan for the new school year and walked into the classrooms for the first day of school, the excitement of the students was overwhelming.

chapter 5

Luckily, I had my stash of Mexican to help me through the early difficult times. It lasted a month.

On my trips into town, I'd heard American rock and roll coming from a tailor's shop where there were always young guys hanging around. With my last three joints, I walked into the tailor shop and introduced myself.

"Hi, I'm Scott. I'd like you to make me two pairs of trousers to wear when I teach at the Christian school. I heard the Beatles music coming from your shop. It makes me feel like I'm home in America."

Pranit, the tailor, and his friends were letting their black hair grow into Beatle-like mops. They wore sharp tailored pants and dress shirts with button-down collars. To my astonishment, they all spoke very good English.

After a few minutes of conversation, I knew my life in Nan was going to get better. They explained Thai culture to me and answered all my questions.

Comfortable, I said, "Listen, I smuggled some Mexican pot

into Thailand. Do you guys want to smoke some *gancha*?"

They clapped their hands. "Pot? Yes, we want to smoke your Mexican. We've never smoked Mexican."

For them, the decent Mexican was exotic. I got stoned, but they got wasted, jumping around, singing and laughing.

Near midnight, we all began to fade. It was time to head home. I bowed to them, as was the custom when parting. I stepped down the wooden steps in front of the open-air shop to pick up my bicycle, I hesitated.

"You know, I don't really smoke that much. But I've got some friends, other English teachers in Thailand. We get together at the end of each semester and hang out. We all like to smoke a little *gancha*. Would it be possible for any of you to score some for me, just to share with my friends?"

Pranit looked at his friends and they all nodded. "No problem. How much do you want?"

Just a little too excited, I replied, "Wow, all I need is … just a little bag. In America, we call it a 'dime bag,' because it costs ten dollars. I'll give you ten dollars. That should be enough."

One of Pranit's friends said, "We'll get you some *gancha*. Give us two baht."

Two baht was ten cents American. A bottle of Coca-Cola cost three baht. That wasn't going to buy me much pot.

"No, ten dollars. That's like an ounce or so. I have ten dollars. Or I could give you 200 baht."

They laughed. "No, give us two baht. We'll get you some *gancha*."

I left the tailor shop less two baht and very disappointed. Now I was out of pot.

When school was over the next day, I returned to my room

and stretched out on my bed. Drifting off into a daydream, I heard someone knocking on my door.

It was Tanat, the office boy from the high school. "Did you go down to the tailor shop?"

Someone had ratted me out.

"Yeah, I stopped by to see if I could get some trousers for school."

With a smile on his face, Tanat handed me a shopping bag. "I'm friends with everyone there last night. They all had a good time. Hope I can be there next time."

My eyes widened. "You didn't tell anyone at the school that I was there, did you?"

"Don't worry. No one knows."

After he left, I walked to my bed, sat down, and looked inside the bag. For ten cents, I had purchased about three quarters of a pound of Thai stick, the highest quality marijuana you could get in the States. I had a few rolling papers left, so I rolled up a joint and smoked it. It was good weed. I didn't have a care in the world.

I heard some noise coming from the kitchen. It sounded like the cooking staff was getting ready for dinner. I gathered myself and headed downstairs to eat, but the dining pavilion was empty. I walked into the kitchen, where the staff was cleaning up the dishes. The Thai stick I'd smoked was so potent that I had lost a few hours and missed dinner. Clearly, I couldn't smoke much at one time. I found a nice one-hitter pipe that became my constant companion. It took me nine months to smoke the shopping bag full of weed.

I learned the Thai phrase *re-ip-roy*—hide your vices. Everyone has vices, but the Thai culture values discretion. I smoked in my room, and even though I was sure everyone could smell the herb, no one said a word.

I was adjusting to life in the tropics. I got the church back in New Kensington to donate $500 to build a water tank so we could all take daily cold showers, though bathing in the river was fun, too. After attending a couple of Sunday church services and weekday prayer meetings, I lost interest in Christian community activities. I was friendly with everyone, taught classes, and spent the evenings with the students, but I was a loner. I read all the paperback fiction I could find and wrote long letters back home to Mom and Dad. I needed the connection back to the Western world. I would toke up and take my bicycle into the countryside, a dreamland of palm trees, rice fields, and water buffaloes, exchanging waves with the farmers I passed.

After a few months on my bicycle, I realized I needed real transportation. My salary at the school was twenty-five dollars (500 baht) a month, not much even in Nan, so I asked Dad for money. Since my letters had turned into exciting descriptions of life in Thailand, Dad was happy to buy me a 100 cc. Honda motorcycle.

My first adventure was to Pua, a small town on a dirt road fifty kilometers north, to visit Mary Ann, a Christian missionary humanitarian. I left one Saturday morning, asked directions to her house, and knocked on her door. She welcomed me. Mary Ann was so quiet, peaceful, and friendly that I felt calm and accepted. After late morning tea, we took a taxi to the Mao and Yao hill tribes' resettlement village where she served the Yao Christians.

Pua was on the hypotenuse of the "Golden Triangle," the Far East's center of opium and heroin production and distribution.

The Mao and Yao hill tribes were farmers from the nearby Luang Prabang Range of 6,000-foot mountains, the perfect place
to grow opium. The Thai government's ineffective solution to
the opium problem was to uproot the Mao and Yao from their
ancestral homes in the mountains, stick them on a barren hilltop
surrounded with barbed-wire closer to civilization, and call it a
resettlement village. It was an ugly internment camp. In the dry
season, the village was arid, brown, and dusty and in the rainy
season, it was a muddy swamp. The Mao and Yao men, unable
to grow food, snuck away to the mountains to cultivate food and
opium there. So much for solving the opium problem. All the Thai
government did was make the hill tribes their enemy.

I visited the hill tribes a couple of times a month, and they
welcomed me into their thatch-roofed huts on three-foot stilts. I
played with the children, chasing the pigs and chickens, spinning
tops, and playing jacks.

My favorite place in the village was the silversmith's workshop. Phoang, the silversmith, seemed ageless. He might have
been in his twenties, full of life, but a hard life had aged him.
He could have been 130, a wise old gentleman. He welcomed
me into his group the moment I introduced myself. He lived in a
stick and grass lean-to, four feet high, eight feet long, and four
feet wide, just big enough for a single bed, silversmith tools, and
cooking utensils, with a firepit in front of it. Each Saturday that
I visited, he would be sitting cross-legged behind his firepit with
four or five Yao men in attendance. A fire was always burning in
the firepit, food and hashish was always shared. I shared my Thai
stick with him and his buddies.

One afternoon, over a few tokes of hashish, the silversmith
produced a small vial of a white sparkling powder. "Have you

ever seen anything like this?"

I was intrigued. "No, what's that?"

He handed me the vial. "Here, this is for you. Take it home with you and sprinkle it on your *gancha* a little at a time. It will make your smoke better. Smoke it all by next Saturday. Make sure you smoke it all in one week. Then come see me in two weeks and tell me what you think. Remember, smoke it all the first week. No more after Saturday. Understand?"

When I got back to my room that evening, I took a little of the powder and spread it on top of my marijuana. It was a very pleasant high. I continued to smoke the powder for the rest of the week. The week seemed to be surrounded by a beautiful blue haze. I felt no pain or anxiety. Saturday morning, I smoked what was left in the vial.

Sunday was a pleasant day. By Monday evening, I thought I might be coming down with the flu. Tuesday morning, I woke up sick with all the flu symptoms: runny nose, mucus in my throat, and watery eyes. My whole body ached with intense pain. I spent the day in the nurse's office at the school curled up in a ball, suffering. Even though Wednesday and Thursday were a little less intense, I began to worry that I would never be healthy and pain-free again. On Friday, I wasn't sure I'd be able to ride my motorcycle to Pua to visit the silversmith. I had no way to reach him to tell him I was ill and couldn't come.

Then, on Saturday morning, I awoke refreshed. I was excited to be well again. I ate a huge breakfast, jumped on my motorcycle, and headed north. I stopped by Mary Ann's house and spent some time with her, then headed up to the resettlement village on my own. I parked my bike and walked over to the silversmith's hut. Phoang looked up and saw me.

"Well, hello. How are you today?"

I sat down and folded my hands. "Wow, the first week was great. I don't think I've ever had a week like that. I was floating on air. Then last week, I don't think I have ever been that sick. I didn't think I'd be able to come up here to see you. Today, I recovered, happy to be alive again. Must have been the three-day flu or something."

He looked at me intensely. "You can't have the first week without the second week. Remember, you can't have the first week without the second week." He would say no more.

I thought about that on the way home. By the next morning, it dawned on me. The white powder had been heroin, and the sickness I had suffered was withdrawal.

Heroin withdrawal is painful, more intense than the euphoria it provides. To avoid withdrawal, you need to use it continually, the essence of addiction. That was the lesson the silversmith taught me. I never used heroin again.

chapter 6

At the end of my first semester of teaching, after three months of immersion, I'd taken a train to Bangkok to reunite with the other American missionary teachers. Arriving at the huge, bustling Bangkok station, I'd hailed a taxi and tested my newly learned Thai. The driver laughed and gazed at me with a look of surprise.

In English, he'd asked, "Where did you learn to speak Thai?"

"My Thai's not good. I didn't get any language training before I came here, but I'm trying to learn as quickly as I can."

"Don't apologize. Where did you learn Thai?"

"I teach English in Nan. The students at the school taught me."

He'd laughed again. "You speak like my grandmother. She lives in Chiang Rai, just north of Nan. She's Lao and speaks Ge'mung, a dialect of Lao. Your students taught you Ge'mung. They don't speak Thai. They're more Lao than Thai."

Apparently, Thai speakers could understand me, but I had a very heavy accent. It was as if I was speaking English with a brogue, or had a Cajun drawl from the Louisiana Bayou.

When I explained my predicament to my missionary friends,

I found out that since I'd started late in the school year, I'd missed out on the language training they'd received before coming to Thailand. They were teaching in less rural cities, so their students spoke Thai as their primary language. For my students, Thai was their second language. English was their third.

I decided if I learned how to read Thai, I could speak it, but despite months of studying, I still hadn't mastered it. My sister Marilyn was the language expert in the family. She spoke German, French, Spanish, and Russian. I'd barely passed introductory German at Amherst. It was surprising that I learned to speak Ge'mung.

I've always been an early riser, waking before dawn to enjoy the sunrise. In Nan, I'd pedal my bike down to the marketplace before breakfast, read the daily English newspaper, and have coffee and breakfast cakes.

The first morning that I bought the Thai newspaper, customers in the restaurant teased me about pretending to read Thai. To prove them wrong, I began reading aloud. Everyone applauded. The next morning when I bought the local paper, a few people asked me to read again. Within days, I had a group who couldn't read gathered around me, listening to the news. Soon, enough people were coming to the restaurant to hear me read that the owner refused my money. His business was booming.

One morning at the restaurant, a monk requesting alms approached me and asked if I would come visit him. Surprised, I said I would. That evening, I went to his temple and had tea with him. He thanked me for coming and explained why he had invited me.

"In all the years a Christian church has been in Nan, none of the foreign Christians have ever done anything for the Buddhist community. They served only the Christian community. You, reading the newspaper in the marketplace every morning, are the first Christian to serve us."

"I'm not really a Christian," I explained. "I'm teaching English at Nan Christian School to avoid the Vietnam War. I'm against killing."

He nodded in agreement. "Would you enjoy learning about Buddhism? I can teach you meditation."

The monk reached into his orange shoulder bag and handed me *What the Buddha Taught* by Wapole Rapula. "Here, read this." With a big smile, he said, "And here are some coloring books from Sunday school. They will explain Buddhism to you."

As I left the temple that evening, I asked my new friend his name.

"My name is Phra Sohm."

Phra is the word for monk. Sohm was the color of his robe. I never thought to translate it. I just assumed it was his name.

I returned a few days later for another cup of tea, and he told me about his life as a monk.

"I meditate in the morning, then walk through the neighborhood asking for alms, rice for my daily food. I have no money. I tidy up the temple, help others when I can, and stay mindful, always aware of what I say and do. I meditate again in the evening. I might remain a monk all my life or I might leave the temple, return to family, and have children. I haven't decided. Whatever happens, my life is good."

Though I never said anything about my drug use, Phra Sohm asked me, "Why do you smoke *gancha*?"

I replied, "Why do you smoke cigarettes?"

He smiled. "Nobody's perfect."

His calmness put my mind at rest. I felt like he was the

brother I never had.

When I returned to the temple for my third cup of tea, Phra Sohm gave me my first assignment, to sit still for a minute.

I asked, "How should I sit, in a chair? How am I going to know if I sat still for a minute?"

"Sit like the Buddha: legs crossed, hands folded. It is a very comfortable position. To know how long a minute is, look at a clock."

I'd moved out of the dormitory above the grammar school classrooms to a room next to the second-story library above the high school open-air cafeteria. It was quiet and I had a beautiful view of the fields and forest, the perfect place to meditate. Each day for a week, once or twice a day for a minute, I practiced, sitting in the lotus position. I could feel myself breathe. A minute was easy.

I returned to the temple. "Phra Sohm, I can sit for a minute."

He replied, "If you can sit for a minute, you can sit for five minutes."

Returning to my room, I learned to sit for five minutes. I got fairly good at relaxing, closing my eyes, then opening them when five minutes had passed.

Phra Sohm's next instruction was to sit for thirty minutes. That was tough. My mind became cluttered with thoughts of time. When I could finally calm that panic, everyday thoughts about school today or tomorrow poured into my mind. Then there were the physical pains, itches, cramps, and the desire to move.

I returned to the temple. "Phra Sohm, I get tired of sitting. My body wants to move. I get an itch and I want to scratch it."

He deliberately scratched his nose. "If you have an itch, scratch it. Your mind is trying to distract you. Patience, your mind will quiet."

I was agitated. "But my body wants to move. What can I do?"

He had simple answers. "Your mind wants your body to move. When your mind becomes quiet, your body will sit still."

"I worry about how long I've been sitting. Then thoughts come into my mind. Sometimes I can't get one thought to go away. Other times, so many thoughts come into my mind I feel like I'm going crazy." I realized I was almost panting.

Phra Sohm looked puzzled. "Worry about how long you're sitting? Time is only a distraction. Your mind is afraid of no distractions. One continual thought? Think it through, then destroy it. Monkey mind? Thought after thought after thought? Separate your thoughts. Hold on to each as long as possible, then dismiss it."

It took me about eight weeks to learn to sit still for thirty minutes. My mind quieted. My muscles stilled. I learned to process my thoughts.

One evening, I came for tea and announced, "I can sit still for half an hour. I process and dismiss continual thought. No more monkey mind."

As if he'd anticipated my success, he quickly said, "Look for the spaces between your thoughts."

A few days later, I sat down for my evening meditation. I crossed my legs, folded my hands, took a deep breath, then another. I sensed my chest rising and falling. With my eyes closed, I peered into the darkness. Within the darkness there was a flutter, a ripple in the stillness, but not an actual thought. The flutter disappeared into the dark stillness. I ended my meditation when I sensed thirty minutes. I opened my eyes. Thirty minutes had passed. As I got up and stretched, I couldn't remember a thought interfering with the stillness, just the fluttering ripples, like waves in the ocean; not separate, but a part of the stillness.

In the following days, when a thought interfered with the stillness, there was no mistake that it was a thought. It was loud and shattered the stillness. I processed it and dismissed it. My mind was slowing down. Either thinking less or thinking more slowly, I sensed an empty mind, a lightness of being that permeated my life with joy.

As I became more comfortable with meditating for longer than a few minutes, a friend from home sent me a book of koans, short Zen Buddhist sayings that, if studied long enough, could push one through to Samadhi, the moment of enlightenment. One evening, I brought the book with me to the temple to show Phra Sohm. He was excited to see it and quickly leafed through it.

"Would you like a koan to study?"

That sounded like a good idea. "Yes, I would."

He leafed through the book again. "The koan on this page is your koan."

It read:

> *When the monkey lets go of the branch*
> *and falls into the pool of water,*
> *the whole world will shine with dazzling brilliance.*

I accepted that koan and studied it. It was a puzzle, something to be solved, like a morning crossword. I saw it as entertainment to strengthen concentration on the ultimate meaning of life. After a while, I assumed there was no answer. Maybe the koan was just a way to introduce me to a life without desire.

I was full of desire: desire not to be alone, for a deeper relationship with my father, for pot, alcohol, anything to block the emotions and vague and powerful anger at my parents for not encouraging me and my ideas when I needed support the most. I was so consumed, it overwhelmed me. I had no way to understand life without it. On top of all that, the drugs and alcohol were clouding my mind, so I couldn't fully appreciate the practice of meditation.

Nevertheless, evening tea with Phra Sohm became moments of peacefulness, occasional words, and long silences. Though the Buddha taught that images of him were of no use, I found comfort in the temple among the statues portraying him sleeping, meditating, and standing. The occasional chanting of the monks resonated in the two-story main sanctuary. The slightly bitter taste of the tea and the pungent sandalwood incense completed my sensory world.

One night as I was leaving, Phra Sohm asked, "Do you have candles and incense at your room? I'd like you to go to the market and buy some tomorrow morning. You can sit still for a half an hour. Very good, but your mind has settled into half an hour. That's a form of thinking, a subtle unconscious thought. You must rid yourself of that unconscious thought. Light an incense stick and end your meditation when the incense burns out."

I asked the obvious question: "And how will I know how long that is?"

Phra Sohm gave the simple answer, "It will depend on the type of incense you buy and how long each stick burns."

The next day, I drove my motorcycle down to the marketplace and picked up some sandalwood incense and five-inch white votive candles. My meditation now began with the lighting of the incense and the smell of sandalwood. I would stick the incense in a small brass bowl filled with sand. The smoke from the incense would curl up and out my window. Meditation took effort, concentration, and patience. Thoughts were like wrong numbers in math or typos in writing; they needed to be corrected. When they wouldn't go away on their own, I turned to my breathing. *Breathe in, one two three. Breathe out, one two three.* Then no thought, just breathing. Then no thought of breathing. Time and space disappeared. For a while, I'd peek to see if the incense was still burning. Soon, I was ending my meditation when the incense stick stopped burning. I'd open my eyes, see the last of the smoke curl off the short stick in the bowl, then watch the smoke rise and fade into nothing. With the incense, my meditation increased from thirty to forty-five minutes.

When I got good with incense, I began using candles to lengthen my meditation to an hour or more. Meditation became a comfortable place without time or space. An occasional thought would wander through. Thoughts of home in America, that was the past and far away. School tomorrow, that was not now. I no longer dismissed thoughts; they just withered and died. At times, I'd hear a pop as the candle burned out, shocking me from my meditation. Other times, I'd open my eyes as the candle popped. The flame would disappear, and the stillness would overflow.

When I realized the focus of my meditation became the end of the candle, I stopped using candles. Without a prop to gauge the length of my meditation, my routine changed. After dinner with the students at the dormitory dining hall, I'd return to my room and catch a couple hours of sleep. I'd awake around ten in the evening and meditate, sometimes with my eyes closed, other times with them open. Whether it was the inner darkness or the stillness of the night outside, I felt a contentment. I was unconcerned with the passage of time. I was just there. Some nights, I would end my meditation and curl up on my bed and sleep. Other times, I'd notice a change in weather, the wind picking up, or the morning light before sunrise. Breathing the cool morning air while listening to the songs of the birds was more than refreshing. I'd head down to the marketplace for coffee and cake. Reading the paper sparked all kinds of conversations with people in town. I was part of the gang.

Meditation, coupled with the potent Thai stick, Singha beer, and Mekong whiskey that blocked my emotions, created a pleasant environment. As insightful as meditation was, I never questioned my need for drugs and alcohol. Addicts never do. They can't. Blocking emotions is too important.

One evening at the temple, Phra Sohm asked, "Do you have a friend who could help you with your meditation?"

"There's one girl, Amporn. She speaks English well and helped me learn to speak Ge'mung. I told her about you teaching me meditation. She studied it at the temple in her village."

"That's good. Ask her if she'll bring you flowers every few days, so you can meditate with them. She'll understand."

Amporn was a student in her last year at school. She was headed to Prince Academy in Chiang Mai for eleventh and twelfth grades, unavailable at Nan Christian School, before she went to college. Her English was excellent. She was from a small village deep in the forests of the Luang Prabang mountains that straddled the Thai-Laotian border. With dark eyes and straight black hair down to her mid-neck, she always dressed in a traditional Thai blouse and sarong, refusing to wear the less modest school uniform. She was a calm presence in the dormitory, well respected by both the students and staff.

The next evening, I asked Amporn. "Phra Sohm wants me to find someone to bring me flowers every few days. Would you do that? Do you know what he is talking about?"

With a little laugh, Amporn agreed. "Certainly, I can bring you flowers. Someone did it for me."

The next afternoon, she appeared with a bouquet of native frangipani flowers. They were five-petaled and had many colors and hues, white with yellow near the center, pink, pink and yellow, yellow, and deep red. I put them in a vase and looked at them. They became beautiful companions. One afternoon three or four days later, I noticed the petals were slowly breaking off. The petals would droop until they dangled, then drop, floating back and forth in the air before finally hitting the floor. The seconds it took the petals to fall to the floor sometimes seemed like hours, transcending time. I was so entranced by the experience, I missed dinner a few times.

I was now six months into my meditation practice. I was calm, peaceful, and focused. The falling petals and the wilting flowers reminded me of Siddhartha's first glimpse of disease, death, and asceticism. I began to think about the end of things, a foreshadowing of completion.

One weekend, I went to visit my fellow English teachers in Chiang Mai and toured the Buddhist temples there. I felt an affinity with all the statues of the Buddha, especially at one temple that had more than 1,000. The foreboding I'd sensed before the weekend evolved into an excitement of approaching discovery, an understanding.

After a meal with my friends, I boarded the night train back to Prae, where I caught the bus to Nan. Stomach cramps during the train ride had turned into diarrhea by the time I got off. The three-hour bus ride over the mountain to Nan was agonizing. I controlled the diarrhea as best I could, but the odor of my farts and the small amount of leakage gave rise to muffled conversations and laughter from my fellow passengers. I remained serene and unconcerned. With no sleep on the train or bus, I reached Nan exhausted. I quickly found a taxi that would take me home.

Heading straight to the toilet near my room, I blasted what was in my system into the toilet. Feeling better, I piled my clothes in the shower, washed them, and hung them on a clothesline to dry. I took a shower and walked to my room to rest.

Lying in bed, I found I was not tired. Sleep was impossible. Realizing I had not meditated at all during the weekend, I decided I would ride my motorcycle up to the temple on top of the hill overlooking the Nan Valley, a peaceful place with a beautiful view.

On the ride to the temple, I felt light-hearted, almost buoyant. I'd gotten through a very embarrassing experience on the bus; I was pleased that I hadn't gotten upset about it, but accepted it as just another experience, neither good nor bad.

When I reached the temple, I sat in a meditative position facing the statue of the Buddha. This Buddha, facing east, had a very serene expression on his face. I'd always wondered what he was seeing that I wasn't. As I sat contemplating his expression, I felt invincible. It was getting light out. I felt energy in my spine. I was on the brink of discovery. All along my spine, my whole back was getting hotter. I felt like I was going to explode. The day was dawning. The sun was rising.

Suddenly, I realized why I was so warm: the morning sun was shining directly on my back. I looked at the face of the Buddha and realized why he was smiling. I rose, turned around, and sat back down. Now I was facing the same direction he was. No wonder he was smiling. I looked out over the Nan Valley, and saw the sun rising, the beauty of the world that the Buddha saw. I was no longer looking inward, contemplating myself. I sat contemplating outward, the way of the Buddha. I grasped how wonderful reality was. In this short moment of peace, I experienced joy, the lack of desire.

That evening, I visited Phra Sohm. He was excited at my discovery and laughed.

"You see reality like the Buddha sees it. You're just a part of it, observing it. Without desire, there's no suffering. There's a way to follow, the Middle Way, the Four Noble Truths, the Eightfold Noble Path. Welcome, you're at the beginning. You have a long road ahead of you. Enjoy the journey."

Over the next weeks, my meditation became restless. I asked Phra Sohm about it the next time I saw him.

"Phra Sohm, I'm having trouble sitting still. I feel like I'm falling into a deep, dark hole. It's scaring me a bit. I don't have many thoughts while I meditate. If that's mindfulness, I feel like I'm carrying it into my daily life. I'm calm and focused, but I feel an uneasiness. I'm not sure what it is."

"You were restless when you started meditating," he replied, "and you're restless again. Maybe it's time to stop sitting, formal meditation. You're carrying your meditation with you. You're mindful in your daily life. That's good. You have my blessing. I can't teach you anything more."

scott hunter

chapter 7

After a year in Nan, I'd become more Thai than American. I preferred sticky rice and vegetables for breakfast over bacon and eggs. I dreamt in Ge'mung. Everyone accepted the *farang*, the foreigner, who read the news out loud in the marketplace in the morning, taught English at the Christian School in the daytime, and hung out at the Buddhist temple in the evening. I was just another local resident.

I spent a few nights each week in the back of the tailor shop smoking pot with the gang. One night, Tommy, a USAID (United States Agency for International Development) worker, came into town to advise the provincial agriculture bureau. We ended up at the shop, and the conversation turned to the Vietnam War and how it was moving closer to Nan. I was used to speaking Ge'mung at the tailor shop, and I slipped into it during our conversation. Tommy didn't understand me.

With a puzzled look, he asked, "What did Scott just say?"

Without hesitation, Pranit said, "Oh, Scott doesn't speak English anymore," and translated what I had just said into English.

Tommy said, "Well, tell Scott he has an interesting perspective because he understands both American culture and Thai culture."

Pranit translated that into Ge'mung. I replied in Ge'mung, and Pranit translated what I said into English.

When Tommy said, "Tell Scott..." and stopped, we all began to laugh at the absurdity of Pranit translating between two Americans.

Tommy saw a side of Nan he hadn't seen before: Americans and Thai people reaching across a cultural divide and enjoying an evening together. What happened when people were unable to get past the divide would soon hit home.

One March evening, after nearly sixteen months in Nan, I was riding my motorcycle through town, headed up to the temple on the hill to visit the Buddha statue, when I noticed a green jeep at the hotel in the center of town. The United States Army was here. With a quick glance into the open-air restaurant on the raised first floor of the hotel, I saw a couple of *farangs* dressed in green camouflage. I turned my motorcycle around and parked next to the jeep.

Two crew-cut gentlemen were relaxing at the center table with their feet up on chairs. I took a deep breath and offered my hand.

"I'm Scott. I'm teaching at the Christian school up the road toward the airport."

Without moving, one of them took a toothpick out of his mouth and pointed it at me. "Jesus, are we glad to see you. You speak English. Anyone else speak English around here? I'm a colonel and he's a sergeant major. We just moved into town, got a house out by the airport. What's going on around here? We can't get service, no how."

All the cooks, waitresses, and waiters were in the back of the restaurant, unwilling to approach the colonel and his sergeant major.

I pointed to their feet on the chairs. "Sirs, the problem here is the soles of your boots are exposed. You should take your feet off of the chairs and put them on the floor. Exposing the bottom of feet and shoes is very offensive in this rural-based Eastern culture. Maybe all the dirt and manure on the ground makes the bottom of feet and shoes unsanitary. It's polite when sitting to keep both of your feet planted on the ground. Your feet perched on chairs someone else will sit on is extremely disgusting to the restaurant staff. I can help you order food, but first, feet on the ground."

The soldiers looked at each other and slowly put their feet on the floor. They understood little of the culture they were invading, but with their feet off the chairs, the tension in the restaurant decreased.

With a slight nod to the staff, I invited the waitress to approach the table and to serve the gentlemen. I ordered a bunch of Thai dishes and ate with them.

The sergeant major said, "Jesus Christ, this is the end of the paved road, all right. We must've done something wrong to get this intel op. First foray into town. How long you been here? Any other Americans?"

I was glad the wait staff couldn't understand him. "I've been here for about a year and a half. It's a nice place once you get to know it. You in-country long?"

This time, the colonel answered. "Been here six months. Been to Bangkok and R & R in Phuket, but first time up country."

They acted like they had been in the country six days. They were either slow learners or this was their first time off the air base. Or they didn't think they needed to learn anything about the people or their culture.

The colonel went on. "Commies spilling out of Laos into Thailand here, just north of Pua. Six Thai Royalist Forces were murdered there. We're setting up base here and advising the Thai army. They got their heads up their asses when it comes to commies."

This wasn't what I had heard. Sure, I had read about the death of the soldiers. The Thai government supported the U.S. war effort in the local paper. There were large American military bases in Thailand now. Tahkli, where the soldiers were from, was the biggest. Thailand was the preferred destination for U.S. soldiers on R & R. I had heard about Air America, the CIA mode of travel and transportation, but they were flying into Laos, not Nan. Nan was a quiet backwater. There was no war here as far as I could tell. The gossip at the marketplace was that higher-ups in the Thai Army wanted a larger kickback from some opium lords. The solders' deaths were a warning.

"I've been to Pua. I have a friend up there, a woman missionary working with the Yao and Mao hill tribes, good lady."

The colonel barked, "Yeah, we met her. Taking care of those…" He hesitated. I waited for the word communists. "She's headed home. Takin' a leave of absence. Too dangerous up there."

I wondered if her presence in the resettlement village was interfering with what the military was doing.

I ventured a thought. "You know, what I heard was that some of the local villages settled a dispute with some obnoxious soldiers. I haven't heard much about communists."

The colonel stared right through me and his face reddened. "Those hill tribes are communists alright. They're all damn communists."

The sergeant major, breaking the tension, joked with a hearty laugh, "Fuckin' surprised to meet an American up here. What are you, Air America? Forward reconnaissance? Using that missionary thing as cover?"

I forced a laugh with the sergeant major. The colonel didn't think it was funny. He dug into his chicken, cashews, green peppers, and white rice. The smile on the sergeant major's face was as good as a wink.

"Nope, just a peace-loving Christian, sir. Staying low-key. This is what I've learned living here for almost a year and a half. The Thai Royalist forces tend to stay out of Nan. They're tolerated here in town, less so in the countryside. It's a quiet province. We see the helicopters overhead and the soldiers out at the airport. Occasionally, an officer comes in and has a drink with the local police. Even the police keep a low profile. The governor is a local guy. He blends in. You don't see many uniforms in town. That's the way of Thai culture: stay low-key, hide your vices. You guys with your buzz cuts, white skin, green camos, you're going to stick out like business suits in a nudist colony."

The colonel was not amused, but the sergeant major was listening.

"I visit the resettlement village in Pua all the time. The Yao and Mao are making the best of a bad situation, away from their ancestral home. They're subsisting on what farming they can do on a barren hillside surrounded by a barbed-wire fence. I understand why somebody might be angry."

The colonel piped up again. "Got to get them out of the mountains. They're opium growers."

I said, "Some of them go back to their old homes, and I bet

that they are still growing opium up there. They're too smart for resettlement. They need the money. I've traveled all over, on back roads and into the mountains. People are just trying to live. Everyone I meet is friendly."

I decided to see how the marketplace rumors would go over with these soldiers. "You know, we're on the hypotenuse of the Golden Triangle. There are drug lords, strong men, a brisk heroin trade around. Maybe that had something to do with the Royalist soldiers' deaths."

The colonel's jaw tightened, his face redder than before. "Boy, there's commie infiltration from Laos. They're coming out of the mountains. Those hill tribes are the front line. We got to stop them here or they'll go all the way to Bangkok."

The sergeant major was concentrating on his Pad Thai. The colonel was getting to me. I figured I would take one last parting shot.

"There's a local radio station everyone listens to. Probably comes from Laos. They play a popular song all the time. The first verse is about a farmer who had a wife, three daughters, and a rice field. The king's army comes to the village, rapes his wife, and takes away his oldest daughter. In the second verse, the French army comes, rapes his wife, and takes away his second daughter. Then the communists come, offer medical attention to his family, and help him plant his rice field. A communist soldier falls in love with the farmer's third daughter, marries her, helps the farmer expand his rice fields, and begins defending the village. The chorus says that the farmer's not a communist because he believes in communism. He's a communist because he wants revenge."

I began to laugh, but the colonel and the sergeant major weren't amused. I pressed on, unable to shut up.

"If the army wants to win this war, you should get some soldiers with picks, shovels, and tomato seeds. Everyone loves tomatoes, but no one grows them. The farmers grow rice to feed their families and make a little money on the side. They don't have time for tomatoes. A few soldiers could clear land, plant tomatoes and other vegetables, and enrich the community. Then the local population would see the U.S. Army as beneficial."

The colonel rose from his seat. With his hands on the table, he leaned forward and shouted, "Boy, you are full of crap. We're fighting a war and we're going to win it. This isn't about helping people. This is about saving Southeast Asia from communism."

That got the attention of everyone in the restaurant. I stood up and held up my hands shoulder high, then backed away. I smiled and bowed deeply to the colonel. The restaurant staff relaxed. I said good night and left. I sensed a shift in the wind.

During the next weeks, I waved to the colonel and sergeant major whenever we passed on the road. Occasionally, I talked with them in town. They surrounded the small house they'd rented with a barbed-wire fence. The colonel imported his Filipino mistress. One afternoon, they careened into the gas station where I was filling up my motorcycle and invited me over to the house for a Friday night American barbeque and movie double-header.

I arrived at their encampment in the late afternoon for dinner. It'd been a long time since I'd eaten French fries and steak and ribs cooked on an outdoor grill. It'd been a while since I drank a Budweiser from a can, too. I liked water buffalo, vegetables, rice, and Singha beer, but there's nothing like an American cookout.

When it got dark outside, we retired to the living room and

watched *Patton* and ate buttered popcorn for dessert. It felt like home in America until I went outside to sneak a few hits of marijuana before the second feature.

I thought about the barbed-wire fence. Here was the visible border between separate realities. America was inside the fence. Nan was outside the fence. A group of children were looking through the barbed-wire. I recognized some of them. They waved. I waved. They had been listening to the first movie.

I returned to the living room. "Colonel, could I invite the kids outside the fence inside to watch the second movie?"

The colonel didn't like my idea. "You're crazy. That's why we built the fuckin' barbed-wire fence. We let those kids come inside, they'll steal us blind."

I put up my hands and said, "Letting those kids in to see the movie, even if they did rob you blind, would be the best thing that could happen to you. First, they'd watch a movie with you and tell everyone how wonderful and kind you are. If they stole from you, you'd then meet their parents when the parents brought the children to return what they had stolen and apologize. These are good people here. You don't understand what's going on. Thanks for dinner and the movie, but I can't watch the second movie with you."

His eyes widened with confusion. "You don't want to see the second movie? It's an oldie, *The Great Escape* with Steve McQueen." Offended, his face reddened. "Well, if you don't like our company, get out."

"Sir, if I stay within this barbed-wire fence any longer, I'm afraid that my reputation in the local community will be in jeopardy. This fence announces to everyone outside of it that you see them as a threat. It defines you as the enemy. I can't continue to associate with you."

I walked outside the fence, sat down with the kids, and listened to the second movie with them. I knew where I was safe.

I didn't associate with the colonel and sergeant major over the next month or so. I greeted them on the street but kept my interaction to a minimum. The community saw them as interlopers. They were the enemy.

A few weeks later, returning from Pua, I took a back road that wound through the hills east of Nan. As I rounded one curve, I came upon a jeep parked across the road with two Thai soldiers standing in front of it. They fired a gun into the air as I nonchalantly slowed to a stop in front of them and turned off my motorcycle. Firing guns into the air was normal procedure with Thai Royalist forces. The soldiers were astonished to see a red-headed American dressed like a schoolteacher.

"This road goes to Laos. You can't go through," they called out.

I thought a second and said, "But in a few kilometers, it comes back into Thailand. It goes down to the new bridge over the Nan River south of Nan, right?"

They then pointed their guns at me. "You are not safe here. Turn around and go back to Pua."

I backed up my motorcycle a few steps. "If you point your guns at me, I'm not safe." I pointed back from where I came. "If I turn around and go back to Pua, I'm going to be riding this motorcycle well into the night, then I won't be safe. I've been to all the villages ahead. It's safe. I'm *Achon* Hunter, I teach English at Nan Christian School. It's okay."

The soldiers lowered their guns. "You teach school in Nan?"

They spoke Thai. I knew they were from Bangkok and southern Thailand. They were more afraid than I was. I laughed.

"Yeah, everyone knows me here." I pointed down the road behind them. "Listen, I'll drive really fast. If you promise not to shoot me, you'll never see me again."

They nodded, then stepped aside. I started my motorcycle and waved to them as I rode on down the road. That experience shook me a little. People were getting nervous.

The winds continued to change. One Saturday, a week or two later, when I was hanging out at the tailor shop after dinner, my Thai friends invited me to smoke some weed with them. We went behind the shop and smoked a couple of joints. I got pretty wasted.

Two young men I didn't recognize appeared from the dark. They had guns over their shoulders. Leaning the guns on the tailor shop wall, they squatted down next to us. My heart was beating a mile a minute. If I hadn't been so stoned, I would've been scared out of my wits.

They smoked some pot with us, then one of them asked, "You're the English teacher at Nan Christian School?"

"I am."

"You're a good person, a friend to everyone in town. You teach English, study Buddhism. We have some friends coming to town. They'll be watching the army guys by the airport. They'll look at you and see an American. They might not understand you're a good American. As the Thai saying goes, 'a tiger is a tiger.'"

The two men shouldered their guns and walked back into the darkness.

Later, back in my room, I realized I'd been given a warning. With the army in town, it was time to get out of Nan. I'd been in the country twenty months; I had four more to go to complete my two-year alternative service. It didn't take me long to decide that I could always serve four months someplace else if my draft board questioned why I'd left the school early. In three weeks, the current semester and school year would be over. It was the end of April. It was not worth staying until September. If I left Nan now, I could enroll in seminary in June, do the summer semester, and complete a master of divinity degree by next May.

When I told everyone at the school I was leaving, they understood. They hadn't taken the presence of the army advisors as a positive sign.

chapter 8

During my last days in Thailand, I applied to McCormick Seminary in Chicago, Illinois. I had an ulterior motive; I had been corresponding with Jill, a beautiful brunette with dark sultry eyes who I'd met at Camp Miniwanca. She was going to Northwestern Law School, across town from McCormick.

In June of 1971, I moved in with my Uncle Karl and Aunt Marge, Dad's younger sister, who lived in Winnetka, Illinois, Jill's hometown. The war hadn't reached Winnetka. There were marches and protests in Chicago, but my life was McCormick, the El train to Evanston, and sheltered Winnetka. Aunt Marge and Uncle Karl didn't watch the news. When I was home with Karl, late afternoons began with gin and tonics until dinner. After dinner, I stretched out on the living room floor and studied Hebrew. I figured if I took the required course in Hebrew during the summer, a heavy course load in the fall and spring semesters, and one course during the winter session, I could complete my master's degree in one year.

The rest of the time, I courted Jill. I'd visited her a couple of times at Vassar when I was at Pittsburgh Seminary, and we'd written weekly while I was in Thailand. We were as intimate as an 8,500-mile separation allowed. Now within touching distance, our relationship slowly evolved, beginning with bike rides to various parks in Winnetka, where we'd sit up against a tree, hold hands, and talk. Gentle kisses would end the evening, then we would bike back to our homes.

In August, the Saturday before my Hebrew final, friends invited Jill and me to an Amazing Grace concert at Northwestern University. Amazing Grace was a local psychedelic rock band. Our friends had some chocolate mescaline, and Jill and I each took a hit. Mescaline was referred to as "organic," a gentle high with fewer side effects than chemically produced hallucinogens. This chocolate mescaline was the most powerful substance I'd ever ingested. During the concert, Jill and I held hands and were engulfed by the music, the August night, a wonderful cool breeze, the rest of humanity swaying with the one large universe. When the concert ended, we found a park and a starry sky where we could be alone. We kissed more passionately than ever before. We talked about making love, but it seemed so incongruous with the mescaline high. We decided to put it off for a more convenient time and place.

We were at one with each other and with the universe all night long, all the next morning, and the entire afternoon. Late that Sunday evening, still totally enthralled, thoughts of the next day's real-world responsibilities began to interrupt our bliss. We thought we could come down more easily and deal with mundane Monday if we went our separate ways.

I spent Sunday night and all of Monday in places well beyond my previously known universe. Monday evening, on my way to my Hebrew final, I was desperately trying to come down. I walked the four and a half miles from Winnetka to the Evanston El station, thinking that would calm me down. At the station, I negotiated the steps up to the tracks. The train arrived, and I floated through the doors.

Watching a swirling and pulsating Evanston and North Chicago fly by, I realized I might be in trouble. All I could do was to go to the Hebrew final and do my best.

I got off the train and descended the steps onto Halsted Street. It was a beautiful August evening; the leaves on the trees danced in a slight breeze, the heat of the summer rose off the sidewalk, and the pulsating red brick and stone buildings engulfed me. I walked into the sterile, cold, gray classroom and sat down at a metal and plastic table on a plastic chair. The Hebrew test was distributed. We were told that we had an hour and a half to complete the test.

I opened the test to find lines and dots moving around on a piece of paper. If I hadn't been so frightened of being found out, I would have laughed out loud. It was all fairly absurd. Outside was so precious, and here I was sitting in a drab room, looking at squiggles. Despite the claustrophobia I was feeling, I sat calmly for thirty minutes. Breathe in, breathe out. Then, I realized I was feeling judgmental. Outside was natural, expansive, soft evening sunlight, warmth, everything good. The cement walls of the classroom, the metal and plastic table and chairs, and the glaring neon lights weren't bad, just atoms and molecules in different forms. The room, the test, and I weren't separate from the outside.

I looked at the squiggles and dots on the test paper. I focused on them, and they stopped moving around. I remembered that dots above the squiggles were the letter 'e'. I recognized a word,

scott hunter

then a phrase. Suddenly, a text from Deuteronomy popped up from the page. I wrote frantically for half an hour and handed in my exam with twenty minutes to spare. I was the first one finished, and I got an A.

When Jill and I saw each other again, we knew we were meant to be together. We decided to live together at the seminary. I told the school I was planning to get married in the fall, so I was given an apartment in the married students building. Jill and I, always the rebels, pretended to be married. We had breakfast together. I drove her down to the Northwestern campus and returned to my classes at McCormick. I picked her up in the evening. We ate dinner and studied. It lasted a week before I noticed something was disturbing her.

"Scott, why don't you want to talk?" she asked one evening after dinner. "All you want to do is drink and smoke pot."

I froze up. How was I going to talk to her if I was afraid of what I might reveal? I was a sinner. How was I going to relax in bed with her, make love to her, without something to block my ugly, evil feelings of guilt?

Before I knew it, Jill had packed up and moved into the dorms at Northwestern. I stood at the door of the apartment, numb, wondering what just happened. I knew she was right. There was something wrong with me, but I couldn't question it. I ignored my sadness, cracked a beer, and lit up a joint.

Breaking up with Jill would've been a devastating loss if I hadn't been so relieved to avoid the sexual intimacy that developed between us. Intimacy wasn't something I could handle. I was a sinner.

I had been a sinner since I was six years old, when I was fascinated with women's bare knees in the vestibule of the side entrance of the First Presbyterian Church in New Kensington. That was a sin, but I didn't know why. I knew all about dresses and looking under them from my teenage babysitter; we played all those games. At that time, all women wore dresses to church, which made it easy for me to bend over a little and look up there. Men wore pants. That hid everything. *If women didn't want me to look,* I thought, *they should wear pants too, right?*

Religion and church were very important in my family, a big production that included a pressed, clean white shirt, an uncomfortable suit coat, pants with a serious crease, and a tie. I was very suspicious about the tie—it was too much like the nooses the good guys hung bad guys with on Saturday morning cowboy TV movies before anyone else was up.

Sunday school started at ten. Mom and all the women ran it, and they didn't have any answers to my many questions about the Bible. How did Jonah get out of the whale's stomach before he was digested? How big were the trumpets that Joshua used to blow down the walls when he fought the battle of Jericho? How did Jesus and John the Baptist keep their white robes clean when John baptized Jesus in the river? How did Moses part the Red Sea? How could the Israelites eat manna in the wilderness for three meals a day for forty years?

When eleven o'clock rolled around, the members of the congregation were ushered into the sanctuary by men. I wondered what the men did during Sunday school. The sanctuary was huge, two stories tall, arched, with exposed wooden rafters. There was a balcony. When I was allowed to sit there, I felt closer to heaven. On a stage up front was a pulpit where Reverend Boswell spoke, wearing a flowing black robe. He spoke THE WORD OF GOD, all capital letters. Behind him the choir was dressed in robes. Robes were like dresses.

There was the big question. Why did women wear dresses? I understood pants. Those exposed knees, nearly at eye level. I couldn't avoid them. And the way dresses swished when women walked. If I bent over, I could look up…so tempting, in church no less. The devil was everywhere. Dresses were a plot to get me to sin.

The story of Adam and Eve getting kicked out of the Garden of Eden for eating apples and being naked, that one really stumped me. I ate apples. I sort of enjoyed my nakedness, except when I was swimming with my butt-naked older cousins in the creek on their farm. Their penises were big and mine was, well… small didn't describe it.

My sinfulness was confirmed by the time I was seven: I developed a hernia. I was skeptical about our family doctor's explanation of the operation. The incision and sutures on my lower left stomach were a little too close to my testicles for comfort. When the first operation failed and my left testicle refused to descend normally, a second operation was performed, suturing my left testicle to my testicle sac, so it would remain descended. My left testicle never grew after that operation. Talk about paying for one's sins. God and Jesus took one of my testicles.

Somewhere between seven and twelve, I concluded that the well-respected Reverend Boswell was important. It was the robe he wore, like a dress over his pants. Women wore dresses, so they must've had a connection to God that men didn't have.

After Sunday services, Reverend Boswell would stand at the main door to the sanctuary and shake hands with his congregation as they left. I felt honored to shake his hand, and he reeked of alcohol. So, that was why they served grape juice during communion! Reverend Boswell was drinking all the wine, the real blood of Jesus. I was impressed. Alcohol, Jesus' blood, gave the reverend power, *and* he was in cahoots with women. He was a sultan with a harem.

A seed was planted that sprouted when I took my first drink. Alcohol was a gift from God like Jesus was a gift from God. Alcohol became an elixir that forgave my sins and allowed me access to women. Now, though, alcohol had taken my woman away.

I plunged into a course on Old Testament History, reading the original Hebrew. I replaced Jill with my new best friend, a huge Hebrew/English dictionary. That was intimacy I could handle.

My professor told us that a few scholars proposed that the seven days of creation were derived from pre-written Hebraic history. He suggested it was a children's story, used to teach basic words and numbers. This resonated with me.

Memories of the stories from Sunday school that I hadn't believed returned. I was in seminary, learning to be a minister, expected to spout these children's stories as fact, the true Word of God. That was nonsense. I had to figure out a way to show my professors, religious scholars, that it was all myths.

As I painstakingly translated the Genesis text, I came upon the word "Eden." It was an Aramaic word, meaning "the garden in the east." Aramaic was a Phoenician proto-Hebrew language, from the fertile Tigris-Euphrates River basin east of Canaan, the land of Abraham—present day Palestine and Israel. I researched the words "Adam" and "Eve" and found they were generic forms of "man" and "woman." Man and woman came from the garden in the east.

I was smoking some very good Vietnamese pot brought over to the States by returning soldiers. In a marijuana haze, I was struck by a revelation: Abraham was living in the Tigris-Euphrates River basin. When he was ninety years old, he and his wife Sarah had a child, Isaac. Unfortunately, Ba-al, the primary God in the Tigris-Euphrates basin, the garden in the east, demanded the sacrifice of a man's first-born son. Abraham didn't want to sacrifice his first-born son to Ba-al. He knew about the fertility gods of the Greeks to the west across the Mediterranean Sea. They didn't sacrifice their first-born sons to anyone. So, Abraham moved west to Canaan, closer to the Greeks, and saved Isaac. He and his descendants became outcasts. (In Aramaic, the word outcast is *habaru*—Hebrew.) Abraham created his own God, Elohim, a blend of Phoenician and Greek gods. Abraham, the Hebrews, and Elohim were the beginning of Judaism.

I had something in common with Abraham. He was a rebel. I was a renegade. He was a leader. Maybe I could be a leader.

It was Chicago in the early 1970s. Revolution was in the air and the marijuana was potent. My heroes of the day were Che Guevara, Ho Chi Minh, Mao, Marx, Engels, Lenin, Fidel, and the Chicago Seven. Near the end of the semester, the obligatory term paper was due. I decided mine would be on Moses. Moses, abandoned by his Hebrew mother in the bulrushes and discovered by an Egyptian princess, I knew was an allegory to connect him to the Hebrews. The descendants of Abraham were the Egyptian proletariat and Moses was their Lenin.

When Moses, the young prince, killed an Egyptian guard who was beating Hebrew slaves, he escaped from the authorities into the desert and found himself in the land of the Midianites. There, he married the daughter of a Midianite priest, and the priest introduced him to "the burning bush." In my mind, there was no way that burning bush could be anything but marijuana. (My Hebrew-English dictionary didn't have any translations, in either Hebrew or English, for the word "marijuana.") The name of the god speaking through the burning bush was Yahweh, "I Am Who I Am" in Aramaic. In my own burning bush haze, I was who I was. I knew exactly where Moses was coming from. I so wanted to be like Moses, leader of his people. I began to think I had a deep connection to God, that I just might be some sort of a prophet.

I had a good stash of pot that got me through the first half of the fall semester and my term paper. I was always looking for LSD. One of my seminary friends had connections at the University of Chicago Medical School. He knew I liked to trip, so he gave me a strip of electrical tape with ten hits of pharmaceutical acid; clear, less than one-eighth of an inch square windowpanes. They had a sparkle to them. Pop one in your mouth and you could see clear through to the mysteries of the universe. I shared six hits of the windowpane with two of my closest seminary friends and three prospective students, coeds from Stephens College. We sat and listened to Pink Floyd. I again awoke to the wonders of the universe. I was Moses. A girl named Alice, a junior at Stephens, had long blonde ringlets of hair down to her shoulders, blue eyes, and a southern accent that melted my heart. To me, she was a Midianite princess.

Though the seminary community didn't accept my portrayal

of Moses as Fidel, Mao, and Lenin combined, leading the children of Israel out of the wilderness into the Davidic Kingdom, I was not deterred in my own messianic vision. If Moses could do it, so could I. My grandmother had an ancestor on the *Mayflower*, my grandfather was dean of faculty at RPI, and my dad was a scientist. That was like royalty, right? On my mother's side, I was working class. I was the epitome of my interpretation of the story of Moses. In the purple haze of the windowpane, why not me? How would the historians write my mythology?

During the spring semester, my two friends and I visited our friends at Stephens. The acid we took there was at least as potent as that autumn's windowpanes. Having fallen in love with Alice in Chicago, I was dismayed to discover her feelings were not as strong as mine. Failed relationships were becoming a pattern. Somehow, my fear of intimacy was pushing them away.

Enduring her rejection, I wandered away from the group and into the Eagle Bluffs Conservation Area overlooking the Missouri River. Like Moses, I was on the mountain with the world before me. Though there was no burning bush talking to me, I experienced the presence of an angel of the Lord. I heard, *Scott, physical love is not important. There is a purer love, a love within you. Forget her, your love will save you.* I was immersed in God, Yahweh, I am who I am.

The strangest thing was I had no idea who I was.

Chicago in the spring. The contrast after a midwestern winter awakened every cell in my body. The effects of the pharmaceutical windowpanes and playing *A Question of Balance* by the Moody Blues every night on my stereo made the spring of 1972 all the more breathtaking. I wanted to be in balance, at one with the universe, normal, not stoned all the time. But I couldn't dare. I had too many secrets.

My time in Thailand alienated me from everyone who didn't have that experience. There was no one to talk to who understood or cared. The people at McCormick Seminary, a bastion of conservative Presbyterian intellectualism, weren't impressed with my missionary service and my conscientious objection to the war. Neither were the protesters. I needed to tell my story.

The final projects for my spring semester course in multimedia presentations were short videos that would be presented at a film festival. I decided to make a video describing what I'd learned in Thailand. It began with me sitting in a classic lotus position, nearly nude, long hair and beard, no body fat, a red-haired Jesus lookalike. The Procol Harum song, *In Held 'Twas In I*, played in the background while I sat in a yoga posture. As the opening soliloquy ended, the opening notes of Leon Russell's *A Song for You* played, and I disappeared. *A Song for You* was a loving farewell to the seminary.

The day before the film festival, I decided to finish editing the video and add the soundtrack for the weekend show. I used up the last of the windowpane. Having chipped the corners off the last hit to stretch out my dwindling supply, I thought what was left wouldn't get me high. When I was done editing, I returned to my room; the acid didn't seem to be affecting me at all. Killing time before dinner, I got lost in doodling small yin yang symbols on a piece of paper. A friend knocked on my door and asked if I was going to dinner. I emerged out of my last yin yang drawing back into reality. Time had disappeared. It was later than I thought.

My friend and I walked to the dining hall and got into the

cafeteria line. Suddenly, I was not hungry.

POW!

The world disintegrated. I was tripping. I usually did acid alone, or with a very small group. I didn't do acid in public. It got really scary. The dining hall and everyone in it began to dance and swirl. I lost it, completely out of control. On the edge of freaking out, somehow, I got to a table and put down my tray of food as nonchalantly as possible. I took a sip of hot coffee, burning the hell out of my mouth. I began to laugh and couldn't stop. No one understood what was so funny. Then someone asked me where my graduation robe was. Senior chapel, a very important event in any seminary, was in twenty minutes.

I escaped the dining hall and ran back to my room to get my robe. I put on my dress pants and white shirt, struggled with a tie, and was baffled by my flowing robe. *Where are the sleeves? Why are they at the bottom of the robe? Oops, upside down.* Somehow, I got my arms into the damn thing. I arrived at the chapel in time to walk down the aisle with my classmates. Amazed by the beauty of the sanctuary with its organ pipes and statuary, I marveled at the pomp and circumstance. I felt empowered by it all. I was Jahweh—I Am Who I Am. I was pulsating with the rhythm of the universe.

The senior class mentor, a young, well-liked, hip professor, conducted the service. His sermon, an analogy of the minister as a vessel of the Lord, was illuminating: "The minister carries the Lord's message to the parishioner as a glass carries water to the thirsty. The vessel that carries Christianity to the people is well represented in Christian symbolism."

I was mesmerized by the significance of the moment. I was graduating from a seminary. From far away, like a still small voice from the wilderness, I heard our mentor's rhetorical question: "Can anyone recognize other vessels in Christianity?"

The baptismal font in front of the sanctuary began to glow. Beautiful swirling trails emerged from it and became three doves. I stood to answer.

"Yes, the baptismal font is a vessel, do you see the three doves above it?"

During the next few seconds of silence, the congregation searched for the three doves. My classmates beside me were trying not to laugh. *Oh, no, Scott's on acid.* They quickly pulled me down and hid me behind the pew in front of us.

Our beloved mentor ignored me, gathered himself, and finished his sermon. Luckily, the senior class led the procession out of the chapel after the closing hymn and benediction. We were out of there before anyone one could approach me and ask about my outburst. My friends spirited me off to the squash courts, where my mind bounced off the walls for the next few hours. No one thought to look for me there.

I made myself scarce for the next few days. I cut my hair and shaved my beard to please my parents, who were coming to my graduation in a week. I thought maybe no one would recognize me at the festival when I presented my film. My video was awarded best in show. Maybe the Christians did understand me.

chapter 9

For the summer of 1972, along with my master's in divinity, I had a new girlfriend, Mary Easter. She said she was an ex-girlfriend of Dick Butkus, the Hall of Fame linebacker for the Chicago Bears. I was impressed. Bewitched by the serendipity of her name and my newly acquired divinity, our intimacy, intensified by a few hits of LSD, was overwhelming and irresistible. Those few weeks of unmitigated sex with her were a short respite from the constant image of my mother's wagging finger and her damning voice—*your fault if you get a girl in trouble*. It was a break from the secrets I held deeply, unarticulated even to myself. It was one of the few times I'd made love unburdened by guilt.

In the midst of that sexual revelry, I received a wedding invitation from a friend, Frank. He was getting married in Fargo, North Dakota. Mary and I decided to hitchhike there. She packed her backpack, I packed my suitcase, and we set out on the road. One of our first rides was with two guys, hippies from New Jersey in a tricked-out van going to something called the Rainbow Gathering in Colorado.

In 1972, the organizers of the war protests in Berkeley wanted to have a party to celebrate the hard work and success of the antiwar movement. They discovered that citizens of the United States had camping privileges in national forests. Choosing the name 'Rainbow Gathering' to proclaim the joy they felt after years of stormy protests, they applied to the National Forest Service for a permit to camp in the Rocky Mountain National Forest near Granby, Colorado, for ten days surrounding the Fourth of July.

When Mary and I climbed into the hippie van, it was as if we fell down Alice's rabbit hole. After a few hits of some very potent marijuana, we nicknamed our two new friends Chipmunk and Squirrel. I was in a dream, along for the ride, not in control of what was happening. Mary was all for extending our trip. I was a little hesitant, but our new friends, enamored with Mary, said they would drive us to Fargo, stay overnight there, and continue to the gathering after the wedding. We stopped in Fargo and stayed overnight. Mary, Chipmunk, and Squirrel slept in the van. I slept on Frank's couch, and in the morning put on a suit, creased pants, a blue dress shirt, and a tie and coat. The wedding was like something out of the Bible. I was Jesus, and the wedding was the marriage at Cana. Afterwards, I took off the tie and coat, but I wore the creased pants and Brooks Brothers shirt for the next week.

Back in the van, as we drove through North Dakota, my mental state began to shatter. Mary and I were passionately making out in the back of the van. It was as if our tongues and mouths were having intercourse, producing simultaneous cerebral orgasms. I experienced energy flowing up my spine and bursting in my head. I was no longer physical, mundane. I was ascending, spiritual. Then, I looked at Mary; she appeared ugly to me. What was I doing kissing her, touching her? She was flesh. She was corruption. I was pure. My destiny was about to be filled. I was a prophet. I had power. Is this what Jesus felt, riding into Jerusalem on a donkey, people throwing palm fronds in his path?

We stopped at a roadside bar for some takeout beer. As stoned as we were, we were intimidated by the row of pickup trucks parked in front. Since I was the least hippie-looking, with short hair and conservative shirt and pants, I was designated to walk into the bar and ask for a couple of six packs. Inside, a row of Dakotan farmers drank.

The bartender asked what kind of beer I wanted, and I said, "Two six-packs of Budweiser, to go."

Suddenly, the men sitting at the bar turned toward me. The hair on the back of my neck stood up. I was in danger. I noticed that everyone was drinking Lone Star.

I grinned and said, "Make that Lone Star."

Everyone relaxed, and I got out of there.

I thought something mystical was happening. I would be recognized at the Rainbow Gathering. My time had come. Chipmunk and Squirrel were my apostles. By the time we got to Colorado, I was physically shaking, unable to put a sentence together or make any decisions. My behavior was bothering Mary, and the tension between us was unbearable. When we stopped at a mountainous lookout and began talking to some motorcyclists going to the gathering, Mary jumped on the back of one of the motorcycles and disappeared. She was gone. What I wanted was coming to pass. Chipmunk, Squirrel, and I continued on to Granby, Colorado.

As we neared Granby, we picked up more hitchhikers. I began to feel claustrophobic. Here were all these long-haired, multicolored children, and I looked straight as an arrow. *What are they thinking? Do they know that I am the chosen one?*

Someone asked, "Are you okay?"

"I think I might be Jesus Christ."

That got everyone's attention.

Someone jokingly suggested, "Well, let's see what the next sign on the road says. It'll tell us if this guy is Jesus."

The next sign was for Troutman Insurance, with a big fish on it. As innocent as it was, everyone, especially me, got the fish connection. The hippies laughed. I sunk deeper into myself. Contact with reality all but disappeared.

Finally, we reached the parking lot in Granby; the gathering was about ten miles up the road, past Granby Lake on a trail up the mountain and into the forest. Everyone got away from me; alone, I got on a bus for the trailhead to Rainbow Central. Without thinking, I'd walked away from my suitcase.

When I reached the main campsite, I tried talking to a few people. I told them I was a seminary graduate from Chicago. People began to avoid me. I kept hearing "Chicago Red." I didn't understand. Weren't these hippies all peace and love? I got angry. I threw a pail of water on the main campfire and put it out. That got their attention.

Before a group of upset and angry people could confront me, a Hispanic guy with long black hair and beard corralled me.

"Brother, your short hair and Brooks Brothers shirts don't fit in here. You're telling everyone you're from Chicago. The cops at the 1968 Democratic Convention were called the Chicago Red Squad. Everyone thinks you might be an FBI agent undercover. Your red hair, Chicago Red, get it?"

My new friend was Felipe Chavez. I told him about my prophetic vision. Realizing I was either extremely stoned or crazy, he countered my story.

"Listen, maybe you know me. I'm the nephew of Caesar Chavez of the National Farm Workers Association. Alright? Hear me? You can trust me."

That and his firm gaze into my eyes steadied me.

He suggested, "Go to the lost and found and be found."

As frantic as I was, that was brilliant logic. Suddenly, I fantasized that I would find a beautiful female companion, we would fall in love, and she would take care of me forever. That swiftly became terrifying. I might reveal my sins, my guilt. I feared relating to anyone.

Felipe then said, "Or you can go back to the parking lot and make some decisions there, my friend. I don't think you should stay around here. You got a lot of people angry, and there ain't much trust left."

I thanked Felipe and headed back down the trail. Walking a few miles along the road bordering Lake Granby improved my state of mind. I relaxed and breathed. I was no longer Jesus, just alone in the country, on Earth, walking towards whatever lay ahead. When I got back to the parking lot, I located my suitcase in a pile of camping equipment. Feeling myself coming together, I got something to eat at a diner, checked into a motel, took a shower, and got a good night's sleep.

In the morning, as if emerging from a dream, I began to feel normal again. After another shower, I went to my suitcase to get fresh clothes. My initials on either side of the handle, S and H, were upside down—H and S. *Oh, my god, my initials backwards are the initials of the Holy Spirit.* I was Jesus, again! Leaving my suitcase with all my belongings in the motel room, I hitchhiked out of town. A black guy who didn't like the white vibes at the gathering was returning to New York; he picked me up and drove me to Chicago.

During the rest of July and August, I hid in a friend's Chicago apartment. I had trouble making decisions, became extremely anxious around others, and continued my Christ fixation. When my friend tired of my behavior and asked me to go someplace else, I decided I needed to talk with a therapist. My aunt recommended one in Winnetka. He suggested I find a hobby working with my hands to channel my energy into an activity.

I decided to return to New Kensington, my childhood home. There, everything got back to normal, though Mom and Dad must have thought I was a little off as I related my summer experiences. I bought leather-working tools and began to channel my energy into leather. Thoughts of being Jesus Christ were far from my mind. I wanted to reunite with friends and meet new people.

Even though I was in a familiar environment and had begun to reestablish contact with reality, crazy things still happened. One afternoon in September, I returned to Chatham College, my old haunt while at Pittsburgh Seminary. I placed an acorn on a library shelf and pleaded with God for a sign of my returning health. As I walked out of the library, I met a coed and began a torrid one-week affair.

Hitching home on the day that affair ended, I was picked up by the director of the Pittsburgh Playhouse. When I told him I had minored in dramatic arts, he offered me a job. I worked the first few weeks of September backstage and looked for an apartment in Pittsburgh. A secretary said I could move in with her. Fearing intimacy, I panicked and left the theater (and a paycheck) behind.

I knew something wasn't right. I wanted to be loved, but what did that mean? I was in a physical relationship for a week with a beautiful woman, but I pushed her away. I had a chance to begin a platonic relationship, but even that was too frightening. What was wrong?

Mom and Dad started to ask questions: "What happened to that Chatham girl?"

My only answer was a downcast, "Oh, I guess it didn't work out."

Dad asked, "Weren't you working at the Pittsburgh Playhouse?"

I mumbled, "Ah, all I was doing was painting scenery. It wasn't going anywhere. I need to find something that will challenge me."

I was full of shit. I was heartbroken over breaking up with the Chatham girl and walking away from a position as stage manager for an upcoming play. I had no answers.

I had to get away, but where? My greatest success was graduating from Amherst College. I would head back to New England. That would be my heritage.

I had never been to Boston. An old friend of mine from high school was living there. I called him up. I was coming to visit.

chapter 10

I stopped in Troy on the way. My grandfather had died while I was in high school and my grandmother had passed away over the summer, so their house was empty. I got the key from the next-door neighbor and spent the night sitting in the living room on all the Oriental rugs and old Victorian furniture I had loved as a kid. I spent time in the third-floor attic amidst the tops of the tulip and silver maple trees, remembering.

Grandmother Hunter was a descendant of John Howland, who came over on *The Mayflower*. She was a member of the Daughters of the American Revolution. Grandfather Hunter was from New Zealand, graduated from King's College in London, and was the dean of faculty at Rensselaer Polytechnic Institute. They'd lived in a three-story, dark-cedar shingled house on a dead-end street.

My grandparents' house was special. As kids, we'd visited them for two weeks every August, and my sister and I had been the center of attention. My grandfather had worn white shirts, ties, and suit jackets to every meal, including breakfast. We'd heat donuts and dip them in powdered sugar; there was nothing as grand as melted powdered sugar on warm donuts. There was a woman who'd helped Grandma cook and clean, a servant, but Grandma had brought the food into the dining room on a cart with wheels and served it herself, like it was very important.

The wisteria-draped front porch was the cool place. We'd all sit around mornings and afternoons, talking, and talking, and talking. I hadn't understood much of what was said, but I'd been determined to learn all about it and take my rightful place as head of the family someday. I was a prince, the first-born male, the heir apparent. From a very early age, especially at my grandparents' house, I'd seen myself as some sort of royalty.

Life hadn't turned out like I'd thought it would. I'd stopped believing my ideas were good. Mom and Dad had forgotten to teach me how to identify and follow my dreams. When I'd wanted a piccolo for Christmas, I was told it would be too expensive. I went from first chair flute in eighth grade to sixth chair flute in ninth grade. In the early '50s, I'd wanted one share of IBM, but Dad said you could only buy shares in lots of 100, even though that wasn't true. I began to think I wasn't wise, that I couldn't understand the way the world worked.

The next morning, I headed to Boston, stopping to check out Amherst College on my way. I ran into an old roommate, a fraternity brother. He was living at the former house of the Congregational minister in Belchertown, ten miles away. He told me of an available room at the manse, and I moved in October 1, 1972. I never got to Boston.

Joanne, one of my new housemates, was a psychologist at the

Belchertown State School. She told me there was a job opening for an attendant in G Building, where she worked. I had a bachelor's degree in psychology; a job at a mental hospital as a nurse attendant would be a snap. I filled out an application and the next day, without an interview, received a telephone call: "Report for a physical tomorrow morning." Their next phone call was just as brief: "You're working the second shift, four to twelve. Show up on Monday."

I was happy and excited. I had my first real work, real work helping others that paid $412 a month.

Belchertown State School, opened in 1922, was made up of large red brick New England Victorian buildings on a sprawling campus, and inspired a feeling of H.P. Lovecraft eeriness. G Building, a bland three-story 1950s cement structure with large rectangular windows set back near the woods away from the main campus, was a stark inconsistency.

I was assigned to the adolescent men's floor in G Building, the bottom rung of the school's employment ladder. If you could cut it in G Building, you could work your way up to more desirable positions. If not, you walked away. No one was ever fired.

That Monday, I went out the back door of the manse, crossed the yard, walked through the fields behind the house, down the hill, and across the railroad tracks to the Belchertown State School. I arrived at G Building about a quarter to four, and I was ushered into the nurse's station on the men's floor.

The nurse locked the door behind me, saying, "Why didn't you show up at the orientation session during first shift?"

I was surprised. "I was told I was working the second shift, so I arrived at the start of the second shift. No one said anything about orientation."

She looked worried. "I'd send you home if I didn't need someone to work this evening. I hope you're ready for this. I'll have Bob, an attendant on low-grade, take you to your station."

She introduced me to Bob. Without a word, he walked me to a door at the end of the long hall and unlocked it. I walked into the low-grade retarded dormitory room. He closed the door and locked it behind me.

The young adults housed in G Building were the most severely retarded residents at the school. In reality, many were likely autistic. Autism wasn't listed as a disease in the Diagnostic and Statistical Manual of Mental Disorders (DSM) until 1980. In 1972, the diagnoses of the residents were high-grade retarded and low-grade retarded. High-grade meant the residents had underdeveloped language and communication skills, limited social interaction with the staff, limited emotional responses, and were engaged in repetitive motions. Low-grade meant no language skills, compulsive repetitive motions, difficulty with bodily functions, and self-injurious behavior. Communication with the staff was difficult, resulting in grunts and hand gestures. When their needs were not met, they became angry.

The demeaning labels of high- and low-grade matched the living conditions. Eighty young adults slept in the four dormitory rooms, twenty in each room. There was no privacy at all; twenty beds in four lines, with three feet between each bed. The bathrooms were open areas with no doors for the toilets or curtains for the showers. In low-grade, all the clothes were stored in a communal closet; the residents had no clothes of their own. They were marched to and from meals three times a day. Meals lasted thirty minutes. The most functional residents could eat and use the bathroom on their own and, generally, respond to the psychologist, nurses, and attendants. The least functional were catatonic.

That first day, I was in a large room divided down the middle by a waist-high wall. There were five beds on either side of the center partition and against each of the outside walls, with a passageway between the rows of beds. For a moment, everyone stopped what they were doing. Twenty pairs of eyes stared at me. I sensed that even the catatonic residents knew I was there. Then, what I came to learn was normal activity in low-grade began. Some of the residents walked around and around the passageway between the lines of beds. Some stood still, whacking themselves on their heads. Others sat on their beds or the floor, rocking back and forth.

I took my time surveying the room and my new friends. I turned and looked at the door. It was locked, and I had no key.

I began to walk around the room, trying to make eye contact. A few residents gave me head nods. After twenty minutes circling the room, I decided that, like Thailand, everyone in the room was a student and I was the teacher. I needed to learn the language everyone spoke, then I could teach them what they needed to learn. I calmly sat down and began rocking back and forth, mimicking some of the residents.

Suddenly, there was a cacophony of sounds from the group. I assumed they were talking about the new kid on the block.

I uttered a chirp or two, just to let them know I could communicate. I changed my position in the room, so I could observe all the residents. I wanted them to know I was one of them, a friend.

Two hours later, Bob unlocked the door. "Two hours in low-grade by yourself? Very good. I see you've met all my buddies. It's time for dinner. Let's take these kids down to the cafeteria."

We gathered everyone together and led them to the cafeteria.

As Bob and I assisted the residents who had difficulty eating, we talked. "You caused quite a stir this afternoon, not showing up for orientation," he said. "Everyone thought you bailed. Then when you showed up for second shift, it was, 'Let's see what this guy's got. Lock him in low-grade for a couple hours.'"

I smiled. "I guess I passed the test. I'm still here. Are all those guys locked in one room all the time?"

Bob nodded his head and looked sad. "That room and the day room. G Building is a warehouse. Not much goes on here."

I knitted my brow. "What about Joanne, the psychologist? Doesn't she do some therapy or something?"

Bob looked up to the ceiling and rolled his eyes. "Joanne's my girlfriend, but I've got to say that she shouldn't be the psychologist here. Yeah, she has a BA in psychology from UMass, but that's nothin'. She's afraid of low-grade. She can barely deal with high-grade. This is a sad, sad, place."

After dinner, Bob and I took the residents back to the dormitory room. When everyone was inside, Bob, with a big smile on his face, turned to me and said, "And now your next test. See ya in a couple of hours."

Around ten o'clock, Bob unlocked the door and I got a fifteen-minute break. I peeked into day rooms and the high-grade dorm room. Residents were sitting or standing. Some were pacing. The nurses and a few of the attendants were gathered in the nurse's station. Not much was going on.

At the end of my break, Bob locked me back into low-grade. "You're doing good. Let's see if you can get them to go to bed."

Some of the residents knew the routine, while others had to be dressed in their pajamas and led to their beds. Turning out the lights and quietly sitting in a corner, I curled up into a lotus position and took a couple of deep breaths. I was a long way from the psychosis I felt at the Rainbow Gathering. Having found a good source for marijuana, I was still smoking pot, but without an acid connection, I felt normal. I was going to keep it together and succeed. Looking over all my sleeping friends, I hoped we were going to be a family here in low-grade.

Just before midnight, Bob unlocked the door, and with a nod of approval, said, "You put all the kids in bed by yourself. A very successful first day, Scott. Time to go home."

I found the nurse who had scolded me earlier in the nurse's station and said, "Wow, that was a great day. I apologize for missing orientation, but those guys in low-grade are really cool. I can't wait to hang out with them again. More fun. See you tomorrow."

With a skeptical look, she said nothing and returned to reading a chart. I walked home full of confidence.

The next day, I met the head nurse, Christine McNamara. Tall, heavy-set, and unattractive, she could have easily played Nurse Ratched in *One Flew Over the Cuckoo's Nest*. She ruled G Building. Known as Big Nurse behind her back, she had worked as the head nurse at the state school for more than fifteen years. Her authority wasn't questioned. She wasn't pleasant.

"I can't believe you missed orientation. That was stupid. I expect more from you. That's all I have to say."

Bob walked me to the dorm door. With a big smile, and lifting his eyebrows a couple of times, he playfully said, "She likes you, Scott."

I was locked in again. Walking around and acknowledging all the residents, I looked into their eyes. I put a reassuring hand on some of their shoulders. Others, if I got even the smallest response, I hugged them. Some gave me a little hug back. On my second circuit of the room, I noticed eyes following me and a few smiles on some faces. On my third circuit, I made physical contact with each resident. Each accepted a hug. With some, I talked, slowly adding a chirp or two. It wasn't the actual the sounds I was making, it was the attempt to communicate that was important. By the end of the week, I was thinking, *These guys aren't retarded, they're misunderstood.*

The residents didn't go to school. There was no concept of rehabilitation or integration into community living. There were a few conscientious employees, but most of the staff were "ham and eggers," working to collect their paychecks and health insurance. They put in their time, stopped at the Buck and Doe Bar at the end of the day, went home, and slept. I wanted to be different, to make a difference.

Being locked into low-grade with the residents didn't bother me. I spent time with each resident each day. I learned and said their names to them each time I talked with them. They were real people inside of their stiff bodies and repetitive motions. I'd once read that painters of colonial portraits focused on their subjects' eyes because the Puritans thought that eyes were the gateway into the soul. The only way into my new friends' worlds was through their eyes.

Around six o'clock every evening, Bob arrived with his key, unlocked the door, and we herded everyone to dinner. We discussed them while they ate.

I leaned forward, and in a hushed tone said, "Bob, I think I can communicate with these guys. I look into their eyes and there are people there. It's non-verbal; I understand what they need. A resident will take me by the hand and lead me to a problem, a broken chair that needs to be fixed, an altercation between residents that I can calm, or a lost item I can retrieve. We fix the problems. Things get done. I'm amazed. Does Joanne understand what's happening? She's a psychologist. She should be creating educational programs for these guys."

Bob stood up and then leaned on the table, his face near mine. With a little bit of anger in his voice, he said, "No, Joanne hangs out in the nurse's station with the nurses. I see the same thing in the dayroom. These kids don't say much, but they communicate. I just help them out. Do the best I can."

"What if we created a normal living environment, more comfortable, some privacy? The toilets don't have doors on them."

"Listen, Scott, there's not much that we can do. Big Nurse runs G Building. She's been around since the '50s, and only understands discipline and order."

For the two weeks I worked without a key, the residents began to see me as one of them, a member of their community. When I got the keys to the doors, my relationship with them changed little. To them, I was a resident with keys.

chapter 11

One evening, after smoking a joint behind the Buck and Doe, Bob and I sat in a booth surrounded by loud conversations, loud music, and mounted deer heads. I was enjoying my beer, feeling like one of the BSS gang.

Bob was frustrated. "Okay, Scott, I feel like I'm wasting my time in the dayroom. Maybe there is something we can do. There are opportunities to teach these kids, but Joanne won't create programs for even basic skills. She won't even try, too much bother."

Bob took a big swig of his beer and finished it off. He looked me in the eyes and said, "Thorazine." He paused to let the word sink in. "Thorazine. It's the drug they give them to control them. It makes them dead inside. These kids are overdosed on Thorazine. They're trapped in their bodies. They want to come out. If it weren't for the daily doses, they could function. I swear to God. You can see it in their eyes."

I drained my beer, motioned to the waitress to get me another, and replied, "You're right, Bob. When I stand next to the catatonic residents, I sense they want to talk. Their babblings and jerks aren't random. They're really trying to communicate. Son of a bitch."

Bob sipped his beer. "I wonder how much Thorazine they're actually getting."

Excited, I said, "Bob, why don't we find out? Tomorrow afternoon when our shift starts, I'll distract everyone away from the nurse's station. You look up their doses on their charts."

The next afternoon when I saw only the shift nurse in the nurse's station, I said. "Dorothy, one of the kids has a bad cold. I don't want it to spread and affect the whole ward. Anything we can do? Can you take a look?"

Over my shoulder, I saw Bob walk into the empty nurse's station as I walked Dorothy into the dorm room.

"Michael's the one who's sick."

Dorothy found Michael and checked him out. "He just has a cold."

I stalled for time. "Could you check on a couple of others, just to make sure it hasn't spread?"

Afterwards, I looked for Bob. He was in the low-grade dayroom.

"You won't believe the doses," Bob blurted out. "Two hundred and eighty milligrams of Thorazine twice a day. It's amazing that these kids are able to stand upright. Their families don't know what is going on here. They just put them here and forget them. That's the history of retardation; institutionalize them, abandon them. The medical treatment these kids are getting is criminal. We're their only friends. We've got to do something."

Bob and I had the same idea at the same time: "Let's see what happens if we teach the kids to not swallow their medicine."

The next Sunday night, I approached a gentle black kid,

Henry, who was on a very high dose of Thorazine. He drooled all the time. His feet were rooted to the floor as he twisted and stumbled, trying to move. It seemed to me that he was always trying to communicate, but could never really complete a full sentence. I'd talked with a few aides who'd worked in G Building for a long time. They said that Henry was a good kid who occasionally became violent when his needs were not met. His outbursts would encourage others to act out. Big Nurse had increased his medication a few years ago, and he'd stopped being a problem.

With Bob watching me, I walked up to Henry, looked him in the eyes, pointed under my tongue and said, "Pills."

I stuck my finger under his tongue and said, "Pills."

I pointed to the palm of my hand, pretended to spit into it, then smiled. "Pills."

The staff nurse distributed the medicine after dinner. When she left, Bob walked over to Henry and held out his hand. Henry put a huge 280 milligram Thorazine pill into it. For the next few days, we were able to cut Henry's dose in half. Later, after an evening round of medication, Henry handed me two pills. He had saved his morning dose.

Henry stopped drooling and began wandering around the ward. Bob and I discovered he could talk and began having simple conversations with him. He learned our names and would ask how we were doing when we entered the bedroom. Bob moved him from the bedroom to the day room during the day. Henry began taking part in activities. He understood us when we stressed that he shouldn't become violent. We encouraged him to come to us if he needed anything. Not only did he become friends with us, he also assumed the role of resident attendant, pointing out problems and calming other residents when they became upset.

When he asked Bob for a bucket and mop and began cleaning the bathroom daily, we joked with him about applying for an attendant's position.

Henry laughed. "Get… me… application."

Having freed one resident, we turned to a few others we felt were on inappropriately high dosages. Whenever we got one of them to tongue his pills and give them to us, we kept a close watch on him during our shift to make sure he didn't act out. We explained to Henry and the others that not taking drugs was a secret. The rest of the staff could not know. Bob and I learned that other residents had language skills, though not as strong as Henry's. Henry was very good at communicating with the others in our drug reduction program. Non-verbal was his first language, English his second. He agreed to help us to keep everything peaceful when Bob and I weren't on the ward. As long as the residents got attention when they were upset, no one acted out.

The ward became animated. More residents left the bedroom and moved into the day room. We got out equipment in the day room closet that was never used and taught the residents games using balls and blocks. Some of the ritual motion guys learned to bounce balls. They got good at it. We taught others to stack blocks, knock them down, and laugh. We brought in Hula-Hoops, paddles with balls attached, and soap to make bubbles. We heard from the day shift that the low-grade dayroom was more fun than ever. They didn't actually understand what was going on, but they told us that the residents seemed happier. We showed their improved behavior to Joanne, but she was uninterested. It was all we could do to get her to agree that soap bubbles were a good thing.

One of the second shift duties, after the clients were tucked in bed, was to fold towels, shirts, and pants, and to pair socks that had been washed and put them in the closet cubby holes. One night, Henry came over to watch me, interested in what I was doing. I showed him how to fold a towel. He learned quickly. That night, he folded all the towels. Soon, I had him pairing socks and other residents folding towels.

Bob and I became the managers of the laundry folding crew. It was contagious. Even some less-functioning residents took on jobs doing what they could. After a couple of weeks, we were supervising the residents. They learned to clean up the day room before dinner and tidy up the dormitory before bedtime. Henry had help cleaning the bathroom.

Life in low-grade was going along smoothly. I was learning more non-verbal language, meeting residents' needs, anticipating and alleviating problems before any outbreak of emotion attracted attention. The few times violence threatened the ward, Bob and I, with the help of our crew, calmed things down. The residents were responding.

Since the residents of low-grade were functioning well, I was asked to substitute in the high-grade area, working the dayroom when attendants were out sick, on vacation, or had scheduling conflicts. The high-grade dayroom was like a carnival compared to the low-grade dayroom. The high-grade residents needed and sought attention. They interacted well with the staff.

As I got to know the high-grade residents, I became aware of their hierarchy. There were alpha and submissive residents. When I wasn't interacting with them on my terms, I would always sit and mimic the behavior in the room, rocking, picking my nose, and hitting myself. That broke down some barriers between us. If I was having a bad day, one of the alpha residents would come over and comfort me as they did the other residents. The submissive ones would come over to me and sit by me, laying an arm on my leg or leaning their head against my shoulder.

One evening, Bob had his day off and I was subbing in high-grade. The attendants taking over for us hadn't worked low-grade in a while. After dinner, one of them approached me.

"There's a problem in low-grade. Can you help us? It's bed-time, and some of the residents want to stay up and fold laundry."

I shrugged him off with a smile. "Oh, that's not a problem. Bob and I taught some of them how to fold towels and pair socks. Watch."

I waited with the other attendants while the residents worked. When all the towels were folded and the clothes were neatly stacked in the cubbyholes, the attendants were both amazed and suspicious.

A few evenings later after the crew had folded the laundry and the residents were in bed and quiet, Bob and I were sitting in our chairs, leaning up against the wall, talking. We heard a key in the locked door to the corridor. Big Nurse appeared.

"Will you two come into the hallway? I need to talk to you." Outside, she continued, "It's come to my attention that the residents are helping with the laundry."

"Oh, yeah, we taught them to fold the towels and pair the socks. They really like doing that. Henry likes cleaning the bath-room. Have you noticed how neat the day room is? The residents put away the toys before dinner."

Big Nurse turned, walked down the hall, and left the building.

A few days later, Dorothy came in and handed me an envelope. It was a warning for insubordinate behavior. I had violated insurance regulations by having residents work. Bob received one too.

Before bedtime, we explained to our crew that they could not fold laundry. They understood the disappointment in our voices. Lowering their heads, they calmly walked to their beds and went to sleep.

Later, I became angry. I got up early the next morning and waited in the kitchen for Joanne. She appeared just out of the shower, her long brown hair straight and wet. Cat Stevens sang about wanting a hard-headed woman instead of a fancy dancer; Joanne was hard-headed. She was in control and making her way in life. I didn't care for her because she was too demanding. I lost most of our debates, conceding before things got too hot. She was beautiful, though, and I understood why Bob was in love with her.

"Bob and I just got fucked over. Big Nurse gave us a warning for insubordinate behavior. We taught non-functioning residents a meaningful activity. The low-grade residents are functional, and with caring educational programs, they could be taught to live in society."

She brushed me off with a tight smile. "Scott, I'm late for my shift. I don't have time to talk. It was not my decision anyway. If you need to talk with someone, why not go to Big Nurse? I'm sure she'd love to talk with you."

I didn't tell Joanne the residents were being misdiagnosed and overmedicated. I didn't go talk with Big Nurse either.

Our insubordinate behavior was the talk of the state school staff. The workers who liked us and tried to help the residents were sympathetic and quietly supported us. A few days later, as I walked to work, a man about my age with a full red beard and long, straight, shoulder-length red hair came over to me and introduced himself.

"Hi, I'm Alfred. I work over in B Building with highly functional adults. I heard what happened over at G Building. There are a lot of people who know about you and think you are doing good work. Don't let the administration get you down. We all deal with it the best we can."

Alfred and I quickly realized we had pot in common. I ended up spending many afternoons with him and his wife, Harriet, smoking way into the evening. He was my closest friend for many years.

The residents were also my friends. They would walk up to me, touch me, and walk away. I got hugs at bedtime. There were quick glimpses and smiles. Some of the high-grade residents would meet me at the ward door when I showed up for work and walk down the hall with me to low-grade, holding my hand.

I was struggling with my own demons. I was unable to be more intimate than a one or two-night stand. I couldn't deal with emotions that I did not understand, and I needed an unending supply of drugs and alcohol. I was caught in a G Building of my own, unable to get out.

One afternoon, I noticed a few of the residents staring out the windows. I approached Dorothy, the shift nurse.

"How often do low-grade residents get to go outside?"

Though she'd been cold to me when I'd first arrived, Dorothy was a sweetheart. In her mid-forties, she was like a mother to all the residents and the staff. She was the one person on the nursing staff I could relate to.

"Never, where would they go? The only times they leave the building are trips for medical care at the school hospital."

"They never go outside?" I asked again, stunned.

She shook her head. "Never. I don't remember anyone ever going outside this building."

"No wonder these guys are retarded." I twisted my mouth in a smirk.

A resident's world consisted of four locked rooms, a hallway, stairs to the first floor, and a cafeteria where they ate three meals. The residents were in jail, but the state school was the criminal.

The next day, I brought it up with Bob in the low-grade day room. "Bob, how about a field trip? Let's take these kids out for a walk. I saw some of them looking into the woods. Do they even know there is an outside? Maybe they think the windows are big pictures. It would blow their minds, walking around on the other side of the windows."

"Scott, if you can get Dorothy's permission, I'll cover for you."

I walked out of the day room and found Dorothy studying the day medicine chart. I sat down on the swivel chair where she usually sat, folded my hands behind my head, stretched, and smiled.

"Dorothy, I have a proposition for you. I will do anything you want me to do, anytime. No questions asked."

Dorothy looked up from the chart and knitted her brow. "I know I'm going to regret this."

I gave her a big smile and looked around, making sure no one else could hear. "Low-grade. They never go outside. Can you imagine never going outside? I want to take them outside for a walk around G Building."

Dorothy sat on the nurse's station desk and folded her arms. "Scott, you're trouble. I think you're too smart for your own good.

Who do you think you're going to take outside?"

"I'll pick seven of the kids I trust the most. Henry's the smartest. Clifford and Wayne are always trying to get out the front door at dinner time; let's give them a chance to see what's out there. Johnny C. is so curious about everything. I can't take Johnny C. without Johnny John, they are the best of friends. Malcolm is my buddy. And Craig, he seems so sad, maybe it will cheer him up. If you're worried about any of them, chose someone you think will benefit from a walk outside. It'll only be for a short time, half an hour or so."

Dorothy thought about it. I'm sure she was thinking about repercussions if Big Nurse found out.

I begged, "I'll say I did it on my own. I didn't ask you. You knew nothing about it."

With a deep breath, Dorothy raised her hands to her face and rubbed her eyes. "Okay, but we never had this conversation."

"Never."

I knew I was taking a big risk. I was already on shaky ground at the school. But to give a few kids an adventure, kids that had nothing—what good was this job if I couldn't take that small risk?

I found coats for seven kids, dressed them warmly, and took them down the elevator and out the front door. They were a little apprehensive at first, but when I took them around to the woods that they could see from the dayroom windows, they relaxed and began to explore. They walked over to the trees and felt them. They bent down and touched the ground. They spent an hour outside. Two of them peed their pants, but they might have done that on the ward. No big thing.

That evening was wonderful. Bob and I got hugs from our seven adventurers as they calmly prepared for bed. They were happy.

We never got the chance to take the residents outside again.

On the Tuesday evening before Thanksgiving, low-grade retarded was quiet. I realized the call for dinner was late. I unlocked the door to the main hallway and peeked out. There was a commotion in high-grade, shrieks and screams coming from the dayroom. A crowd of nurses and attendants had gathered, including Big Nurse. I left Henry in charge of the bedroom and strolled up to the crowd.

I asked, "What's up?"

An attendant whispered, "One of the residents broke a window in the dayroom."

"I'm not surprised at that."

Big Nurse turned and confronted me. "And why are you not surprised, Mr. Hunter?"

I cheerfully explained, "Well, it's Thanksgiving. All the pictures of ghosts and pumpkins on the walls and windows for Halloween created a lot of excitement. For Thanksgiving, pictures of turkeys, pilgrims, and Indians went up. I'll bet you that there was a picture of something taped to the window that was broken."

One of the attendants piped up. "How did you know?"

I didn't answer the question. I knew these kids. They wanted to do everything the staff did. They didn't distinguish between staff taping a picture on a window or wall and pounding a fist on a picture on a window. They didn't know the window would break.

"And I bet everyone has been eating sugary treats all day. I know what the sugar in a pint of ice cream does to me. I avoid straight candy because it gives me a whole lot of energy, makes me crazy. Twenty minutes later, I calm right down. I see the residents running around like crazy after they're allowed to eat the candy that's around for holidays. They are no different than I am."

That gave Big Nurse pause.

I went on. "With the activity and emotional levels in the ward, I think one of the residents saw an attendant taping pictures on the windows and decided to tape a few up himself. He probably pounded a few windows with his fist, hit one too hard and broke it. Not a big deal. I'm sure it wasn't malicious, just an accident."

Big Nurse asked, "And I suppose you know who did it?"

"I can find out. I have a good relationship with the guys. All I have to do is ask them."

With her feet planted apart and hands on her hips, Big Nurse was not a small presence. She was a big woman—not as tall as me, but she outweighed me. She stared me down for a moment, then said, "Okay."

"If that's what you want, I need all the staff to leave the dayroom and all the residents to remain. I need to go in there alone. Lock the door behind me and wait until I come out. And you have to promise me that whoever broke the window will not be punished."

I didn't present a strong front to strong women often. My mother's dominance in the family hadn't helped with my confidence when challenged by anyone, let alone a powerful woman. Occasionally, though, the courage to stand up to authority kicked in. I stared Big Nurse down.

She conceded, "Alright, Mr. Hunter, go in there and find out what happened."

I went into the room alone and heard the door lock behind me. Some of the residents were grouped together in the corners, talking and chirping. Some were yelling, running around, whooping it up and having a good old time. Others were by themselves, performing the ritual behaviors they displayed whenever they were uncomfortable and uncommunicative.

I found a place by myself, pulled up one of the plastic chairs, and sat down. Staff never sat down, always standing in a dominant position. Sitting, I became just another resident. I began watching for the non-verbal cues the residents used as language.

Soon, everyone was watching me. It was hard to follow all the cues being tossed around. There was a lot of eye contact, gestures, sounds, and movement. I got up, slowly arranged some chairs together, sat in the biggest one, and continued my own ritual behavior, rocking back and forth, moving my head from side to side. Sitting in the chair where the alpha residents usually sat, I was one of them—the alpha male.

Soon, everyone became quiet and calm. I knew the residents were getting hungry, waiting for dinner. I waited. After minutes went by, the most functional of the residents, Joshua, whom I affectionately thought of as Boss Man, came over and sat next to me. His facial features were those of a Down syndrome child: small chin, slanted eyes, and flat nose. He was heavy-set, more jolly than flabby. He was helpful and always happy. He looked around the room, almost regally, caught my eye, then continued to look around. He caught my eye again, raising an eyebrow. I raised my eyebrow as a question. He looked in the general direction of a group of residents who were huddled together in a corner.

I noticed that Tommy, a shy little kid who usually sat by himself, seemed more frightened than the rest. I walked over, sat down, put my arms around him, and hugged him. He buried his head into my shoulder.

After a short time, I stood up, pulled Tommy up, and walked

with him over to the window. I looked into his eyes and gave him a big hug.

Quietly, I repeated, "It's okay. It's okay."

He looked up at me.

I touched the window and said, "Ouch." I laughed and made a funny face.

He made a funny face.

I asked, "You?"

He lowered his head, then nodded.

With a big hug, I said, "Everything is going to be alright."

I heard soft murmurs from the residents in the dayroom. Everyone was at ease. I walked Tommy back to his group, and we all had a group hug. I went over to Joshua and gave him a big hug. I turned back to the residents in the dayroom, smiled, bowed, walked to the locked door, and knocked. It opened.

"It's time to eat."

The attendants began ushering all the residents into the hall, through the doors, and down to the dining area.

Big Nurse glared at me.

I walked over to her and got a reassurance. "You promise me the resident who broke the window will not be punished, right? Everyone will be treated as if nothing happened, right?"

"Yes, Mr. Hunter, everything will be taken care of."

I told her, "It was Tommy."

The next evening, as I strolled through the high-grade wing of G Building, I noticed that Tommy was not on the ward. I asked Dorothy where he was.

She let out a big sigh. "Big Nurse moved Tommy to another building."

The next day, I walked past the secretary and into Big

Nurse's office.

"You moved Tommy to another building? You're punishing Tommy."

Her eyes turned hard. "Thank you for discovering who broke the window. But you don't make the rules. I make the rules. Moving Tommy to a new building isn't punishment. It's precautionary."

I was undeterred. "To Tommy, moving out of G Building was more than punishment. You took him away from his friends, away from the only home he knew, out of his comfort zone, to a foreign place. You don't understand what the lives of the residents are like. You warehouse them in crowded dormitories and dayrooms with no activities, with no way to better their lives. They never go outside. They're drugged so that they won't cause problems."

Big Nurse stared at me, scowling. "You may leave now, Mr. Hunter."

The next evening, an envelope was waiting for me. I was being blamed for breaking the window, a second warning of insubordinate behavior. Even though it was a lie, what could I do? Big Nurse made the rules.

Christmas and the New Year were observed with decorations and parties, but we managed to keep everything peaceful. On the third Sunday of January, I arrived at work looking forward to spending time with my friends. The floor was very quiet as I entered the nurse's station to sign in. I greeted Dorothy.

"How was the weekend?"

She looked up from the charts in front of her. Her eyes were slightly red. She looked like she had been crying. "You didn't hear what happened?"

I felt a chill up my spine. "No, what?"

"Gerald died. He choked on his food last night and died."

I was shocked, devastated. Gerry was one of the least-functioning residents, but he was a good person. I had worked with him for three months.

"How much Thorazine was he on?"

By the look on her face, I knew that was the wrong question to ask, or the right one. She stared at me for a moment, glancing at the charts she'd been looking at when I came in.

She didn't answer the question. "Scott, go down to low-grade, lock yourself in, and stay out of sight."

I found Bob in the dayroom of low-grade, leaning against a window. He had worked the weekend and looked sad and tired.

"Bob, what happened?"

He shook his head slowly. "Last night was very calm. We walked the residents down to dinner, the usual unappetizing stew—chunks of meat, lumpy mashed potatoes, over-cooked vegetables. Dessert was a soggy piece of cake. Gerry was eating when he began to cough. By the time we realized he was choking, he was off his chair, on his back, struggling to breathe. A couple of us tried to clear his throat, but couldn't reach all the food. By the time help arrived, Gerry had stopped breathing. The medical staff whisked him away. Later, we learned he died." Bob turned and looked out the window. After a couple of heaves of his chest, I knew he was crying. He wiped his eyes and looked up. "Scott, it was a combination of Thorazine and the shit food Gerry was eating."

The next Sunday evening, I went back to work and found out that Melanie, one of the low-functioning female residents, had choked on her food and died. Everyone was devastated. I quickly went to the dayroom and found Bob. The story was the same.

Neither Gerry nor Melanie were in on our drug-reduction therapy. We'd heard talk that Gerry had a history of anger, but he was so low-functioning, we were not sure why he couldn't have been cared for without Thorazine. Bob talked to a friend who worked the second floor. She confirmed that the nurses handed out a lot of medicine to the residents and that Melanie had gotten doses of something twice a day.

Monday morning, I was eating cereal at the kitchen table when Joanne came down stairs and began making coffee. When she finally looked at me, I could see her eyes were red. She'd been crying too.

"Joanne, this is horrible. It's almost too much. Gerry was such a good kid. Never any trouble. What's your take? They choked on some food?"

Joanne sat down across from me and folded her hands. "That's what the report will probably say. You're lucky it happened on your day off. I know Big Nurse, I mean Christine, blamed you for the broken window in the day room. That was wrong. The first thing she said to me on Sunday day shift was, 'Was Mr. Hunter working last night?' Everyone's upset and she's looking for someone to blame."

She took a deep breath. "Bob and I are quitting. We're talking about getting married, moving to California, and starting our life together there. You should quit too. It's not worth working at the bottom of the Belchertown ladder. There are better jobs with better pay. And the shit's about to hit the fan."

It was the first decent conversation with Joanne since I'd

moved in. She took a couple of sips of her coffee. I ate my cereal. We sat in silence. When Joanne finished, she got up, washed her cup out, and put it into the dish drainer. Then she walked over to me and put her hand on my shoulder.

"I have to get to work. Scott, I know what you and Bob have been doing. It's good work. I guess I should have supported you more. I've been working there eight months. Everybody else has been there forever. No one wanted to hear what I had to say. I'm sorry I took it out on you."

I took her hand from my shoulder and squeezed it. "Joanne, I understand. It's a bad place to work. Like you say, everyone who has authority has been there too long. Change will come. Take care of the residents. I'll be okay."

I finished my cereal and went out into the backyard and smoked a jay. Joanne and Bob were quitting. I wondered who else. I wasn't going to go quietly. They would have to fire me.

On Wednesday, we found out what was going to happen. Bob and I got warnings for smoking marijuana during working hours. We'd never smoked at work. When I told Alfred, my friend in B Building, he said, "A lot of the staff in my building smoke pot. The other buildings, too. You don't have to go far to find pot at the school. I think you're being set up."

By the weekend, Joanne and Bob had given their letters of resignation to Big Nurse. They heard that since I was refusing to quit, I would be urged to resign. I told them the school would have to fire me.

Luckily, I had become friends with the union representative over beers and joints at the Buck and Doe. Michael had worked at the school forever, supported the staff, and was very sympathetic toward the residents. When I saw him sitting at a booth,

I bought two beers, placed one in front of him, sat down, and took a sip of mine.

"Michael, you know those deaths were waiting to happen. The food is terrible, but that's only half the problem. The staff has no training. The nurses are giving the kids huge doses of Thorazine."

Michael was in his forties, short hair, always dressed in button-down shirts and nice slacks. You wouldn't know he was a pot smoker by looking at him. He was a family guy with a couple of young kids. He worked with the highest functioning residents in A Building.

He looked surprised. "Thorazine?"

"You don't know that they hand it out to the residents like candy to keep them in line?"

Michael looked around to see if anyone was listening. I leaned closer to him across the table.

"Bob and I found out how much Thorazine the kids in low-grade were getting. We taught some residents to tongue their pills. They started to wake up. We had nothing to do with Gerry's death. He wasn't on our team. Because of the three warnings I've received, I'm sure I'm going to get fired. Michael, people have to know what's going on."

When I finished, Michael lifted his glass, touched mine with a clink, raised it to his lips, and took a large gulp.

"Well, Scott, if you had been working at the school long enough to have union representation, I would be able to advise you to appeal your firing and demand a hearing. But you haven't. Sorry."

He took another gulp of beer and continued, "If you get a hearing from the secretary at the director's office, you have to get what you think on the record. People have to know. I can't represent you, but I can show up and be there for you, unofficially, of course."

A few days later, an impatient Joanne approached me: "Have you written your letter of resignation? Christine doesn't want to have to fire you."

It was obvious whose side she was on. This conversation wasn't as friendly as the one over coffee and cereal. I could be tough, too.

"Screw Big Nurse. Tell her I want a termination hearing."

The next day, I was called over to Christine's office and given a letter of termination. I refused it and demanded the required termination hearing. Thursday evening when I appeared at G Building, I was told to go home. I was fired.

I went to the main administration building and found the wood and glass door to the director's office and demanded a termination hearing.

Dr. William Jones, who'd been the director of Belchertown State School for less than a month, scheduled my hearing a week out.

Over the weekend, I was stretched out on my bed reading when Joanne poked her head into my room. She looked scared.

"Scott, Nurse McNamara asked me to be a witness to your third warning for smoking pot on the ward. I know it's bogus, and that you're being framed, but Christine is going to give me good references when I leave if I do this. If I don't, she won't. I don't want to do this, but..."

I interrupted her. "Hey, don't worry. I understand where you're at. Big Nurse will screw anyone who goes against her. We've had our differences, but we're friends. I got the hearing all planned out. You get up and say what Christine wants you to say."

"I'm sorry, Scott."

The day of the hearing arrived. Dr. Jones, in his early fifties, refined and well-dressed in a dark suit, his dark brown hair beginning to gray, sat behind a big desk in a high-backed leather chair. Christine, radiating contempt for the hearing, sat on his left with Joanne. A group of people I didn't recognize sat on his right. They were introduced as members of the Friends of Belchertown State School. The Friends, which began in 1954, had become an advocacy group for patients when the father of a resident was elected president in 1969. I was happy to see some possibly neutral people in the room. That was to my advantage.

Dr. Jones opened the proceedings, "Thank you all for coming. This is a termination hearing for Scott Hunter. I'd like to introduce Christine McNamara, the head nurse and administrator of the school's nursery and G Building, where high and low-grade residents live, and where the latest two deaths occurred. She will speak first."

Big Nurse stood up. "I have issued three warnings for insubordinate behavior to Mr. Hunter. That's grounds for firing. The first warning was for disregarding insurance regulations. The second was for destroying state property. I would like Joanne Kovak, the psychologist in G Building, to speak to the third warning."

Joanne stood up. "Mr. Hunter received a third warning for insubordinate behavior for smoking marijuana on state property. Thank you." She sat down.

Dr. Jones turned to me. "Mr. Hunter, Massachusetts state employment regulations stipulate three warnings of insubordinate behavior are cause for termination. You are no longer an employee of the Belchertown State School. This case is closed."

I stood up. "Wait. I have something to say."

The room was dead silent until Christine protested, "He hasn't worked for six months. He's not entitled to question his termination."

"I'm not questioning my termination. I'm fired. I'll leave the property and never return. I just want you to listen to what I have to say."

Michael spoke up. "I don't represent Mr. Hunter, but I've talked with him. What he has to say needs to be heard. I think it's very important."

When Big Nurse began to protest again, Dr. Jones stopped her. "Mr. Hunter's request is not unreasonable." With a nod of his head, he said, "Proceed."

I took a deep breath and looked at everyone in the room. "Thank you all for coming today and allowing me this opportunity to explain what I've experienced as an attendant in the low-grade retarded section of G Building. I spent the first two weeks in a single large room with no privacy where twenty residents sleep. I wasn't provided with keys to lock or unlock the door. For those two weeks, I felt more like a resident than an attendant."

One of the Friends asked, "Why didn't they give you a key?"

I smiled. "I think you need to ask Nurse McNamara that question."

Christine responded angrily, "I knew nothing about that. This is the first I've heard about it."

I continued, "I had hours with nowhere to go until someone unlocked the door and I could leave, so I observed the residents' body language, the sounds they made, and their relationships with each other. As I interacted with them, I began to see them as people with mental health issues and learning disabilities, rather than high-grade and low-grade retarded patients. I thought if they were provided with educational programs, they could become functioning members of society. The psychologists weren't interested in my understanding of the residents' mental health. I was told I was an attendant, not paid to think."

Another of the Friends spoke up: "What were the psychologists doing while you were locked up?"

"I was working second shift, four to twelve. Miss Kovak worked the first shift. You need to ask her."

Joanne squirmed in her seat. "We conducted educational programs in the morning and afternoon. Mainly, I worked with the residents in the high-grade section. They were the most functional. We were able to obtain observable results with them. The low-grade residents, the ones Scott worked with, were low-functioning residents. Their ability to learn was minimal. We felt it was more important to work with the more functional residents."

I countered Joanne. "The reason why the low-grade residents are so low-functioning is that there are no programs to educate them. They're not encouraged to do anything. There's no stimulation in their environment. They're living in a warehouse, one big room. They have beds without partitions, no pictures on walls, stark day rooms with plastic institutional furniture, barren hallways and stairways, open toilets and showers. They're served institutional food. It could be healthier. They have no possessions, no clothes of their own. They never go outside unless it's to the hospital."

I noticed the reactions of the Friends. They were distressed, unaware that the residents never went outside. They began to talk among themselves.

I took a deep breath. "There's another problem. The residents are given high doses of Thorazine that affect their abilities to function and communicate."

Christine began to stand, but Dr. Jones motioned for her to sit down. Joanne began to fidget. The guests in the room became wide-eyed.

"Overmedication is the real problem in G building. With lower doses of Thorazine, more attention from the staff, and more educational programs, the residents' quality of life could improve dramatically."

The Friends began to ask questions all at once. I put up my hand to stop them.

"Please, let me continue. Another aide and I took it upon ourselves to teach a few residents not to swallow their Thorazine pills and give them to us for disposal."

At this confession, I heard a collective gasp and felt Christine's eyes on me.

"I admit this was an egregious act of insubordination, but it created a positive result in the residents' lives. Their behavior improved substantially. The violent behavior used to justify the use of Thorazine was avoided by paying more attention to the residents when they needed it. As we weaned the residents off their medication, they became more conscious and expressive. They stopped drooling. These residents can learn meaningful activities. I was given a warning for insubordination for teaching them to fold towels and sort clothing. I'm sure you are aware that two residents of G Building recently died. I suspect that high doses of drugs may have assisted in their inability to swallow their food."

The Friends were visibly shaken and began to cry out: "Is this true?" and "Why are you giving the residents Thorazine at all?"

Christine and Joanne dropped their heads. Dr. Jones leaned back in his chair, one hand cupping his chin. I'm sure he was thinking about the work that was ahead of him.

I finished, "I know Gerry's dosage was extremely high because I looked at the nurse's charts after he died. I don't know Melanie's dosage, but I suspect it was also very high. Considering the medication and the quality of the food, I'm surprised that more residents don't choke on their food." I bowed to everyone, as a sign of respect. "Dr. Jones, friends, Nurse McNamara, Miss Kovak, Michael, thank you for the opportunity to speak."

The deaths of the two G Building residents and two other deaths were added to a 1972 class-action suit on behalf of the residents against the Massachusetts Department of Mental Health. That suit led to the closing of Belchertown State School and the creation of a system of residential housing within the community for those with disabilities. The language used to describe the former residents of G Building and all people with learning disabilities changed.

I was deeply affected by my time at G Building. I'd felt compassion for the residents and had worked hard to improve their lives. I emerged from Belchertown State School with no direction. Lost and alone, I smoked more pot. Though it erased many of my difficulties and cares, avoiding reality didn't solve any of my problems.

chapter 12

Even though I was now unemployed, I was not without money. I got stock dividend checks in the mail from a small inheritance I'd received when my grandmother died. Since my only expenses were rent, food, and marijuana, I didn't need much to live on. Without a car, I hitchhiked everywhere. I was growing my beard and hair again, so I didn't need shaves and haircuts. The spring of 1973 arrived; I was about to turn twenty-eight, and I began to look for something meaningful to do with my life. I moved into a house across town, further into the woods. I spent my mornings swimming in the creek below my new home and most afternoons smoking pot with my friend Alfred from BSS and his wife, Harriet. My evenings were spent with members of the band Home Comfort, either at their house or the gig they were playing in town.

One afternoon I saw an ad in the *Valley Advocate*, the local alternative newspaper, for managers of the Blue Moon Food Co-op. My fantasy of leading a revolution reared its head. A revolutionary army needs food. And a co-operative? It sounded like healthy socialism to me.

When I went to the co-op in a back alley off the main drag in Amherst to get an application, I learned that it was in financial difficulty. Their way to solve their problem was to hire three managers. That didn't make sense to me, but I showed up at the membership meeting that Saturday to interview in front of the members. Discovering I was the only applicant for the three positions, I figured I had a job.

It wasn't that easy. The president of the co-op, Chris, tall, bearded with long hair, dressed in a multicolored tie-dye outfit, chaired the meeting. He looked at me, a stranger, and spoke to the membership.

"We don't even know this guy. Doesn't anyone in the co-op want to manage us?"

I spoke up. "I graduated from Amherst College and have a master's degree in divinity. If I can get through Amherst and graduate school, I can handle a co-op. Food is very important, and we need to get food to the people inexpensively. Co-ops are the way to do it."

Finally, two other guys, Sam and Mike, volunteered. Sam, the current manager with three kids hanging all over him, wanted to quit and start his own soap company. Mike, with a full black beard, was the cross-country coach at the high school.

Sam said, "If Mike will be the other manager, I'll stay on."

Then, Chris raised the question, "Do we need three managers? Can we do it with two?"

After a short, closed discussion between Chris, Sam, and Mike, Chris addressed the meeting, "Well, we're going to have three managers, Sam, Mike, and Scott. Let's take a vote."

The three of us were voted in as managers. I felt a little awkward, almost not getting the job despite being the only candidate, but I was determined as ever. I spent the rest of the meeting introducing myself to all the members.

The following week, I found out why I was hired. Sam and Mike didn't show up much, except to pick up their paychecks and to forage for free food. I wanted to question them about their behavior, but they intimidated me. Because I was new, I had neither the confidence nor the courage to stand up to them. I learned a lot as a manager, but too many people were stealing food. Chris, the president, and his girlfriend, the treasurer, controlled the checkbook. I saw what needed to be done—raise prices, waste less, and keep hands out of the cookie jar—but I had no real power. Sam and Mike always outvoted me two to one.

At a Fourth of July Home Comfort concert, I got the idea to hold a benefit concert in August. The bands would be Home Comfort, to whom I was supplying dope, and two bands they gigged with, NRBQ and Big Screamin' McGrew. *Food and concerts,* I thought, *what better way to organize America?*

I talked Amherst College into providing their observatory lawn for the concert for free. They must've figured when I eventually grew up, I'd be a rich alumnus and would remember their kindness to me as a young aspiring hippie.

On the day of the concert, I stationed myself with some helpers at the entrance to the observatory and collected five dollars from everyone. Fifteen hundred concert goers, $6,000. I talked Home Comfort and NRBQ into playing for $750 each. Big Screamin' McGrew, the headliner, got a thousand. After expenses, the co-op might make $3,000.

Toward the end of the concert, we were cleaning up around the entrance. The president of the co-op showed up, excited about something.

"Where's the money we made? I want the money."

I was busy and not really paying attention. "Chris, calm down. I've got everything under control. We made a ton of money. I arranged to pay the bands after the concert, then we'll figure out how much we made."

Chris wouldn't have it. His eyes lit up and he yelled at me. "I want the money. I'll pay the bands. I'm the president. I'll put it in the bank on Monday."

The people helping me clean up stepped back when they heard Chris yell. His anger frightened me, and I wilted in front of him.

I pulled the wads of money out of my pocket and said, "Here. I already told the bands how much they were going to get."

He snatched the money and headed up the road to the concert site without a word. I turned to the other co-op members and shrugged my shoulders. It was out of my hands now.

On Monday, I stopped by Amherst College grounds crew's office and said, "I want to thank you guys for all of your help. The concert was great, and the co-op made some money."

The head of grounds replied, "We're happy to help the local community and alumni. Our only expense was $100 for the fencing. If the co-op could cover that, we'll call it even. Okay?"

This was a very reasonable request for their generosity.

"No problem, sir, I'm on my way to the co-op now. I'll be back this afternoon."

We shook hands over a job well done.

When I got to the co-op, I was all smiles. Sam and Mike had frowns on their faces. Chris and his girlfriend weren't around.

Puzzled, I asked, "Why all the frowns? We made a lot of money."

Sam looked up at me. "Chris thought we made more money than we did. The bands talked him into paying their expenses on top of what they agreed to with you. And then there were our expenses. We made less than a thousand dollars."

I was shocked. "What expenses did the co-op have?"

When they mumbled something, I tried to press them for a better answer, but they shut me down: "It's none of your business, Scott. It's just the way it is."

I wondered if someone hadn't taken some money for themselves, but I didn't have the courage to confront them.

I went and talked with my friends in Home Comfort. They felt no responsibility for taking more money than we had agreed on. I was pissed at Chris and felt used by my friends in the band. I planned to raise hell at the annual meeting and tell the membership my four ideas to lower expenses: get rid of two managers (specifically, Sam and Mike); call out Chris and his girlfriend about their control of the checkbook; deal with food spoilage and theft; and raise prices to cover expenses.

At the start of the meeting, Chris beat me to the punch: "Scott is not a good manager. He won't co-operate with Sam and Mike. They've tried to teach Scott how to manage the co-op, but he has his own ideas and won't listen. His concert didn't make any money."

Before I could react, a motion to fire me was quickly raised from the back of the crowd. I was stunned. The motion was quickly seconded and approved. I looked at Chris, Sam, and Mike. We traded daggers. I scanned the membership. They seemed unconcerned. No one would look at me. As the vote was being taken, I walked out of the meeting. That was the last they saw of me.

I was unemployed again. How could this keep happening to

me? Did the world have it out for me? Was it something I was doing to myself? Whatever the answer was, I wasn't going to let it get me down. I had Mom's persistence. I had Dad's intelligence. I had to figure my way out of this predicament.

While working at the co-op, I discovered Llama, Toucan, & Crow, Inc., the natural foods distribution company in Greenfield, Massachusetts. I had met a couple of their truck drivers. Deep in my mind, I set my sights on a class-one driver's license. Maybe I could organize America from the cab of a semi-trailer, like the camel drivers atop the caravans who'd helped the Israelites conquer Palestine.

I walked uptown from the co-op meeting and wandered into a concert on the Amherst Common. I shared some pot with the members of Seagull, a soft rock band. Seagull lived in the Dexter House, a three-story Victorian with a large barn in Wendell Depot, a crossroads in the middle of nowhere. There was a wonderful room available on the third floor. Without hesitation, I rented it.

When I arrived on Labor Day to move in, my new housemates gave me a hit of LSD, the first since my experience at the Rainbow Gathering. I sat on the front porch listening to Seagull perform for their friends. On one of the posts supporting the roof over the porch, someone had carved the initials H. S. I flashed back to the upside-down initials on my suitcase at the Rainbow Gathering. I was a far cry from the panic in that hotel room in Granby, Colorado. No longer scared and alone, I was among friends, where I was supposed to be, happily stoned at home.

Though I felt relaxed and at home at the Dexter House, I needed something spiritual to counter the guilt I felt all the time.

The day after the Labor Day weekend, I walked into the Wendell Depot Post Office, a two-room building; one side a five-stool café that served coffee and donuts to the locals and the other side a tiny office stuffed with mail bags and boxes around an early twentieth century bank of 100 P.O. boxes.

After I rented a P.O. box, I sat down at the café counter, asked for a cup of coffee, and met Elwood Babbitt, who said he was a clairvoyant who channeled knowledge of past lives. A wizened, weather-beaten old man, Elwood could have been as old as some of the past lives he channeled. After talking with him for a while, I hoped he could provide some spiritual direction, but as he described his modus operandi, going into a trance and telling people they used to be princes and princesses, I decided he was a bit too much even for my drug-addled mind.

I left, still desperate for spiritual guidance.

I searched shelves at The Sirius Bookstore, a new spiritual bookstore in Amherst, built with boards from the Dexter House barn. I found *How to Construct a Teepee*. It seemed perfect. I would sew together a teepee, a conical structure that concentrated spiritual energy, and move, legally or not, into Wendell State Forest, the most convenient wilderness. It didn't matter what religion I latched onto—Christianity, Buddhism, or Native American spirituality—I would be in nature. I decided I could only find meaning in the wilderness. That was where Jesus found his calling, after all.

That autumn, I also read two books by Carlos Castaneda, *The Teachings of Don Juan: a Yaqui Way of Knowledge* and *A Separate Reality*. His introduction to Yaqui witches and warriors and the Yaqui way of life sounded like the Druid beliefs I had read about in *The White Goddess* by Robert Graves. I began to sense that there were basic spiritual truths common to all beliefs. I embraced parts of Castaneda's story.

Castaneda had one experience, burying three seeds and encountering the Yaqui Spirit, that really caught my attention. He was not getting anywhere with his spiritual development, and asked Don Juan, his spiritual guide, about the Yaqui Spirit: "You say it appears to guide people who are lost and confused. I am struggling, Don Juan. I think if I met the Yaqui Spirit, it would help me."

Don Juan replied evasively, "Carlos, it is very difficult to meet the Yaqui Spirit."

Bewildered and distraught, Carlos pleaded, "Don Juan, I am desperate. I'm stuck here. How do I get to a higher understanding?"

With a sigh, Don Juan relented. "Ah, Carlos, you need patience. But I see that you're struggling. Find three seeds. Plant them. Ask the Yaqui Spirit to appear. Within three days, the Yaqui spirit will appear to you in the form of three people to guide you."

Castaneda found three seeds, planted them, and asked the Yaqui Spirit to reveal itself. For two days, nothing happened. On the third day, Castaneda was driving along a deserted road when he noticed a commotion ahead blocking the road. As he got closer, he saw three people, two men and a woman, disheveled and dirty. They were jumping around, yelling, and acting crazy, forcing him to stop his car. They ran up to him, pounding on his car hood.

"Take us to the next town. We need to get there fast. Help us, please."

The next town was 120 miles down the road, and Castaneda was hesitant about traveling with three crazy people. He decided to not give them a ride.

Shortly after driving away, Castaneda remembered the three seeds he had planted three days earlier. Suddenly, he realized the crazy people were the Yaqui Spirit. He turned his car around and raced back to the spot where he had encountered them. When he arrived, there was no one to be seen.

I decided to empirically test for the existence of Spirit, maybe the Wendell Depot Spirit. A three-day Veteran's Day weekend was coming up, and I was going to visit friends in Boston. I went to the Hadley Garden Center, bought three tulip bulbs, and took them back to the Dexter House. On Friday morning, I knelt down and planted them in the garden near the front porch. I raised my arms to the sun, palms up.

"Spirit, I pray to you. I am a seeker of the meaning of life. I am struggling. I am lost and confused. I bury these three bulbs in the hope that in three days I will meet the Spirit and it will guide me to understanding. Thank you very much."

After I bowed my head in a moment of silence, I climbed up the hillside over the guardrail on the Route 2 bridge over Wendell Depot, hitchhiked into Boston, and spent the weekend with my friends.

On Monday morning, I headed back to Wendell Depot. My first ride let me off at the rotary near the Alewife Station in Cambridge on Route 2, a difficult and dangerous place to hitchhike. I walked down the road to a place where it was a little easier for a car to pull off and pick me up. As I turned and stuck out my thumb, a horn beeped behind me. A Volvo sedan had stopped. I ran to the car as its back door was opening and jumped in. Immediately, the car pulled away from the curb.

"Hey, thanks for the ride. I'm headed to Greenfield, Massachusetts, about sixty miles down the road."

I settled into the back seat and looked up. Sitting next to me was a beautiful brunette dressed in a full skirt and colorful embroidered blouse. Two rugged-looking young men sat in the front seat, staring straight ahead.

The woman replied, "We're going right through Greenfield on our way to Saxon Bridge, in Vermont."

As I did with everyone who picked me up hitching, I began to tell my story: "I'm heading into the wilderness to discover my spirituality. I plan to sew together a teepee and live in the forest. The teepee is a conical structure that will focus the spiritual energy into me. I want to find my spiritual self."

They were stealing glances at me now with strange looks on their faces.

I rambled on, "Hey, you're three people. I planted three bulbs three days ago and asked to meet the Spirit, like a spirit guide to help me." I told them about the teachings of Don Juan and the story of Castaneda and the Yaqui Spirit. I laughed, "So the three of you, you must be the Spirit I'm supposed to meet."

The three of them looked at me with amazement. The driver turned back towards the front and concentrated on his driving. The other man in the front seat and the woman next to me continued to stare.

Finally, the woman said, "We have a business in Saxon Bridge. We teach people to sew teepees together."

Now, I was amazed.

She continued, "I'm Roselyn, Maxwell is driving, and Frank is the best sewer of the three of us. You should come to our farm and live with us for a few days.

"You'll do well to live in a teepee. We'll teach you how to sew, use a sewing palm to protect your hand from the needle. Ten-ounce duck canvas, sail cloth, is very thick; sewing it will make your hands strong. We will sell you the equipment you need, order the canvas for you, and deliver it to you. The cost to you, $120."

I almost yelled, "Sign me up. I'm going to live in a teepee."

At the end of January, I went to Saxon Bridge and learned to sew. Seams in the canvas were formed by interlocking each piece, so when you sewed the canvas together, you sewed through four layers. Then you waxed the seam, so water didn't seep through. It was laborious. Thousands of stitches were going to make my hands strong.

After learning to sew, I returned home. The next week, Roselyn and Maxwell dropped off the canvas for my teepee at the Dexter House, along with the equipment to put it together. When they left, I stood by the garden in front of the Dexter House where I buried the bulbs and prayed.

"Thank you, Spirit, for introducing me to Roselyn, Maxwell, and Frank."

I spent all of February, from a new moon to a new moon, sewing together a sixteen-foot diameter canvas teepee. In the spring, a bouquet of beautiful tulips appeared in the garden.

chapter 13

While sewing my teepee together, I thought about the paper I had written on Moses and the Israelite revolution. The Israelites had conquered all the Pharaonic city-states along the Palestine coast of the Mediterranean Sea by utilizing the commercial transportation system of that time, donkey and camel caravans, as a communication infrastructure to infiltrate each of the city-states. If I learned the modern-day commercial transportation system, I thought I could be the technician who engineered the ground game for the new American Revolution. I wasn't Lenin—writer, speaker, motivator of others. I was more of a nuts and bolts guy. The mechanical side of the revolution was where I belonged.

In August, before I'd moved into the Dexter House, Mom and Dad had stopped by to belatedly celebrate my June birthday and Dad's in August. They had been in Troy to close on the sale of my grandparents' house. It was a sad time for Dad, but we celebrated our birthdays with a dinner at The Lord Jeffery Inn. The white linen tablecloths gracing the tables at the inn sparked memories of meals in the dining room at the old house. I wonder now what they thought about my long hair and beard. They said nothing, but I'm sure they were concerned.

When there was a lull in the conversation, I found the courage to ask, "Mom and Dad, I'd like a special birthday present this year. I've always wanted to drive tractor-trailers. I need a thousand dollars for the tuition to the New England Tractor-Trailer Training School. I know that's a lot of money, but that's what it would cost to get a class-one driver's license. It would mean a lot to me."

Mother's eyes opened wide. She looked around the room and then back to me. "You want to drive tractor-trailers? You have a degree to be a minister. I thought you wanted to...be... be a minister?"

I replied, "Mom, I've always wanted to drive tractors on the farm, like cousins Bobby, Jackie, and Johnny. Tractor-trailers are bigger and better."

When I was a kid, we'd spent weekends on the two farms owned by Mom's parents and her brother John. Baba, Lithuanian for grandma, was scary. She was a big plump ball of a grandmother. She spoke Lithuanian, no English. When we played canasta, she got angry when she lost. I knew not to cross her. At her egg farm in Slippery Rock, Pennsylvania, she spent all day cooking over a huge cast iron coal stove, like the one I imagined was in the gingerbread house where Hansel and Gretel met the witch. Her first two husbands died, worked to death in the steel mills of Pittsburgh and the coal mines of western Pennsylvania. Her third sat on the porch, spat tobacco juice, and swore. He looked like someone who had worked in a coal mine all his life and had suffered for it—dirty, bent, and misshapen. He never said much, but when he did, there was hell to pay. I never crossed him either.

Baba's farmhouse was tiny—one floor with a kitchen, living room, and three small rooms big enough for a bed and dresser. No bathroom, just an outhouse in the front yard. I made sure I pooped before we left home. Pooping in the outhouse was impossible, and long weekends were the worst.

Uncle Johnny, my mother's brother, and Aunt Esther's farm was three miles away. They had an indoor toilet, a complete lifesaver, but their farm was not the happy place I wanted it to be. My cousins, three brothers all older than me, ran the place. They were workers—strong, determined, in control. I was the bookworm, a weakling, a weekend wannabee, the butt of their jokes. It had always been my dream to drive the tractor through the fields and down to the swimming hole on Slippery Rock Creek. I'd never been strong enough to find a hand and foot hold on to it. I'd run behind it down to the creek and watch my cousins jump into it naked. I was too skinny and afraid to let them see me.

"Mom, Bobby, Jackie, and Johnny drive tractor-trailers now. They make a living. I understand the importance of food to peoples' lives. I learned a lot managing the food co-op. I heard about a company up in Greenfield that delivers food all over New England. Maybe I can get a job there."

Dad was quiet, sitting with his hands folded on the linen tablecloth. Mom looked at him. "Scott, what do you think?"

Much to my relief, he said, "Emmy, I think it's a good idea. If Scott wants to drive tractor-trailers, I think we should help him do that."

I was surprised that I was going to get a birthday present that

I wanted. That rarely happened. I'd usually gotten school clothes. I suspect that Dad might have wanted to drive tractor-trailers, too.

In September, I began classes in a dirt lot at the training school in Westfield, about an hour and fifteen-minute drive from Wendell Depot, but I hitchhiked. Hitching in the early '70s was easy. I never had to wait too long. Breathe, focus, and wait. Sharing stories, my enthusiasm, and pot, I was good at it. I would walk out to Route 2 around six o'clock in the morning. Training started at eight o'clock sharp. I was never late.

Two months later, on the Wednesday before Thanksgiving, I took my class one driver's test and passed it.

I was so proud. What an accomplishment, better than graduating from seminary, and almost as good as graduating from Amherst. Now I could tell cousins Bobby, Jackie, and Johnny that I had a class-one license, too. I was a kid again, playing in the sandbox, zooming trucks around. Now, I was a big kid. I was going to get a job and drive big rigs.

I heard that Llama, Toucan & Crow was looking for a class-one driver to deliver in New England. Delivering food, I would meet all the important people and establish a reputation as a provider. With knowledge of the roads in New England, I could direct the rebel troops to avoid the army when the revolution came.

The next day, I walked into the warehouse and introduced myself to Bill Duckworth, the head guy: "I just passed my class one driver's license test. I'm ready to drive tractor-trailers. Need me?"

Bill was stressed out. He had a clipboard in his hands with papers sticking out every which way. I followed him from his cluttered office into the warehouse. He was doing too many things at once.

One of the warehouse guys yelled, "Hey, Bill, we need three

more tins of tahini on the truck to Maine. And where are the fifty-pound bags of organic whole wheat flour? We just got a call for twenty-five more bags going to Provincetown, Mass."

Bill turned to me. "You drive semis?"

Truthfully, I said, "Sure! I've been driving them for three months now, five days a week." I neglected to tell him the semis were the practice vehicles at the school.

I followed Bill back into his office. He looked around, opened a filing cabinet, pulled out some invoices, sat down at his desk, and began filling in a blank invoice.

"It's crazy here. Everyone wants natural organic food. I can't keep up. I need some herb. You got any pot?"

I nodded my head. "Interestingly enough, Bill, I just happen to have some sweet tasting Columbian Gold, fresh off the boat. You got any papers?"

With a big smile on his face, Bill leaned back in his chair, put his feet up on his desk, and opened the desk drawer. "Scott, I just happen to have some Zig-Zag Extra Larges right here."

I rolled two joints. "Let's smoke one of these now and you can save one for later."

We puffed on the joint until it turned into a roach.

Bill said, "So, you've driven semis? Ever been to New York, south of Canal Street? That's where all the warehouses are for pickup."

I lied. "I've mainly driven western Massachusetts, local stuff. Once you get the hang of it, all the roads are the same. Stay on your side of the road and lay on the horn when there is an ass-hole in front of you." We laughed. "Just kidding. When you're on the road, safety comes first. Courtesy is right up there. Stay in control, never hurry, fill out your time log, and respect the road."

Bill's feet came off the desk. "Meet me here early Thursday afternoon. I'm picking up a rig at Ryder Rental in Springfield. We'll drive down to Stamford, Connecticut, stay at my parents' place for the night, and head into Canal Street in the morning. You're driving, Scott. And thanks for the smoke." He concentrated on the invoice in front of him.

I saw LT&C as my destiny. I began signing all my invoices "Roger Goldfinch," the saffron bird, in honor of Phra Sohm, my Thai meditation teacher.

I showed up at 1 p.m. on Thursday. Bill was at his cluttered desk, shifting papers around. He was eating a McDonald's cheeseburger and fries and drinking a Diet Coke. He looked up.

"Good, you're here. Sit down. I got things to do."

For an hour, I watched him race around. I wandered around the warehouse and introduced myself to a couple of hands, then sat in the office and waited. When Bill finally returned to the office and threw down his clipboard, he looked at me.

"Ready?"

I nodded. He reached into his desk drawer, grabbed something, and went into the bathroom. He returned to the office wiping his nose and sniffing deeply, and stuffed whatever it was into his pocket.

"I'm ready. Let's go."

We drove to the Ryder Truck Rental Company in Springfield, Massachusetts and picked up the biggest tractor-trailer I'd ever seen, 13' 6" tall, the only one on the lot. I tilted my head back and surveyed the top of the trailer. I swallowed the saliva that had pooled in my mouth. I took a deep breath, climbed into the cab, and started the engine. We were off to New York City to pick up the week's produce. I drove the truck to southern Connecticut, where we stopped at Bill's mother's house. We didn't eat any dinner. I slept on the living room floor.

At four the next morning, after an uncomfortable night's sleep, without breakfast, Bill and I jumped into the semi and drove to the warehouse district below Canal Street in New York. Driving a huge tractor-trailer was difficult enough, but the warehouse district was not exactly designed for tractor-trailers. There, it was wicked hard. Somehow, I made it through traffic to the first stop, where we waited for our misplaced order to be found and filled. I ate some bread. It was not a decent breakfast, but I was ready to do whatever it took.

The loading dock at our next stop was recessed into the warehouse. The ceiling of the recess was twelve feet high, so I couldn't back the trailer into the dock. Bill and I created a twenty-foot platform into the truck out of metal skids and ramps. We began loading fifty-pound bags of flour and grains, sixty-pound tins of peanut butter and tahini, and tons of other groceries. Bill helped load for about fifteen minutes, then disappeared with his friend, who owned the warehouse. They returned to check on me, talking, occasionally sniffing and laughing at something, while I loaded the truck alone. Having been around coke heads, I knew what was going on. My Yao silversmith friend had taught me to avoid white powder.

I was finding out what real physical labor was. Bill's friend didn't have dollies at his warehouse, so I loaded the truck by hand, carrying each bag and tin the twenty feet into the truck. I started loading the truck around 10 a.m.; it took me more than five hours to finish. The truck was full, and I was exhausted. Bill showed up around the time I was finished.

"You have one more stop at a Connecticut warehouse to pick up cheese. Then drive the truck to the warehouse in Greenfield. I'll meet you there this evening and we can unload."

I have no idea how I found the cheese warehouse. When I got there, I was confronted with a long reverse drive down a long, thin driveway and a right turn, backwards, into a loading dock. I couldn't keep the trailer on line; I began to panic. Luckily another driver, waiting for his trailer to be loaded, walked up to my truck.

"Looks like you're having trouble."

Near tears, I said, "My first day on the job. Spent the day south of Canal Street. Haven't eaten since yesterday. I'm cooked."

He motioned for me to get out of the truck. "Lemme back that thing up."

When I jumped out, he got in. It took him one minute and one try to get the trailer into the dock. I was very grateful for his help.

Around 1 a.m., I pulled into the Greenfield warehouse, backed the truck up to the dock, went to the office, and fell asleep on the floor. The next morning, Bill was angry that I'd arrived so late and hadn't helped unload the truck. I didn't care. I returned the truck to Ryder Rental and hitchhiked home.

Like they say, the first days are the hardest. It took me a couple of trips to New York to figure out the route and routine. Each time, it got easier and I returned to Greenfield earlier. I got stronger and I began to help unload the truck at the Greenfield warehouse.

Just when I got good at the New York run, Bill told me I was going to drive the Maine route. The driver who'd had the route drove his truck into a bridge abutment on the Maine Turnpike and was no longer able to drive. Since Bill was paying me so little, he decided that it was cheaper to hire a professional driver for the one-day New York City pickup route and put me on the week-long Maine distribution. I was actually happy to be done with New York. Maine sounded like less traffic and more days driving.

Though driving semis was easier now, it was still difficult. Thoughts of the revolution took a back seat to learning a trade. Backing semis up took mental gymnastics. Everything was reversed in mirrors. Dealing with traffic was frustrating. I was good at finding alternative routes to avoid traffic, though before GPS, guessing at better routes was not always successful. Remembering times and places when filling out logs was a challenge too. I made a lot of stuff up. It was all exhausting. Downtime between runs was feet up, good herb, and rest.

I arrived at the warehouse on Sunday afternoon for the Maine run. Since there was only one truck now, Bill wanted me to drive to Brunswick Sunday night, find someplace to sleep, start delivering early Monday morning, and be back Thursday afternoon in time for the New York pickup. He handed me invoices for sixteen food co-operatives and stores. Each invoice had an address and telephone number. I was on my own.

I drove to Brunswick, found a payphone, called the local food co-operative, and asked if I could deliver their order on Sunday evening instead of Monday morning. That worked for them. The co-op was in a large community house. I was invited to eat dinner with the housemates who ran the co-op and offered a couch to sleep on.

If you think Maine is rural now, even Portland was rural back then. Route 1, hitting all the small towns along the coast, was a crowded two-lane road. The Maine Turnpike was good for through traffic, but useless for delivering food to places on the coast and off-the-beaten-path, like Millinocket and Presque Isle, which might as well have been in other countries.

Each morning, I would wake up early and get out the door to my next delivery. I found that if I arranged my last delivery of the day to a community co-operative, usually a group of friends buying food wholesale and avoiding retail, I could find a convenient place to sleep with a member of the co-op. If I could arrange a delivery to a co-op before the natural food stores opened in the morning, I could finish my first stop before nine. Hitting a couple of food co-ops after the stores closed at five or six, I could work a twelve-hour day, making six or seven deliveries in a day. When I returned to the Greenfield warehouse early Wednesday evening, everyone was shocked to see me. Having cut nearly two days off of the Maine route, I felt like the king of the road.

On each of the next Maine runs, I would be given more invoices: eighteen, twenty, twenty-three, twenty-eight. Each week, I would arrive back at the warehouse early Thursday afternoon at the latest. Long hours and good analytical skills helped. Bill was so astonished, he called customers to make sure I was making all the deliveries. I was at the top of my game. I had places to stay on the road and the occasional adventures every truck driver dreamed about.

LT&C expanded during the six weeks I delivered in Maine to a fleet of trucks. I arrived at the warehouse one Monday morning to find that I wasn't going to Maine. Instead, I was going to do the Eastern Massachusetts run.

When I looked through the invoices to plan the run, something didn't add up. The Eastern Massachusetts route had fewer deliveries than the Maine run, and they were all closer together. Why did it take so long to do so few stops?

Then it hit me. I had been to Boston a few times and the traffic maze there was confusing. A driver could spend hours trying to find routes and directions in and around the city, with its one-way streets and alleys, cars, and tight quarters. The joke was that even the locals couldn't get there from here.

I settled into the driver's seat, high above the warehouse parking lot, pushed in the clutch, ran through the ten gears, then reached for the key and turned the Cummins Diesel engine on. I took a deep breath and began to repeat my mantra: *I can do this.* I headed east toward Cambridge.

Nearing the Alewife Station rotary where I'd met my teepee sewing friends, worried about finding my first stop, I noticed a hitchhiker on the side of the road. I hit my brakes, slowed up next to him, and stopped. A young kid, maybe eighteen, twenty at the most, a jacket too skimpy for the winter weather, no gloves, reached up and struggled with the door. He got it open and climbed up and into the passenger seat.

My first question was, "Are you from Boston?"

Blowing into his hands to warm them, he said, "Yes, thanks for the ride. It's cold out there."

I ran through the lower gears and turned the truck onto the road when there was a break in the traffic. "I've hitched a lot. Just returning favors." I looked at him out of the corner of my eye. "Do you know your way around Boston?"

He perked up. With a smile, he said, "Yep, I've lived in Boston all my life."

"What's your name?"

He stuck out his hand to shake, then realized I was busy. "Joseph. Friends call me Joe."

I downshifted, and the engine purred. "I'm Scott." I shifted again and asked, "If I gave you an address in Cambridge or Boston, could you direct me there?"

"Sure!"

"Do you smoke pot?"

With a big smile, he said, "Sure do!"

When I came to a red light and stopped, I turned to Joe and asked, "What are you doing today?"

With a shake of his head, and looking a little puzzled, he shrugged. "Nothing."

The light changed, and I ran through my gears. "Okay, I have good herb. If you spend the day with me, showing me the places where I have to deliver, you can smoke all the pot you want."

Joe leaned forward and put his hands on the dashboard. "You're on, where are we going?"

I handed him a joint I'd rolled back in Greenfield and told him the address of my first stop.

We made three stops in Cambridge, two in Somerville, and four in Boston. I couldn't have done it without him. He was a living GPS, directing me on back roads and side streets. Because he knew all the addresses and was able to navigate the one-way streets, we were always headed in the right direction as we approached a store. I never had to turn around. He knew the cross-town streets to the next stop; we avoided all the traffic. He helped me unload the truck at each stop. At the end of the day, he explained how to get out of town to Plymouth. I gave him some pot, thanked him, and bid him adieu.

I made it to Plymouth in the early evening, made a delivery, and finagled dinner and a couch to sleep on. The next morning, I headed back to Boston and made my last delivery there at nine in the morning. When I left the natural food store and found myself headed the wrong way out of town, I knew I had been more than lucky to find Joe. I got lucky again, finding a policeman who set me in the right direction. I zipped out of town past Plymouth and out to Cape Cod. I made five deliveries on the Cape and one evening delivery to a co-operative in Rhode Island on Tuesday. I made two deliveries in Rhode Island and two in Connecticut and headed back to Massachusetts late Wednesday night. I slept at the Dexter House and returned the truck to the warehouse on Thursday morning. Again, everyone was surprised to see me. I never told anyone how I slipped through Boston so quickly. When I returned on Monday for the Eastern Massachusetts run, I found out that the driver on the Maine run had returned Saturday afternoon.

LT&C continued to expand. On one weekly run, after Boston, the Cape, and southern New England, I ended up in Syracuse, New York. When LT&C expanded into Vermont and New Hampshire, I drove that route once. When I arrived at the warehouse Monday morning to do the Vermont route, Bill was complaining.

"I'm out of pot. My dealer got busted and I don't know where I'm going to get more. Scott, where do you get your pot? Can you help me out?"

"Hey, I got a little stash. I'll roll you couple of joints. That should get you through a while. I'll give you a number to call. You'll be all set."

Before I could get into the cab and drive away, Bill yelled

across the yard, "Scott, you can't drive to Vermont with pot on you. It's illegal. You might get stopped and busted. Then we'll all be in trouble. You got to give me your pot."

He ran over to me and held out his hand. I looked him in the eye.

"Bill, I can't drive without pot. Driving trucks is like twelve on a ten-point difficulty scale. Without pot, it's impossible."

Unfazed, he said, "I don't care. Gimme your pot."

Intimidated, I reached into my pocket and pulled out my half ounce in a plastic sandwich bag. As I contemplated discovering routes and stops in Vermont where I had never been, I looked at the pot in my hand. I thought, *There's no way I'm going to deliver Vermont without pot.* Bill grabbed the pot out of my hand. With a big smile, he turned and walked back to his office.

"Thanks, Scott. I don't want to get in trouble with the cops. We got a business to run."

I had been driving for LT&C for less than five months. Often, I was in way over my head. Not only was the driving difficult, but I had to do all the unloading myself, and then find places to sleep at night. I was given no travel expenses, so I had to either find a place to sleep with customers or spend the night sleeping on the front seat of the truck. None of the tractor-trailers had sleepers behind the cab. I needed pot to drive big rigs and to stay alive. Smoking pot was just the way I kept my life together. It kept my emotions suppressed. In the driver's seat of my semi, atop all the power of the Cummins engine, pot relaxed me, made the job fun, and gave me confidence that I was actually a road-eo cowboy. But now I left Greenfield without any pot and headed to a back-country village northwest of Brattleboro on Route 30.

My first mistake was to drive by the storefront that was my

first delivery. I didn't even know it was there and wound up on a dead-end road. Turning around in a residential driveway, I pulled down wires between the house and a telephone pole. I returned to the store I'd passed earlier and realized it was the natural food store. Vermont was a totally different animal than Maine, Boston, and the rest of New England.

After a long day of deliveries, I ended up near Rutland, Vermont. Exhausted, I felt too exposed to park in a shopping mall parking lot, plus there were no bathrooms. I headed north toward my next stop. Having trouble keeping my eyes open, I pulled off the road into a dirt parking area where I could pee behind an old building. After sleeping on the front seat of the truck, I awoke the next morning to find that the building was a burned-out ice cream stand. I was burned out too.

I completed a few more stops and headed across the state to Montpelier, made one stop there, then went on to a co-op before a pick up at Cabot Creamery Co-operative. The co-op was a private residence on a side road. In the 1970s, Vermont wasn't known for its road signs. I flagged down a car and asked directions. The driver told me to take the next left. He meant the next major left. The next left was a small road to a covered bridge. I should have known better, but I tried to cross the covered bridge. The trailer was too big. It hit the bridge. I backed out of the small road and surveyed the damage. The bridge was barely nicked, but the trailer had a huge hole in the roof. Since the trailer was refrigerated, I had to patch the hole. I ripped off some plastic pallet wrapping and duct-taped it over the hole. Praise the Lord for duct tape. I drove on and found the left I should have taken and made my delivery.

With a deep breath, I headed to Cabot Creamery. The driveway into the docks at the creamery was a long U-shaped road. There was no place to turn around near the docks, so I had to back the truck the eighth of a mile into the dock. Since I'd done so well backing out of the small road away from the covered bridge, I figured I could do the eighth of a mile on the driveway easily. As I was backing up, a green Plymouth Duster sped by me. *What an asshole*, I thought. As I approached the dock, I was able to see it clearly in my driver's side rearview mirror. However, I couldn't see the right side of the trailer in my passenger side mirror, since the driveway curved dog-legged left into the dock. I successfully lined up to the dock, but was having trouble backing up the last few yards. I gave the truck a little gas. The tractor-trailer seemed to go up hill.

I got out of the truck to see what the problem was. The driver of the Plymouth Duster had parked his car directly in front of a no parking sign, partially blocking the right side of the dock. The rear double-wheels of my tractor-trailer had creased the Duster and were sitting on its roof. I pulled off the Duster, went into the office, and found the driver.

"You need to get a tow truck to move your car, so I can get my semi into the dock."

The Plymouth Duster was so crumpled it was funny. All the employees of the creamery came outside to look at the car. They couldn't help but laugh. The owner of the car was crushed.

He screamed, "What the hell happened to my car? It's three months old. I just bought it."

On one hand, I was embarrassed that I had just ruined the guy's new car, but I was pissed and deadpanned, "You shouldn't have parked it in front of a No Parking sign."

I knew I was in trouble and sensed my driving days were

over. I turned to the crowd on the dock.

"Someone should call the police. And is there any way we can get the cheese I'm supposed to pick up loaded onto the truck?"

A Vermont State Police officer arrived and wrote up the information about the accident. He noticed the patch job on the trailer and asked, "Do you know anything about the truck that damaged the covered bridge?"

I told him, "That's me."

He chuckled, "You're having a bad day."

Crestfallen, I agreed.

"Don't be too upset. It happens to everyone. I've got to write you up for the covered bridge, but I'll let you slide and get on with your deliveries. When I was driving for St. Johnsbury Company, I drove a tractor-trailer off the road into a river. I was fired, but then I became a state policeman. Son, every cloud has a silver lining. You gotta make good out of bad experiences."

With the support of the officer's words, I completed my route. It was the last one I would make in a tractor-trailer. LT&C's insurance covered the cost of bridge and truck repairs. There was an argument between insurance companies as to whose fault the car was. I convinced Bill he should downsize to large class-two trucks; smaller, less expensive to run, and easier to maneuver. I delivered a few more weeks in a class-two box truck, but the adventure was over. Like a pin puncturing a balloon, the Vermont trip deflated my dreams of leading the revolution in a semi-trailer. Though unemployed, I had my teepee to set up and live in. Maybe the meaning of life was there.

chapter 14

In the spring of 1974, I had my teepee sewn together and was ready to find poles and a forest to live in. With permission from the owner of a hemlock grove, I cut down sixteen trees for the poles. Betty, an old friend from Mt. Holyoke College who was living at Woolman Hill, a Quaker community in Deerfield, told me that Jimmy's Popcorn Farm in Wendell, next to the state forest, was looking for people to live and work there.

I drove over to the farm and met Jason, a portrait painter who owned the farm with two other Amherst College alumni: his girlfriend Tracy, a wannabe opera singer, and Kurt, the farm manager. After agreeing to their anarchistic philosophy that everyone should do what they want, I moved into a cabin at the end of a farm road for the winter. I would wait until spring to begin my forty-day wilderness adventure. Behind the cabin, a path led to a clearing at the edge of the property where the Wendell State Forest began. My plan was to turn my back on civilization, sit in front of the teepee, and stare into the woods until God spoke to me and told me what to do.

As winter progressed and becoming a prophet loomed ahead, I was overwhelmed by all the responsibilities I would encounter. As a prophet, I would have to speak to the people, guide them to a spiritual life. I wasn't sure I was ready. And what if all my sins were discovered? Then I would be in trouble. Damn, I didn't even know what my sins were. They were just feelings that I did something wrong. My embarrassment would be too much.

The conflict between the need to achieve and the need to keep my secrets hidden was unbearable. To distract myself from my anxiety, I decided to hitchhike across America and visit Marilyn, who was living in Los Angeles, California. Since my sister was political, I'd explain what was going to happen to me in political (rather than religious) terms. Like Nguyen Tat Thanh, who'd traveled around the world to gain experience before he became Ho Chi Minh, the leader of Vietnam, I'd take a trip across America to acquaint myself with my country before I led the revolution. Maybe she'd understand and be able to explain me to Mom and Dad.

On January 2, I packed a knapsack and set out for the West Coast. I hitchhiked south on Interstate 91, through Connecticut and New York on 95, then west on the Pennsylvania Turnpike. As it was getting dark, I assumed it was much later than five o'clock. I panicked. My ride was getting off the turnpike in the middle of nowhere. I saw myself on an entrance ramp, waiting for a ride all night long and freezing to death. When we stopped at a service area, I thanked the driver for the ride.

"I think I'm going to look for a ride here. It's cold and dark outside. It's warm in here."

He showed some concern. "Are you sure you want to stay

here? It might be easier to get a ride at an entrance ramp."

"I'll be okay here. Hey, I hitchhike all the time. Service areas are good places to catch rides. Thanks again for the ride."

A few minutes later, I realized that service areas were the worst places to get rides. I walked out to the exit. Cars sped past me. I returned to the door of the cafeteria. I found myself begging for rides. It wasn't a pleasant experience, pleading for help: I was either ignored or told 'no.' Standing at an entrance ramp, I could be patient, allowing the driver to decide whether to pick me up or not. Wordlessly asking for a ride was a stronger position than begging aloud. Finally, one man offered me a ride going north on the turnpike extension towards Wilkes-Barre, then west on Interstate 80. We drove for a few hours until we reached his exit. He dropped me off on the side of the road.

Now, I was truly in the middle of nowhere. With little traffic, cold temperatures, and a pitch-black night, I decided that progress west on Interstate 80 was a fantasy. I walked down the road into a town called Plainville, Pennsylvania.

Not much seemed to be happening in Plainville that evening. The only sign of life was the bright neon beer signs in the windows of the only bar on Main Street. I walked in and ordered a beer. A row of men at the bar turned and stared. It was as if I was back in North Dakota ordering Budweiser instead of Lone Star. I acknowledged them with a nod of my head. They nodded at me and turned back to their drinks in silence. As I nursed my beer and contemplated my next move, a guy approached me and struck up a conversation. He seemed agitated.

"You're not from Plainville. I saw you walk in here. Hey, I'm Nick. I'm from Boston!"

He was talking a mile a minute, but I was happy to have

someone to talk to: "Yeah, I left Massachusetts this morning, got rides south to the turnpike, then up here. There were no cars on 80 this late at night, so I walked into town. I'm hitching to the West Coast."

Nick continued talking at a rapid pace. "I left Boston in September and, God knows how, I ended up here. I'm living in a room upstairs, paying my rent cleaning the bar every night. Welcome to Plainville. Let me buy you a beer. Actually, I don't have to pay for beer. I get that free. Free room and all the beer I can drink. Hahaha. Drink up. Cheers!"

Nick was making me nervous, but I couldn't walk away. "I'm on my last great journey, visiting my sister before I settle down on a farm. I'm going to live in a teepee and find out what Jesus discovered in the wilderness."

After a few free beers, Nick blurted out, "I am overjoyed to meet someone from Massachusetts. I've got some Black Beauties up in my room. Want to do one? You can help me clean up the bar. Sleep on my couch. We're not going to sleep anyway, haha."

Now I understood why Nick talked so much. "Speed? Don't mind if I do."

On an empty stomach, it didn't take long for me to blast off. Everything became clear. Nick and I chatted like magpies and drank unending beers. After the bar closed, I helped Nick clean up. Somehow, he went to sleep around three in the morning, while I stared at the walls of the large, open, second-floor loft. There was no way I was going to sleep. At dawn, with the sky lightening, I knew that heading west in the morning was unwise. I had done speed before. As with many drugs, the hangover can be punishing. I knew I was going to crash hard and I wanted to be closer to home when that happened, not on the road.

I wrote Nick a note thanking him for the couch, the beer, and the speed. Walking up to Interstate 80, I found out how good Nick's Black Beauties were. *Zip*, I was at the entrance ramp. Heading east, I stuck out my thumb and, *zip*, a car picked me up. After settling in, I noticed a car fly by with a UMass window decal.

I asked the driver, "Sir, could you speed up and pass the car that just flew by?"

When we came alongside of the car with the decal, I rolled down my window and motioned to the other driver to roll down his.

I yelled out the window, "Are you going to Amherst?"

With a big smile on his face, the driver nodded.

"I'm going to Amherst, too. Can I have a ride?"

Zip, both drivers pulled off the road and I switched cars. *Zip*, I arrived in Amherst early in the afternoon. It was very good speed.

I spent the next few days doing farm chores and thinking about why I'd panicked and ended up in Plainville. Realizing I had become impatient and feared what would happen next, I decided that I needed to let life unfold in front of me. No fear. No panic. I also sensed I needed a change in appearance. Clean cut when I drove semis, now my hair was long and I had a short beard. I needed to improve my look. I bought a beautiful, heavy, three-quarter length coat at Wilson's Department Store in Greenfield for thirty-five dollars on sale. I still had that inheritance keeping me afloat, so I bought an expensive chic leather travel bag and Birkenstock sandals. The coat and bag changed my image from down-and-out hitchhiker to sophisticated traveler without an automobile.

When I told Jason I was heading out to hitchhike west again, he said, "I'm driving to Washington, D.C. to sell some portraits I just finished painting. Come with me, stay at my parents' house for the evening, and I'll drive you to Interstate 66. You can start your trip from there."

Jason and I brainstormed my trip west on the way to D.C. He came up with a good idea. "You'll miss February in New England. Smart move. You should plan to be in New Orleans for Mardi Gras."

That would be cool. I'd always wanted to go to Mardi Gras. A bacchanalia of pleasure before Lent and the repentance of sins fit into my spiritual quest.

"Yeah, I'll go to Mardi Gras. I wanted to stop at Stephen Gaskin's farm in Summerville, Tennessee, too. Maybe I can stay there long enough to get to New Orleans by Shrove Tuesday."

Jason didn't know about Gaskin's farm. "Gaskin was a professor at San Francisco State College. During the Vietnam protests when the students shut down the school, he taught a class at the Free University the protesters organized. He called it 'Monday Night Class.' When the protests were over, he quit his teaching job and led a bunch of students on a bus trip around the country to find a place to start a farm. You know, tune in, drop out, grow your own food, live off the land. I want to ask him to come to Massachusetts and give a talk."

Jason wasn't interested in inviting Gaskin to Jimmy's Popcorn. "We don't have room for a whole busload of people on the farm. Maybe he'd be interested in the whole Michael Metelica, Spirit in Flesh thing in Turner's Falls. Spirit in Flesh is a commune like Gaskin's farm. Metelica is a spiritual leader like Stephen. I want the farm to be quiet, so I can paint."

Trying to ease Jason's mind, I said, "I'll manage the farm. You can paint. I'll tell Stephen about the whole Spirit in Flesh thing and he can hang out with them."

After a pleasant ride to D.C. and a comfortable overnight at Jason's parents' house, he dropped me at an entrance ramp to Interstate 66. I headed west to Interstate 81, then southwest. Rides came easily with my new civilized look. With tons of good stories to tell, I traded companionship for mobility. Late in the afternoon in western Virginia, a pickup stopped. The driver, sporting an axe in the gun rack, was a real Tennessee woodsman. We rode into the night, stopping at a roadside diner for dinner in Bristol, just over the Kentucky border into Tennessee.

As we finished our dinner, the cute waitress, with a salacious smile and Tennessee accent, asked, "It looks like you guys could use some dessert. Maybe some pie?"

The glint in her eyes and the emphasis on pie made Billy and me laugh.

"Oh, we're certainly going to need some pie tonight." Billy replied. "Do you have some pie for us?"

"I don't have pie for you, but there is some apple pie and cream pie over there," she said, pointing to the pies in the display stand. "You can have all the pie you want."

Flirtatious Tennessee was not staid New England. With a shiver up my spine, I got the feeling I was about to experience a real Tennessee adventure.

When we returned to the car, Billy decided that he didn't want to drive all the way home that evening. "Let's head over to Eastern Tennessee State University in Johnson City, hang out at the student union, and meet some women." Billy hesitated a second. "You like women, don't you?"

I laughed. "Don't worry, Billy, I like women. Hey, I'm twenty-seven. College girls are just the right fit. Let's do it."

At the student union, Billy began a conversation with two coeds. "Hello, girls, I'm Billy and this is my friend Scott. Aren't we lucky to meet you here! I'm traveling to Knoxville and Scott, here, from Massachusetts, is hitching across America. He's a real Jack Kerouac. We thought we would stop here tonight and make some friends."

The two women, as impressed as I was with Billy's approach, giggled and smiled.

The less shy woman, in that sweet Tennessee accent, replied, "Well, y'all, welcome to Eastern Tennessee State. I'm Stephanie and my dear friend is Marsha. We've just finished studying and were looking for something to do. Isn't it nice that you showed up?"

Billy turned to Marsha. "Aren't you the cutest little girl? I want to get to know Stephanie, but you, you're going to be my favorite."

Billy extended his hand. Marsha took it and held it. Tongue-tied, I was just staring at Stephanie. With a wonderful smile, she was staring back at me, waiting for me to say something. I fell in love with her blue eyes, her light honey-brown ringlets of curls, and her curves.

"It's a pleasure to meet you, Stephanie." I bowed to her and then blurted out, "You're beautiful." I blushed.

With a little laugh Stephanie replied, "That's so nice of you to say. I think you're quite handsome, too. Let's get a soda and you can tell me all about your trip."

The four of us talked until late. When the student union was about to close, Billy stretched his arms above his head.

"Marsha and Stephanie, it's been such a pleasure talking with you. I'm refreshed. Scott and I need to head back out on the road and take that long drive to Memphis tonight."

Stephanie, placing her hand on mine, suggested, "Billy, you and Scott don't have to drive all the way to Memphis tonight. Marsha and I have room for guests to stay at our apartment. You can sleep on the couch and Scott can sleep on the floor." Stephanie's hand tightened on mine. "If Scott is going to live in a teepee, sleeping on our floor will be good practice."

Billy left his truck in the student union parking lot. As we walked over to the apartment, I realized I had talked so much about myself that I knew little about Stephanie. I asked her to tell me about herself. She blushed and smiled.

"I'm from Nashville, so I'm not so far away from home. Mommy and Daddy sent me to a private school, so I got a very good education. Daddy's an executive for Reynolds Aluminum Company. Mommy stayed at home and raised me the best she could."

I couldn't believe the coincidence. "Stephanie, my father is one of two senior scientists at the Alcoa Aluminum Research Lab in Pennsylvania."

Our connection was magnetic. Sleeping on the floor that night, I dreamt of a long-term relationship and everlasting love. In the morning, the attraction between Stephanie and me was palpable.

During breakfast, she hinted, "How long are you staying around campus? I have classes this morning, but my afternoon's free. And I have nothing to do tomorrow."

It didn't even register that she was asking me to stay awhile. "I'm headed to Stephen Gaskin's Farm in Summerville and then to New Orleans for Mardi Gras."

Persisting, Stephanie said, "I've never been to Mardi Gras. If you wait until Friday, we have spring break. We could hitchhike to New Orleans together and get there in time for Mardi Gras. You could stay with me until Friday."

Oh, my God, Stephanie wants to go to New Orleans with me. All kinds of bells began to ring. I saw before me unbridled sex. I saw love blooming, meeting parents, a wedding, kids, and life ever after.

Then, a bomb blew up inside me. I couldn't go through with it.

"Uh, I'm sorry, Stephanie, wait until Friday? I can't. We can't. I can't wait. I have to go to Summerville. I have to ask people there to visit Massachusetts. I live on a farm, you know, in Massachusetts. This is very important. I can't. We can't."

Her face said she didn't understand.

With all the strength I could muster, I ripped out our hearts and stomped on them. I said goodbye to Stephanie and Marsha and left that morning with Billy, the Tennessee woodsman. He was stunned I had walked away from such an enticing opportunity. I didn't quite understand either. I couldn't connect my childhood guilt with my fear when I desired to love a woman.

chapter 15

Forlorn after Billy dropped me off, dreams of bliss faded into reality. Determined to continue my journey to visit Marilyn, my next stop was The Farm in Summerville. Hitchhiking was slow. My heart wasn't in it.

My last ride was a van full of hippies going to an REO Speedwagon concert. Their energy was infectious, almost breaking my sullen mood.

One of them asked me, "You want a free ticket?"

Though I wasn't feeling it, I said, "Sure."

What the heck. A live rock-and-roll concert would take my mind away from Johnson City and Stephanie.

The van was hot, and I'd taken off my coat. As we were getting out of the van in the parking garage, I asked, "Hey, it's going to be hot in the arena. Can I leave my coat and bag in your van and get it after the concert?"

One of the hippies flashed me the peace sign as they ran off. "Sure, meet you here after the concert."

I wandered around the cavernous arena by myself. I felt lost, anxious, and out of place, like I had at the Rainbow Gathering. After the last song, the venue began to empty. When I got to the parking garage, the van was gone, along with my coat and bag. I felt wretched, miserable, woeful, pathetic. My yearning was intensified by the loss of my good coat and bag. I could have been in Stephanie's arms, back in Johnson City. At least I had my Birkenstock sandals.

With no other options, I walked out into the cold February night. Nashville was asleep. I had sixty dollars in my pocket, the shirt on my back, and no clue what to do or where to go.

I rounded a corner and saw a young woman, maybe in her twenties, with a box in her arms. She turned towards me with a bright smile.

"Would you like to buy a box of chocolate bars? I have only one left. It's ten dollars."

I projected my loneliness onto her. How could she be so happy late at night on an empty street corner? I pulled my three twenty-dollar bills from my pocket and gave her one.

"Keep the change."

As I unwrapped one of the bars of chocolate, she asked, "What are you doing wandering around in Nashville at three in the morning?"

A wave of sadness washed over me. Near tears, I needed to share my sorrow.

"I just lost all my possessions. I have nowhere to go. I don't know what to do."

She put her hand on my arm. "It's okay. I'll be your friend. Where are you from?"

I gathered myself together and my story poured out. As I talked, suddenly I felt better, like she was somehow sharing her happiness.

"You're so happy. You're a life saver." I laughed. "Why are you selling candy in the middle of the night in Nashville?"

Her eyes lit up. "I belong to the Unification Church. I am not allowed to return to the church until I sell all my chocolate." She seemed to deflate, exhausted. "It's been a bad day. I started this afternoon and I'm still here." Her smile returned. "You are a gift from God. You bought my last box. I can go home now."

She had a home to go to. Lucky her. I didn't want to walk away into the night.

"You're in the Unification Church? I've heard of that. I'm into religion myself. I went to Pittsburgh Theological Seminary to get my conscientious objector status."

She looked up at me in surprise. "Pittsburgh Seminary? I'm from Pittsburgh."

"Really! I'm from New Kensington. Where did you live?"

Excited, she asked, "Have you heard of Shaler Township?"

I was startled. During my last semester at Pittsburgh Seminary, my student minister position was at a small country church in Shaler. The youth group there wanted to do a Friday night coffee house like the Loaves and Fishes in Shadyside.

"I ran a coffee house in a church in Shaler! The Sacred Cow."

Her eyes widened and her mouth dropped open. "Scott? Oh, my God, you're Scott Hunter. I'm Sharon. I was in the youth group that started The Sacred Cow. I was there every Friday. I'm twenty-one now."

We reminisced for a while, then Sharon said, "Maybe you can stay at the house where we all live. I have to find a pay phone to call the church to get a ride home. A van will come to pick me up. I'll ask the driver if you can stay with us. Wait right here."

She ran off to find a pay phone.

I knew a little about the Unification Church—better known as the Moonies, after their leader, Sun Myung Moon. It had the reputation as a cult.

Sharon returned. "The van is coming soon. The driver wants to talk with you before deciding if you can stay with us. I hope you can."

The van arrived with seven or eight people in it. They stared out the window while the driver got out and came over to Sharon and me. She explained how she knew me.

With a mustache drooping over his lip, the driver looked more street-smart than Sharon or the kids in the van. He ran his eyes over me, then looked at Sharon. He decided to take out his walkie-talkie and make a call.

When he was finished, he said, "Here's the deal. We'll invite you to stay with us if you agree to participate in the Church's activities for three days and listen to the seven introductory lectures all members listen to."

With a sigh of relief, I thanked him. I jumped in the warm van and sat next to Sharon.

When we reached the community house, I was introduced to about fifteen church members, all recently back from selling candy. It was 4 a.m., and the house was a beehive of activity. Didn't these Moonies ever sleep? Finally, after a vegetarian snack, everyone disappeared. I was given a blanket and slept soundly on the living room floor.

The next morning, I met the leader of the group, Dwayne. He wore creased gray pants and a white dress shirt. He was short, thin, and looked young for a leader of a church. Dwayne spoke with authority.

"Sharon says she knew you when she lived in the material world. You were her minister?"

I steadied myself and spoke with as much confidence as I could. "Yes, I have a master's degree in divinity. I was also a missionary in Thailand."

He seemed puzzled. "But now you're hitching to California. And you want to live in a teepee? Sounds like you're a little confused."

His comment made me feel weak and vulnerable, so I changed the subject: "Are you the person who is going to give me the lectures?"

He motioned toward a door and said, "I could give you the first lecture now."

We walked into a small classroom with a blackboard and folding chairs. Dwayne walked to the blackboard and started: "Sun Myung Moon was born in 1920 in South Korea. When he was sixteen, Jesus came to him in a vision and asked him to complete his work as the messiah. Our leader studied the Bible and became a Presbyterian minister."

I interjected, "What a coincidence. I'm Presbyterian."

That threw Dwayne off. He heaved a sigh. "Scott, please don't interrupt. These lectures are very important." He continued, "When our dear leader was forty-five, he published *The Divine Principles,* which is a doctrine of God's purpose for humans and explains the fall of man and woman and their subsequent restoration. When he began to preach his doctrine in 1946, Moon was excommunicated from the Presbyterian Church, imprisoned and tortured by the North Koreans. He then fled to South Korea, where he established the Unification Church."

Dwayne went on to explain how Moon expanded his church

worldwide, calling it 'The Holy Spirit Association for the Unification of World Christianity.'

When Dwayne was finished, he enthusiastically said, "That was so exciting! Shall we keep going? I'm sure you're ready to hear about our dear leader's *Divine Principles*!"

I couldn't explain it, but something was off. Everyone last night (and now Dwayne this morning) seemed too happy. Was this brainwashing? Was this what it was like inside a cult? A constant stream of happiness? I couldn't be that happy.

I sarcastically matched Dwayne's enthusiasm. "Dwayne, that lecture was great. I definitely want to hear about *The Divine Principles*."

I had trouble listening during the second lecture, but Dwayne was so into it, he didn't notice. *The Divine Principles* explained God's purpose in creating humans, the fall, and the restoration of the human race through Jesus Christ. I had rejected that already. Jesus Christ wasn't my personal savior. What I needed was a hit of acid.

When Dwayne was finished and said it was time for lunch, I bolted out of the room. I was eating a vegetarian soup when Sharon sat down next to me.

"Dwayne told me you just received the first two lectures."

I was blunt. "Sharon, do you believe this stuff?"

Sharon was steadfast. "Scott, this is my family now. I've found a home here. I'm so glad to have met you again, but my way of life is the Unification Church."

Her face radiated so much blissful energy that I backed off.

"I'm so glad you have found a group of people to share your beliefs with. I'm happy for you. But I don't think it's for me. I need to be moving on soon. I can't thank you enough."

When I said I was leaving soon, Sharon saddened, but quickly gathered herself to be happy again. Something wasn't right with that. Maybe they weren't allowed to feel their darker emotions. I needed to get out and back on the road away from them. But I owed them for a place to stay and felt obligated to listen to all the lectures.

In the afternoon, I took the third lecture with the group of fifteen Moonies. They all sat transfixed, while Dwayne introduced us to the role of Young Oon Kim, a religion professor at Ewha University in Seoul, Korea, recruited by Moon to establish the church in America. He portrayed the church in America as a crowning achievement. Hardly able to keep quiet, I wondered what would happen if I threw Dwayne a curve.

When the lecture was over, I asked him, "Dwayne, what was Moon's relationship with women in the church? Was he married? Did he have any children? And what are the mass marriages about?"

As the members filed out, Dwayne stared at me, annoyed. "That's not what this lecture is about. It's about glorifying the church. You may have been a minister once, but you aren't now. I'm the teacher here, teaching our dear leader's principles. You're here to learn. Please don't ask questions that don't pertain to his doctrine. It's time for lunch, then we'll all go out into the community, hand out literature, and invite people we meet to join in an evening celebration."

I apologized and caught up with Sharon. We went to Austin Peay State University to talk to students.

When I handed some literature to a local guy walking across campus, he asked, "Are you a believer?"

I laughed. "No way. My name is Scott." I explained my story

to him and how I was infiltrating the Moonies.

He was all excited. "Wow, I live near that house. I've always been curious about those meetings. I'm Don. I'll show up tonight."

Don was one of the three people from the outside to show up for the meeting. The celebration was some sugary drink, vegetables with a tasteless dip, and a brief message from Sun Myung Moon through Dwayne.

After the meeting, Don and I talked out on the porch.

"Scott, that was crazy. Did you notice no one made eye contact with anyone? I tried, but everyone turned and walked away."

I agreed. "Yeah, and they're all happy. Sometimes their expression changes, but they quickly catch it and get happy again. Freaks me out."

Don grabbed me by my shoulder and said, "My wife told me to come and rescue you. She wants to meet you. Tomorrow, you have to sneak out of here and have dinner with us. I'll drive over and pick you up around five o'clock."

Relieved, I said, "I could use some homecooked food and sane conversation."

Back inside, Dwayne was giving a pep talk before everyone went out to sell candy. I crawled behind the living room couch, threw a blanket over me, and got a good night's sleep. No selling candy for me.

The next morning, I participated in the fourth lecture, all about how Moon interpreted the Bible and came up with his *Divine Principles.*

"Dwayne, Moon takes a giant leap here, the way he interprets the resurrection. He says it's awakening to the Word of God? That sounds more like Calvinism, you know, Presbyterian. Are you sure about that?"

Dwayne gave me a cold death stare, then ignored me and went on with his lecture. When it was over, he confronted me.

"Are you questioning my authority?"

I spoke to him candidly. "I respect what you're doing here. You're teaching these kids how to live a Christian life. That's great, but I don't agree with you about Sun Myung Moon and the Unification Church. You're not going to convince me that your church is the true way. I'm sorry, I've had too much education for that. I appreciate the place to sleep, the food, the lectures, and meeting you all, but I'm not going to stick around. I'll listen to the remaining lectures like I promised, but then I'm gone."

Dwayne's shoulders dropped. His head fell forward. Then he looked up and met my eyes. He seemed disappointed that he hadn't converted me.

I spent the afternoon handing out literature with Sharon. When we returned to the house around five, my new friend Don was waiting for me in his car.

I touched Sharon's arm. "Do you want to come with us, for a home-cooked meal?"

She shook her head like she was frightened.

"Could you cover for me missing dinner and the meeting, then? Maybe we can meet later tonight, and I can help you sell candy."

Her face lightened as she replied, "Sure, go hang out with Don. I'll cover for you. I'm so happy and had so much fun with you these last afternoons, I am going to go out and sell my candy real fast. I'll be the first one done. You have fun with Don."

Don took me home for a meat and potatoes dinner, a welcome relief from the vegetarian fare at the church house. His wife, Mary, was an affectionate woman. While we talked before dinner, she snuggled up to Don on the couch and held his hand. That was the kind of woman I was looking for. Don was affectionate, too. When Mary went into the kitchen to finish cooking dinner, the three of us talked there. Don would put his arm around Mary every chance he got. Mary was smart and funny. She had her own opinion about the Unification Church.

"I can't believe you're hanging out with those kooks. If Don leaves me and disappears into that church, I am going to hunt you down and kill you."

We laughed and talked long into the evening.

When Don was ready to take me back to the church, Mary said, "Scott, you're eating dinner with us tomorrow and you can sleep on our couch. You have to get out of that church before you disappear forever."

The next morning Dwayne came up to me. "You missed last night's dinner and the meeting."

I shook my head, "Dwayne, I'm not a convert. Our deal was that I listen to the lectures. Give me the last lectures and I'm out of here."

Resigned, Dwayne went over the last lectures with me quickly. I spent the afternoon with Sharon handing out literature.

I headed over to Don and Mary's for dinner and slept on their couch. In the morning, they gave me a navy pea jacket that was too small for me—a far cry from the coat I'd lost, but better than nothing. I thanked them for their hospitality and returned to the church to say my good-byes to Sharon, thanking her for bailing me out. Both Sharon and I had tears in our eyes.

"I'll pray for you." She gave me directions to the interstate, turned, and went into the house, her home.

It was difficult walking through the suburbs of Nashville out to the interstate. As much as I thought about Stephanie, I realized my relationship with Sharon was deeper. We both were searching for a spiritual life. She found hers in a group of people following a cultish philosophy. I was afraid people would discover my faceless secrets. They wouldn't if I lived my spiritual life alone in a teepee.

My encounter with the Unification Church lead to a reassessment of my prophetic goals. If Sun Myung Moon was an example of a modern religious leader brainwashing young people into servitude, selling candy late at night to make money, preaching doctrines that made no sense, then I didn't want to go there. I believed young people needed freedom to discover meaning for themselves. They didn't need to be force fed authoritarian craziness. No, being a prophet wasn't for me.

I began to look forward to the teepee. I loved being outside. I loved the farm and the farm work. I wanted to prove that I could live in the teepee for a whole year. Winter would be tough, but I was up for it. Nature would be my god. It would make me stronger. I was headed south to Stephen Gaskin's Farm. Gaskin was political, an anti-war back-to-the-land hippie. Maybe that was the way to go.

chapter 16

I arrived at the Farm in late afternoon, full of myself. I wanted to make an impression that separated me from other visitors. I walked from the paved road on a half mile of dirt road and came to a small wooden house with three authentic hippies—long hair, beards, colorful clothes—sitting on the porch as guards.

I strode up and made a flamboyant, theatrical announcement: "I'm Jimmy Popcorn. Just come from Massachusetts to visit you folks. I'm inviting everyone to my farm this summer."

One of the guards, perplexed, asked, "Who are you?"

"Like I said, I'm Jimmy, from Massachusetts. I run a farm just like this with a bunch of friends. There's a great community where I live, the Spirit in Flesh, 2001 Space Center, led by Michael Metelica. Their spiritual leader is a famous clairvoyant, Elwood Babbitt. You might've heard of them." I was just throwing out names.

The second guard spoke up. "We haven't. Are you for real?"

Realizing I must have sounded crazy, I toned it down. "I left Nashville this morning. I'm headed to the West Coast to visit my sister in LA. I thought I'd stop here and tell you about the alternative community in western Massachusetts. Seriously, I'd like to invite you to our farm."

While one guard radioed to someone and waited for a reply, one of the other guards saw my Birkenstock sandals.

"Oh my god, you're wearing leather. No one here wears leather. We're total vegetarians."

Still trying to talk my way in, I said, "We eat meat in Massachusetts." Pointing to my shoes, I said, "These are Birkenstocks. They're pretty comfortable."

One of the gatekeepers broke from his buddies. "I've heard of Birkenstocks. My sister in Oregon swears by them. Do you think I can try yours on?"

The Birkenstocks broke the ice. I took off my sandals and handed them to the guard. While the guards took turns trying them on, word came back from headquarters. Someone there had heard of the Spirit in Flesh commune. I was welcomed to The Farm with handshakes all around.

"When you first got here, you were acting strange. We thought you were some crazy FBI agent or something, trying to get in. You know Stephen's been in jail for a year on a marijuana charge? He was released on parole a couple of days ago."

I was shown to a cabin, where I was welcomed with a delicious eggplant stew and given a place to sleep. My new acquaintances were more laid back than the Moonies. I liked the atmosphere here better than the tension-filled, top-down authoritarian structure at the church. If this was politics, I wanted more politics and less religion.

The next morning, I awoke to a delicious breakfast of pancakes and syrup. I followed all the residents to the main meeting hall, where Stephen was giving his first Sunday sermon since being released from prison. He was given a long and loud ovation when he entered the room.

When he began his sermon, he seemed to be at a loss for words. He stumbled through a couple of beginnings, and then there was a prolonged uncomfortable silence. I had an overwhelming feeling that I should get up and say something.

"I'm Jimmy Popcorn. I've come from western Massachusetts to invite Stephen and you all to travel to my community to talk with us."

There were murmurs from the crowd.

I continued, "Stephen, I'm so happy to welcome you home from prison. I know it's been a long exile. I'm sure it'll take time to adjust to the love and appreciation from your community. Maybe I could say something while you gather yourself?"

Surprised that anyone would interrupt him, Stephen peered at me. "Who are you? Jimmy Popcorn? Oh, yeah, someone said something about you. No, I'm fine. I'm just feeling a bit emotional about being home."

Stephen's followers stood and gave him a long round of applause. I sat down. Stephen regained his composure and gave his Sunday sermon.

The next morning after breakfast, a warm, earthy brunette woman who lived in the cabin where I slept suggested, "Jimmy, you should stay awhile. There's room here in our cabin. We'd like to make you comfortable."

Her smile drew me in. She showed me around, then walked me over to the farm machinery shop.

"You could work here. We need welders. You could learn a trade."

I couldn't tell her I wasn't Jimmy. Anyway, Scott had too many secrets. How could I share a life with such a wonderful, beautiful woman? I made some quick excuses and got back on the road. I had gone to the Farm to connect with Stephen, but he didn't seem interested in what we had back east. I didn't think there was any way to really connect our farms after all.

Stephen and a busload of his companions did come up to Massachusetts in June and stayed at the Spirit in Flesh's 2001 Center. He gave a speech at an outdoor concert in Turner's Falls. I tried to reconnect with him and his people, but no one remembered Jimmy Popcorn. I was just another face in the crowd.

chapter 17

I was nearly broke, but in good spirits when I left The Farm. The weather was clear and warm, and I was headed for the biggest party in America, Mardi Gras. In New Orleans, I quickly found my way to an eight-block-long crowd milling around, drinking plastic cups of beer on Bourbon Street. It reminded of a Saturday night at my old fraternity basement bar, except outside and larger, with drunks everywhere. At the end of my stroll, I found myself in a quiet, nondescript residential area. It was eerie, eight blocks of drunkenness in the middle of calm.

As I turned back to Bourbon Street, the unreserved hedonism conjured up my mother's wagging finger. I was at the edge of Hieronymus Bosch's *The Garden of Earthly Delights*, Dante's hell. Deep inside, I knew I should avoid drinking alcohol on Bourbon Street. Of course, I only had a few dollars, but I sensed that if I drank, I'd be in trouble. Mardi Gras frightened me to death. I spent the rest of the afternoon and evening in a universe parallel to all the revelers, unable to communicate with anyone. I couldn't go into any of the barrooms. I bought dinner from a street vendor and ate it sitting on the curb. I was consumed with sadness, an alien in a celebratory world.

Mardi Gras slowed around 2 a.m. The police walked down the street shooing everyone away, followed by the street sweepers cleaning up the trash. Soon, New Orleans was empty, and I needed a place to sleep. I wandered away and found myself in Jackson Square, a large park with circular roads and large trees. Knowing I'd be conspicuous if I slept on a bench, I climbed one of the trees, found a comfortable fork in a large branch, and settled down for the night.

I arose with the morning light without much sleep and walked out of downtown New Orleans to an Interstate 10 entrance ramp. Vance, a drug courier, picked me up. He was driving from Miami to Phoenix after dropping off a load of herb. He produced a joint of very good marijuana and we were on our way. We drove all day and through the night. When we reached Phoenix in the morning, exhausted, I was introduced to Sal, the head drug dealer. He was unhappy about my sudden appearance, but when he learned I'd helped with the driving, he allowed me to get some sleep. I lay down in a small bedroom and slept from noon to the next morning, nineteen hours.

Over an early breakfast, I told Sal about driving tractor-trailers. He was so entertained by my stories that he gave me a hit of acid to aid my trip west.

It was dark when I reached southern California. Cudahy was one of the three poorest cities in the United States. The two others, Bell and Bell Gardens, were adjacent to Cudahy. This is where Marilyn lived with Brian, her husband, Ethan, their five-year-old son, and Katie, their three-year-old daughter. Marilyn taught in a bilingual primary school and Brian worked in a steel mill.

With only a street address and without a dime for a phone call, I strolled the streets of L.A. asking people for directions. Finally, I found Marilyn's small house squeezed between and behind two other larger houses. There were no lights on, so I sat by the front door and waited. Marilyn knew I was coming, but not when.

Eventually, I heard talking near the street and stood up. "Hey, Marilyn, it's Scott."

She let out a scream. "You scared me to death. I almost dropped Katie."

She handed Katie to Brian, who was also carrying Ethan, and gave me a big hug. Brian, who wore a Fu Manchu mustache and long, black stringy hair passed Ethan and Katie to Marilyn and gave me a bear hug. After Marilyn put the kids to bed, Brian brought out a bottle of Jack Daniels and we sipped the warm L.A. night away, talking politics and religion.

Marilyn and I were always close, so when she met Brian, a Korean hippie card shark, in 1967, and introduced him to our parents, Mom and Dad enlisted me to find out why she'd gone crazy. I'd invited myself to New York City to meet Brian and, after sharing a quart of Twister, a peppermint rotgut wine, and a football game, we all became friends. I told Mom and Dad that Marilyn wasn't crazy.

Six months later, I went to Marilyn and Brian's wedding in New York, and a week or so later, they came to my graduation from Amherst. They were headed to the Montreal Expo World Fair for their honeymoon, and having nothing to do, I tagged along.

That had been five years ago, and Marilyn and I hadn't seen each other since. Luckily, Marilyn's school was on winter vacation, so we spent all day playing with Ethan and Katie and catching up.

She introduced me to her new friends from L.A. over a home-cooked Mexican dinner.

The next night, she hosted a potluck for her transplanted East Coast friends, whom I'd met in New York. I was amazed at how many friends she had.

We spent a day walking arm-in-arm to the corner store, to the school where she taught, and to the steel mill where Brian was the shop steward. On my last night there, Brian, Ethan, and I visited some jazz clubs while Marilyn stayed home with Katie. We could not have squeezed more love into three days if we'd tried.

After sweet farewells in the morning, I headed 400 miles north to San Francisco to visit Michael, a linguistics professor I had known in Thailand. I popped in unannounced shortly before dinner and asked to stay overnight with him and his family. With my long hair, beard, and days on the road, I looked and probably smelled more like the local homeless guy. The next morning, Michael gave me some hits of LSD as a bribe to get me out of their house.

Headed east on Interstate 80 over the Donner Pass, a few rides got me to Reno, Nevada, close to dark. I decided to do one of the hits of acid and get something to eat with the money Marilyn had given me. As I walked into a casino, the transition from the dark cold night into the neon world triggered the LSD. The sounds of the slot machines engulfed me. A homeless hippie walking past the gaming tables attracted the stares of all the gamblers. I believed that if I walked up to the blackjack table and put down money, I'd win big. I'd no longer be homeless, but rather living large in the penthouse suite, surrounded by the pleasures of the world. Paranoia and panic surrounded me.

I tried to eat but couldn't. I rushed from the casino and found myself standing on a dark and cold entrance ramp. Inconspicuous again, I relaxed.

A truck slowed and stopped. Two guys and a dog sat in the cab, and the driver offered me a ride in the bed of the truck. Despite the acid, I calmed my mind and laid still through the cold night.

At daybreak, I was in Salt Lake City, surprisingly well-rested. It took me a day to get to St. Louis, and then, after hitching for hours at an impossible place, I got a ride in the late afternoon. We drove through a snowstorm all night, and when I got dropped off in East Stroudsburg, Pennsylvania, it was a warm, bright, dry, wonderful February morning. I walked backwards with my thumb out, breathing in fresh country air. A few cars passed me before Dave, a musician driving home from a gig in eastern Pennsylvania, gave me a ride to Waterbury, Connecticut, and invited me into his home. I met his wife and we relaxed in his living room. They reminded me of Don and Mary in Nashville.

Dave said, "Scott, what you need is a little pick me up. You've been a long way since you left Massachusetts, and your stories helped me stay awake this morning. I wouldn't have made it home without you. I have some pure mescaline. Would you like a hit?"

How could I refuse? With a big smile on my face, I popped it in my mouth and swallowed. "Thank you very much."

Then, Dave said with a mischievous smile, "Do you play chess?"

Maybe it was the mescaline, but the way he said it scared me. It wasn't sexual, but was he trying to seduce me? A very dark feeling came over me.

"I'm sorry, I'm feeling tired, dirty. I haven't showered since California. I don't know if I'm ready to play chess."

He was already setting up the chess board. With a gleeful chuckle, he said, "After a game, I'll call a girlfriend of mine. You can shower with her later at her house."

Suddenly, I was hallucinating. Dave was the devil and I was at a crossroads, about to sell my soul. If I played chess with him and won, I'd live in the lap of luxury with women and riches. I was consumed with guilt—I didn't deserve pleasure, success. From my unconscious mind, no words, but feelings. I panicked, again.

"Dave, thanks for the ride. Thanks for the mescaline. I have to go. Please, let me go. I can't stay around here."

I grabbed my coat and ran out the door. I didn't stop until I was standing at the top of the entrance ramp heading east. My heart was beating wildly. My shirt was soaked clear through. I'd just escaped from mortal danger. I took a breath, another. All I had to do was stay calm. Everything would work out.

I longed for but feared the erotic. Any thought of it was surrounded by guilt. Intimacy was forbidden. What was wrong with me? It happened again and again: East Tennessee State, Gaskin's Farm, Mardi Gras. Sexual feelings put me over the edge. It was getting worse. Psychedelics certainly didn't help. I couldn't afford companionship. I was desperate to be alone, but also lonely.

When a fat man in a Cadillac smoking a huge cigar finally picked me up, I was relieved. He was a caricature, a good spirit, almost Santa Claus, the antithesis to Devil Dave.

The day had turned gray when my friend let me off in the middle of the interstate, north of Springfield, Massachusetts. The world was not all colors and joy, but I was happy to be nearing home. Another ride got me to Miller's Falls, and I walked up the hill out of town. At the end of Davis Road, the lights in the farmhouse were a cluster of stars in the cold dark night.

chapter 18

When I opened the kitchen door, I was hit with the wonderful warmth and smell of a maple wood fire.

Tracy looked up from the stove and called out, "Scott's back."

Jason, Kurt, Betty (my friend from Woolman Hill), and friends from Montague Farm (Jimmy's Popcorn Farm's sister farm) were waiting for the roast beef dinner that Tracy was cooking. They looked surprised. Jason was the first to speak.

"What are you doing here? We thought you were long gone."

Kurt sounded irritated. "You came back? What for? There's a whole world out there and you come back to this end of the road?"

Tracy shouted, "Dinner's ready."

We moved into the dining room and chowed down. I was feeling like Odysseus, the returning hero, having survived a month on the road across America. Everyone else seemed to be suffering from depression. Jimmy's Popcorn Farm in February, sitting in a north-facing sheltered valley, was a dreary and uninspiring place.

Halfway through dinner, one of the Montague guests asked, "Why *did* you come back? There's nothing here!"

I thought of the teepee I had made. "Just you wait until spring. I'm going to build my own castle."

In a few weeks, the thaw came. The weather grew warmer. The makeup of the farm changed dramatically. Kurt moved and I became the farm manager. Jason and Tracy stayed on. By year's end, there were thirteen of us.

Frank, just graduated from UMass, was an idealist without a clue about life on a farm. He moved in with Mary and Meredith. Mary was in love with him, but they broke up when Frank fell in love with a local girl. Mary withered away. Meredith wanted to be a farmer. She was my sidekick until she learned to milk the cow and tend the chickens. She took over the animals, while I became the vegetable farmer. When Bruce, brother of the owner of the bookstore where I'd found the book on teepees, and Carol moved in, Meredith and Bruce became a couple and Carol hooked up with Andy, a local guy just out of the Army. Meredith and Bruce had a baby boy and named him Jesse James.

Carol and Andy moved into the cabin where I'd spent the winter when I moved into the teepee. All Andy did was buy booze and drink. I have no idea where he got the money, but I enjoyed drinking with him. Carol married him and became a true farmer on Andy's parents' farm until she died when she flipped a tractor on top of herself plowing a field.

Les, a local drug dealer who was driving trucks for LT&C, moved onto the farm. He brought Lucy and Joe, two ex-heroin addicts, with him. Lucy got pregnant and had a baby girl and named her Jimi Popcorn.

One of Andy's friends, Allen, moved onto the farm. We all smoked pot, drank, and did what we wanted to do.

We each paid twenty-five dollars a month into a common

pot. That went to the mortgage and to our communal food. The mortgage was $150 a month, which left $500 for food and farm supplies. In the '70s, that went a long way. Andy's older brother owned a junkyard, so we had an endless supply of old cars to rattle around in. I bought a '63 Chevy station wagon that became the farm transport. My inheritance covered my alcohol consumption, and we also grew pot. When the homegrown ran out, Les always had a stash. We cut the electrical lines to the farm, installed a hand pump for water to the kitchen, and built a composting toilet. We were off the grid.

I saw it clearly then. The stage was set. I would move into the teepee and there would be twelve people on the farm, my twelve disciples. Whatever I discovered in the teepee, I would tell the group on the farm what I'd learned, hopefully less like Sun Myung Moon's *Divine Doctrine*, and more like Gaskin's peace, love, and back to the earth.

On the farm, I worked my butt off, cutting and stacking firewood, plowing and tilling the fields. I created new gardens by cutting through grass turf with a pick and shovel. I cut out a hidden field in the woods and planted a marijuana crop. Farming was the perfect way to get strong.

I set up the teepee and slowly moved into it over the spring, summer, and fall. It was exciting, but I wasn't ready for a forty-day experience in the wilderness that would catapult me into all-knowing. They crucified Jesus at thirty-three years old. I was only twenty-eight. I had plenty of time. Though frightened to hell to be alone, I was sure I was in the right place. My teepee was at the base of Jerusalem Mountain, named by the nineteenth century Mormons who'd lived on top: what could be clearer? In the words of Brigham Young himself, "This is the place."

By the end of March, I was out of the cabin, my material possessions stowed away in a crawl space above the farmhouse kitchen. I worked the farm all day. In the evenings, I would walk up the hill past the cabin and onto the path that led to the teepee. That was scary. When I passed the cabin, I would take a deep breath, wait until my eyes adjusted to the dark, and calm my fear. I was afraid something out there would attack me. Every noise portended danger. Eventually, I realized there wasn't anything out there, just me and the trees. I had a laugh one night when I remembered the hermit who lived in the coal mine near our house growing up. Mother would always say, "Don't wander too far from the house. You don't want the hermit to get you." I was the hermit my mother told me to be afraid of.

When I had a fire going and felt safe, I would take some deep breaths, look around at the inside of my canvas teepee, and smile. I would feel a surge of power. I saw myself as savage and strong. I was home.

The first spring and summer in the teepee were a struggle. I was learning to manage a farm. It hurt when our milk cow's calf died. I tried to be graceful when I watched the vegetables of my labor being consumed by everyone who'd done so little work to produce them. I spent too much time drinking alcohol in the five bars just down the road. When I did spend nights in the teepee, I sat by the fire, listening, thinking, waiting for revelation. I never got close to forty days in the wilderness. Revelation didn't happen. I dwelt on my failures in life, not on spirituality. There were clear moments when the night sky was cloudless and the millions of stars or a bright full moon would spark feelings of confidence, but I never felt good about myself. I was lonely, not knowing how to be an adult. I missed Mom and Dad.

Mom was raised Catholic. I'm glad I wasn't. I was guilty enough in my own mind. The emphasis the Catholic Church put on guilt would have led me to suicide. Dad took catechism classes and was going to convert to Catholicism, but the priest wanted him to sign a pledge to raise his and Mom's children Catholic. He said his word was good enough. Then, they wanted to get married on a Sunday so Dad's parents could make it to the wedding. When the priest told them he wouldn't marry them on a Sunday, Mom got so angry she became a Presbyterian, Dad's religion. They got married on Sunday in a Presbyterian Church.

My mother was persistent. She was a doer, always cleaning the house, doing laundry, working in the garden, cooking, and washing the dishes. I liked to stand next to her and dry. Before she was married, Mom was a phys-ed teacher. She was the first and only one in her family to go to college, Henry Clay Frick Training School for Teachers in Pittsburgh. She actually met Frick, owner of the coal mines and coke factories that supplied Andrew Carnegie's steel mills with fuel. She had a personal interview with him when she applied to the college. Frick was the devil incarnate, who had probably helped kill Mom's father (who, without money to buy the good stuff, died drinking wood alcohol) and her stepfather (who worked in the mines). They were paid nothing, while Frick made millions. But Mom got her education. She got a good job teaching, which didn't pay much, so she had a second job at Kaufmann's, the big department store in Pittsburgh. That job probably didn't pay much either. She had a friend at Kaufmann's who was dating

Dad's friend. Mom's friend set her up with Dad, because Dad had a car. Mom and Dad would sit in the front seat and talk while Mom's friend and her date would neck in the back seat. That, at least, was the story Mom told.

Mom had to quit her job teaching when she married Dad. That's the way it was in the '30s: married women couldn't teach. So, Mom ran the house. Nothing was dirty or out of place.

Our two-story brick house was on Carl Avenue, a dirt road. The New Kensington Highway Department would spread the coal ash from the local power plant on the street and cover it with oil. There was no way to avoid tracking dirt and grime into the house. Mom spent years trying to get Carl Avenue paved. She was always on the phone with some local official. When City Hall got tired of Mom's browbeating, they told her the only way the city would pave the street would be if seventy-five percent of the street's residents signed a petition. She got the owners of all but two of the forty-four houses to sign the petition in one summer. (The two who didn't sign were away on vacation.)

Mom never let Marilyn and me get away with anything. After school, we were allowed to go out and play before dinner, but after dinner, we finished our homework. School was our work.

Play was something Mom didn't have time for. It didn't mean she wasn't good at it. Once when my friends and I were shooting hoops in the driveway (Dad had attached a basketball hoop on the side of the house above the garage), Mom stopped on her way to the clothesline to say hello.

One of my friends asked, "Mrs. Hunter, do you want to shoot some hoops?"

My friends chuckled.

Mom replied, "I've got laundry to do. You boys shoot the

basketball. I don't have the time."

My friend continued, "Mrs. Hunter, you were a phys-ed teacher, right? Did you ever play basketball?"

More chuckles from my friends.

Mom put down the laundry basket and motioned for the ball. She hit seven or eight out of ten flat-footed set shots from beyond the three-point line, before there was a three-point line. Mom then picked up the laundry basket and hung our clothes out to dry.

Marilyn and I got hugs, but there weren't outward signs of affection. I'm not sure Mom knew how to do that. She definitely didn't learn to be affectionate from her mother, a real battle-ax. She didn't encourage us. We were supposed to do well in school. We knew to keep our rooms neat and clean. We behaved in public. Mom was quick to criticize, and it wasn't gentle criticism. A distinct look on her face accompanied comments like, "That is so disgusting," and "How dirty and nasty that is!"

She expressed the same distaste and discomfort towards sex, uncomfortable talking about it. I never saw her show affection with Dad. When there was kissing on television, she would cringe. Whenever she talked to me about sex, it was nasty and going to get me in trouble. I was confused. Kissing looked fun and exciting on TV.

Dad got his master's degree in metallurgy from Carnegie Tech (now Carnegie Mellon University). He was an amateur ham radio operator. He had his own call letters, W3NCF (Nancy, Charlie, Fox), his own transmitters and receivers, and a huge twenty-foot antenna. No one else in town had an antenna like that. He spent a lot of time in his den talking to people all over the world. He had awards for talking to more people than anyone else on ham radio contest weekends.

Dad built our first television, a black and white seven-inch from a Heath Kit. All the kids in the neighborhood came to watch TV at my house until they got their own. Heath Kits were Dad's thing. He built all his radio equipment with them.

Dad repaired all the TVs in the neighborhood and around New Kensington, so our phone was always ringing. He took me along with him on house calls at night. I met a lot of people I otherwise never would have met. I saw the inside of many houses, different people and the different ways they lived. It was an education, watching Dad help people. I learned kindness. No matter if a person was rich or poor, black or white, if you could help them, you did—no questions asked.

When Dad wasn't building something, he sat in his favorite chair in the living room with a book. I would sit next to him on the couch and do homework. When homework was finished, there was always a book to pick up and read with him. Even when everyone else was glued to the TV, Dad would have a book on his lap. Most of the time he was quiet, but during meal times around the kitchen table, he would hold court. He would talk about everything: politics, current events, chemistry, history, economics, sports. I think I learned more over dinner than I learned in school.

Dad's job at the Alcoa Research Laboratory was to study aluminum with an electron microscope. He flew to Massachusetts to tell Sprague Electric Company all about capacitor foil. He flew to Tennessee and Alabama to tell the U.S. Air Force how to make their fighter jets stronger.

I wanted to be like Dad, but I also wanted him to spend more time with me. Even though I wasn't mechanically minded, I wanted Dad to teach me how to build things. Dad wanted to turn the screwdriver himself. I couldn't figure out why. It sucked the confidence right out of me and made me angry at him. I was angry that he never took me camping so we could huddle by the fire and talk about why Mom was always on my case.

I loved my parents. I wished they would have given me more guidance; Mom telling me about the birds and the bees instead of frightening me, Dad and I having man-to-man talks about man-to-man things. That never happened. The only time my parents visited me at the teepee, they were speechless, disappointed by their bearded, long-haired son, lost in the woods, surrounded by poles and canvas.

It was not until late that first autumn that I began to realize how unprepared I was to survive through the winter. When it got cold, it was very cold. When it snowed, it got worse. I moved back to the farmhouse for the winter.

In a snug, warm loft above the kitchen, I read *The Golden Bough* by Sir James Frazier, a comparative study of pagan beliefs incorporated into the Christian mythology. The pagan beliefs of using the spirit of the natural world as a religion appealed to me. I wanted to become a Druid priest, a warlock, a male witch, sorcerer, El Brujo, the good old Yaqui spirit.

When winter passed, I moved back into the teepee. Stronger after a year and a half on the farm, surrounded by nature, I felt my confidence surge. I took a motorcycle trip to Salem, Massachusetts, the witch capital of the world, where I bought a cast iron kettle and skillet. They were sturdier than the cheap frying pan I had used the first summer.

One Thursday afternoon, it started to storm. By evening, my clothes were soaked through. Everything in the teepee was wet. Still, nothing was going to force me to walk down the hill to the farmhouse. I built the fire to a roaring blaze until inside was warm and toasty. The rain continued through Friday and the weekend. Feeding the fire constantly, I reached a balance between wet and dry. When wet clothes chilled me to the bone, I removed them. Fetching wood naked was easier than drying wet clothes. I discovered a full-length gray flannel skirt left behind by a visitor, which dried quickly; useful attire for the rain. I found a thin old gray Dial Tone Lounge T-shirt. It dried quickly, too. The Dial Tone Lounge was a '70s bar in Hatfield with telephones on each of the tables. If you noticed a good-looking person at another table, you called them up and talked; *Match.com* before the Internet and cell phones. Smoke from the teepee fire gave my gray skirt and t-shirt a wonderful burnt wood smell.

I waited out the storm. By Sunday night, the weather cleared to a beautiful starlit night. I slept soundly and awoke Monday morning bolstered by my achievement. I headed down to the farm to see how everyone else was doing.

When I got to the bottom of the hill, everyone was getting into cars. Jimmy's Popcorn Farm was headed to Springfield Superior Court for Les' trial. He'd been busted with marijuana and charged with intent to distribute.

When Les saw me, he shouted to me in the Patois he'd learned in Jamaica, "Scott, I and I are going to Springfield for Jah trial. Justice will serve. Jah judge, his name is Lester Friedman. Les is a free man. There is no way I will convict. You must come as I and I. Give thanks and praise to the most-high, Hail I him, Selassie I, Jah, Rastafari."

Les could have been a mischievous elf in a fairy tale. He was short and round, always jolly, always entertaining. He would vanish for a time, then show up to share and sell intoxicating drugs. I never really trusted him, but I couldn't help being bewitched when he was around. He was a fancy dancer, always looking out for himself. Les personally introduced me to Rastafari, its history, philosophy, and its Patois. He had been to Jamaica a couple of times. The last time he was there, he'd spent a few months isolated in a small four-foot by six-foot, underground cell in a Savanna la Mar jail for a drug-related arrest. A revelation there led to a name change. He became Les Homme, loosely translated, the man. There was something attractive about his self-confidence. His talent for manipulation was captivating. Plus, he always had excellent marijuana.

I looked at my gray flannel skirt and ripped Dial Tone Lounge T-shirt. "Les, I'm not exactly dressed for Superior Court."

Les insisted, "Never mind, Jah smell like fire and brimstone. I and I brother wear Jah gray flannel suit, court perfect. Jah hair and beard are dread Rasta. I and I must oversee Jah's court. When Jah's judge sees and smells I and I together, he will intoxicate. Him forget about I. He sees only the dread Rastafari, hail I him. My dear friend, Jah cannot miss Jah trial. Positive vibrations. It will be superior."

I had spent so much time with Les, I actually knew what he was saying. "Irae, Les, positive vibrations. Jah, the most-high, Rastafari." How could I say no? I jumped into one of the cars and enjoyed the ride into civilization.

Les was right. When we walked into court, all eyes turned to look at the ragamuffin crew including a wild man with long matted red hair and beard, dressed like a woman. My wood-fired BBQ aroma permeated the courtroom. We sat down on a bench a few rows behind Les and his lawyers. The stares and whispers subsided with the appearance of the judge. After a flurry of activity in front of the bench, the judge, with Les and the lawyers, disappeared into the judge's chambers. After a long absence, they all returned to court, the judge made some quick pronouncements, and court was adjourned. To our astonishment, Les walked out a free man, just like he predicted.

At the party celebrating his release at the Springfield penthouse apartment of the real drug dealer, Les, his Patois evaporating into standard English, told us what happened in the judge's chambers: "One of my pre-trial conditions for the dismissal of the charges was the identification of the higher-ups in the western Massachusetts drug world. In chambers, my lawyers argued that I fulfilled the terms for my release by bringing you, Scotty, into the courtroom. The judge and prosecution lawyers were so flummoxed that a dirty, aromatic barbarian in women's clothing might be a drug boss, they dismissed the case."

We all had a good laugh, pretty sure that he was bullshitting us. Actually, I didn't believe Les had fingered me. His story was just a ruse to draw us in. I suspect he became an informant that day, since he never again appeared in court whenever he was busted.

Anyway, if the judge, the prosecutor, or the DEA wanted to come and talk to me about drugs in America, I would give them an earful. I had my First Amendment Constitutional Rights defense all planned out: marijuana was the Eucharist, a vehicle for Holy Communion with God, for the Rastafari. It was all a justification to block my negative feelings about who I was, a sinner. Marijuana was a lifesaver. I couldn't drink alcohol in the morning and stay drunk all day. Hits of acid were hard to come by. Marijuana? It was readily available, and I could smoke all day, happily do all the work on the farm, and never have to worry about feelings.

The next year, I spent two weeks in Jamaica with a couple of students from Hampshire College who happened onto the farm and invited me to go with them to Negril. A long walk out of Negril, we ended up in Spring Garden at the home of Seymour, a true Rasta. We slept on the ground next to his firepit the first night, then helped him build a shelter where we slept the following two weeks. I sharpened my Jamaican Patois and solidified my understanding of Rastafari beliefs.

I told my story of Moses as the revolutionary leader of the proletariat Israeli army and how Haile Selassie was the descendant of the first-born son of King Solomon and the Queen of Sheba, whom she secreted away to her relatives in Ethiopia to protect him from anyone who might want to do him harm. Seymour agreed that Haile Selassie, the Emperor of Ethiopia, was a descendant of that union. He told me that when Selassie arranged to come to Jamaica and greet the Rastafari, the religious fervor among the Rastas was so great that their storming of the runway prohibited Selassie's plane from landing.

That summer, I bought eighteen sheepskins for $180 from a leather company in Chesterfield, New Hampshire, and sewed them together by hand to make two huge thick blankets. I bought some more tent canvas and sewed together an ozan, an inner lining for my teepee. I cut up cordwood and surrounded the teepee bottom with a five-foot wood snow barrier. I spent the day growing and storing vegetables, milking the cow, making cheese, and cutting firewood for the farmhouse. At the teepee, I carried wood and fetched water. By autumn, I was ready for winter.

When the cold weather arrived, nights were pleasant with

sheepskin blankets and a sleeping bag on a hard wood platform I'd nailed together. I ate pan bread, squash, turnips, and popcorn cooked in a stone firepit over an open fire in the center of my tee-pee. I spent some afternoons smoking pot by the farmhouse stove, sharing occasional evening meals with my farm-mates, and more than a few nights at the local bars numbing myself with alcohol. I spent many long and lonely days and nights in the teepee. I got through the winter.

When spring came and turned into summer, I worked on the farm and spent my free time at the teepee. Not many people came to visit. My only companion was a red fox. When I was eating breakfast, he would appear out of the woods and sit fifteen yards away on the edge of the tree line, watching me. He stayed around until fall, then moved on.

In the late summer and fall, I had another visitor. When I returned from working my gardens late in the afternoon, a squir-rel would appear and sit on a rock near the tree line, watching me. I would smoke marijuana in my little pipe and just be with him. Life at the teepee was meditation. I worked the farm, ate when I was hungry, slept when I was tired, and enjoyed the day. Pot kept me free from feelings, especially the guilt I had in the presence of women.

One day, I imagined what the squirrel saw while he was sitting there. Was he wondering what I was doing with the plastic bag full of something, placing some of it in a piece of wood, lighting it with fire, putting it to my lips, and then exhaling smoke? That day, like always, the squirrel ran off when I rose to walk down to the stream to fetch water. I took a good-sized bud of marijuana and placed it on the rock where he sat. When I returned to the teepee, the bud of marijuana was gone and, in its place, was an acorn. That acorn became sacred.

I had tasted acorns before. The tannic acid made them taste bitter. A month or two later, while sitting in my teepee tending the fire, as I rolled the acorn around in my hand, I noticed it was cracked. I opened it up and popped the meat into my mouth. It was very tasty. I realized then why squirrels store acorns. They ate last year's stash. In storage, the acorns ripen and lose their bitterness. I added roasted acorn meat to my diet.

I was thinking, *Hmmm… I'm enjoying hanging out with fox and squirrels more than humans.* If I hadn't needed alcohol, I would have forsaken the bar scene and humans altogether. I was comfortable with my animal companions at the teepee, though I did enjoy it when someone would visit me. We would talk a little and share some weed. It didn't take long for them to feel the need to get back down the hill, back to their lives. There wasn't much at the teepee for them to do. There was a lot for me to do at the teepee; eat, sleep, fetch wood, and carry water.

Farming was good for me. Before I moved onto the farm, I saw myself as smart but physically weak. My plan on the farm was to work as low-tech as possible and become strong. I got good at pick and shovel work. At the end of January 1976, my first full winter in the teepee, an old farmer who lived in a trailer on Mormon Hollow Road told me how he used to get sap from the sugar maples and make syrup. I decided to make maple syrup the old-fashioned way.

I bought a double-bladed axe. Each morning in early February, I crossed over the creek below the farmhouse to the pine grove covering the opposite hillside and chopped down all the dead trees in the grove, lopped the branches off, and turned the trunks into long logs. I dragged the logs down the hill and across the creek to a cooking site I made in the center of the sugar maple grove. With a bow saw, I cut them to three-foot lengths. I cut down a couple of three-quarter-inch sumac saplings and made four-inch long maple syrup taps, hollowing out the soft core of the sumac. There were sixty sugar maple trees on the ridge halfway up Jerusalem Mountain. I drilled holes in them and inserted the sumac taps. During maple season, one tap yields a gallon of sap. Most of the trees had two or three taps. Forty gallons of sap produced a gallon of maple syrup. I had about 150 taps, so I figured I would make three and a half gallons. My plan was coming together. Free maple syrup for my people, everyone on the farm and all the neighbors. That sounded better than manna in the wilderness.

Bruce, the other Popcorner who was partially committed to farming, decided that he would tap 120 trees in a hillside sugar maple grove between the lower pasture north of the farmhouse and the large vegetable garden. I was looking forward to his company while we boiled the sap. However, he abandoned his trees after a small branch stuck him in the eye. I suspected he realized how much work old-fashioned sugaring was and wimped out. Since it would have been a waste of sap and an injury to the trees if I hadn't taken over his taps, I worked the trees he'd started and mine, 180 in total.

I found a fifty-gallon oil drum that had never been used at Andy's brother's junkyard and cut it in half length-wise. I built a firepit and put both halves of the drum over it, using one half to boil the water out of the sap and the second half to continue the boiling process toward real maple syrup. When the sap began to flow in late February, a typical day would start before sunrise. I'd light a fire underneath the primary drum and fill it with the sap I'd collected the previous evening. Then I'd head out to one of the two maple groves and collect more sap. Collecting sap from the trees near my teepee was the most fun. My sap transport in the snow was a metal garbage can on top of a red plastic sled. With a full garbage can on the sled and using one foot as a rudder, I'd race down the snow-covered path and farm road, across the driveway, then down the next hill to the cooking area. I'd stoke the fire underneath the primary drum, then expand the fire to heat the finishing drum. Then I'd transfer the boiled-down sap from the primary drum to the finishing drum, fill the primary drum with new sap, and head out for more sap. When the day's sap was collected, I'd stoke the fires and spend a leisurely afternoon watching the sap boil down.

With temperatures in the thirties and forties during the day, I'd strip down to my bare chest and stay warm by the fire. At sunset, when the sap was thick, a consistency near syrup, I'd collect it into new, clean, five-gallon buckets and carry them up to the farmhouse. I'd finish the process on the wood stove in the kitchen.

Amazingly, the color of the maple syrup was always a reflection of the light in the sky when I emptied it out of the finishing drum. If I finished early and the sky was still bright at the end, the syrup would be a light amber. If I finished later when the sky was dark, the resulting syrup would be a darker hue. The maple syrup tasted of hard work and a day well spent. All the exercise, accomplishment, and a few joints made me feel at one with the universe. I slept soundly at night.

Despite some anger at being the only farmer on the farm (now that Meredith was caring for her baby), every day was filled with wonder. I would start with a breakfast of raw eggs, fresh milk, and homegrown maple syrup—you know, eggnog. Homegrown vegetables for lunch and dinner throughout the year were the best. Warm fires to sit around when it was cold couldn't be beat. Daily exercise—planting, weeding, and harvesting the garden during spring and summer and gathering wood in the fall—was fulfilling, physically and spiritually.

I sold bumper crops of vegetables to local and Boston restaurants. Milking Daisy the cow twice a day was an almost folkloric chore. She produced more than enough milk for us to drink, so I learned to make cheese in a wood cheese press and churned the milk into butter with a real butter churner. Toasted cheese sandwiches for lunch were a treat. After giving blocks of cheese to our neighbors for goodwill, they began to insist on paying for them. Chickens supplied the farm with eggs and an occasional chicken dinner. I slaughtered a couple of one-year-old calves for meat. At harvest time, we canned tomatoes and applesauce and gathered and stored winter squash. The farm bought fifty-pound bags of whole wheat flour and twenty-five-pound boxes of spaghetti from LT&C.

chapter 19

I was most proud of my small marijuana field hidden in the woods—some serious bud. When Les discovered the field, he decided the police helicopter flights over the farm would find them, so he harvested the buds. Angry as hell, I confronted him.

"Les, what the fuck did you do? You harvested my pot crop? I spent all year working it and you come in and pick all the buds?"

Indignantly, he replied, "Scott, I had to. The police helicopter saw the field. I knew it. We had to harvest immediately. I did you a favor. I saved the crop. It's communal bud, and we have good stuff to smoke now. You should thank me."

His endearing Jamaican Patois was gone. He was in his intimidating mode. It worked on me.

I was bummed, but said, "I guess it's all of ours. Let's dry it and smoke it."

Les controlled the buds. He shared them with the farm as if they were his own. Despite my anger, I did have a feeling of accomplishment. I had grown some righteous weed. The buds lasted until Christmas. All I had left to get through January and

February was a half-pound of chaff.

Once a week, I would head over to the post office in Wendell Depot to pick up my mail. The breaking news over coffee was the marriage of Emily Babbitt, the divorced wife of Elwood Babbitt, the local clairvoyant, and Harvey Matusow, recently arrived from New York City.

Harvey's actual claim to fame was that he was the chief witness for Joe McCarthy, Roy Cohn, and the House Committee on Un-American Activities. After destroying hundreds of people's lives, Harvey admitted his testimony under oath was false. He was a rat. To separate himself from his infamous past, Harvey changed his name to Job. Instead of being God's faithful servant, in my humble opinion, this particular Job was an anathema, the epitome of evil, and a harbinger of bad luck. Upon the death of his mother, Harvey had moved into a bus in the woods. He'd inherited her estate and began throwing money around.

For a wedding present, Harvey bought Emily Jack McCracken's old junkyard across the river from the post office. Phil, a regular at the post office café, suggested that he and I help Emily get the junkyard into shape. We figured it would be fun to see what McCracken had collected over the years, and it would fill my time until the maple sap started to flow. Emily welcomed our help.

The next Monday, Phil and I began cleaning out the main shack. We separated tools, car parts, and usable junk from the grease, dirt, and crap. There were a few wooden boxes with papers and greasy rags in them. We moved them to one side, near a window.

For three days, Phil and I worked in the bitter cold. Nights were colder. It was not unusual for the temperature to plunge to fifteen or twenty degrees below zero on clear nights.

When I arrived at the junkyard for the fourth day of cleaning up, I found a pile of ashes in place of the shack. The Wendell Depot gossip was arson. Maybe, one of the many people who disliked "Job" for stealing Emily from Elwood had probably set the fire intentionally. My first thought was the wood boxes of paper and greasy rags we'd moved near the window had somehow ignited during the bitter cold night.

Since the junkyard was no more, I didn't think about it much until a police detective showed up at the farm a few days later. I welcomed him into the kitchen. Short and clean-cut, he could have been ex-army.

"I'm Lieutenant Chris Johnson. You were working at Emily Babbitt's junkyard. Did you see anyone suspicious hanging around? Someone who might want to commit arson, hurt those two? This Matusow have enemies?"

I answered straightforwardly. "Sir, I don't think it was arson. Phil and I moved some wooden boxes of paper and greasy rags from the back of the shop to the front, near a window. I never thought about anything catching fire in such cold weather. If it's anyone's fault, it's Phil's and mine. Do you know if the fire started on the east or south side? That's where Phil and I moved those boxes full of flammable rags, close to a couple of windows. Those rags could have spontaneously combusted. It might have been an unfortunate accident."

Lt. Johnson was looking around the kitchen, taking it all in. "Maybe. How many people live here?"

I told him about the farm and offered to show him around, but he declined. He may have dismissed arson as the cause of the junkyard fire, but he'd discovered Jimmy's Popcorn and began surveillance. He noticed the LT&C truck at the farm, occasionally parked in the driveway overnight. Les would stop at the farm during his route to deliver the natural food we'd ordered. Sometimes he'd drive home after he finished a delivery route and return the truck to LT&C in the morning. Johnson decided that the unmarked class-two truck was transporting huge loads of marijuana to and from the farm.

Johnson contacted the Wendell Chief of Police, Ted Hawkins, and learned it was common knowledge we smoked pot at Jimmy's Popcorn. At 5 a.m. the next Saturday morning, the Orange and Wendell police departments invaded Jimmy's Popcorn dressed in SWAT uniforms. They arrested five of us, Les, Joe, Lacy, Bruce, and me, on marijuana charges. We were placed in handcuffs and carted off to the Orange jail.

From the back of the police van, I asked Chief Hawkins, "Why are we in handcuffs? Why are you so enthusiastic? What's with the SWAT uniforms? I'm impressed with the camouflage gear and the guns, but, fuck, aren't we friends? We talk all the time at town meetings."

Ted seemed very angry. "Scott, you better be quiet. You're under arrest, remember."

I persisted. "So, that's what the handcuffs are for? I know you're just doing your job, but Ted, this is crazy."

Ted swerved the van as he turned around to face me. "Shut the fuck up, Scott, or I'll charge you with…just shut up."

I wouldn't quit. "You know I smoke pot. Everyone knows we smoke pot on the farm. You know people who come over on Saturday night and smoke with us. If you wanted to know about how much pot we smoked, you could have asked your friends any time."

Ted sped up and finally slammed on the brakes in the parking lot of the Orange police station. We spent about forty-five minutes in our jail cells and were released on our own recognizance. Ted was standing by Lt. Johnson as we left the station.

I asked him, "That's it? We can go home? Don't we have to stay in jail until we go to court? Don't we have be arraigned?"

Curtly, he said, "Go home, Scott. Your friends are waiting for you outside."

He and Johnson were discouraged.

When I went over to the post office to pick up my mail the following week, I received a standing ovation from Phil.

"Jimmy's Popcorn made the front page of *The Greenfield Recorder*! You're putting Wendell on the map!"

Even Fredrick, an old, conservative farmer, was supportive: "Jesus Christ, those idiots busted you guys for smoking pot. If they do that to all the pot smokers in this town, they're going have to build three more jails in Orange."

A few weeks later, we went to Orange District Court and were arraigned. We hired a lawyer, Morris White, a fellow Amherst College alumnus who was practicing law in Warwick.

In the fall, with our Superior Court trial date approaching, seven months after our arrest, the four of us met with Morris to discuss our strategy. Les had disappeared, saying since he was involved in the drug trade, he did not want to be associated with any trial or publicity. He never told me where he went or how he avoided a warrant for not showing up for the trial. It deepened my suspicion that he was working for the cops somehow. He showed up at Jimmy's Popcorn after the trial. Morris assured the four of us that nothing would happen at the trial. At worst, we would be found guilty, fined, and put on probation. There was no chance of jail time.

Lacy and Joe were expecting a baby girl. Meredith and Bruce were taking care of their baby. With families, Lacy, Joe, and Bruce wanted to plead guilty and settle everything with as little fuss as possible. I was left alone to fight for my First Amendment right, the freedom of religion.

By now, my hair was matted into Rastafari dreadlocks reaching to the middle of my back. My beard, blowing in the wind as I rode my 650cc. Triumph Bonneville motorcycle around the countryside, had formed into two dreadlocks. My two weeks with Seymour in Jamaica convinced me that marijuana was sacred to the Rasta, like the wafer and wine was to a Christian. I looked like a Rastafari, smoked pot like one, and spoke Patois as good as any American Rasta, but I didn't find a deep spirituality in it. For me, the real truth was that it was just an excuse to justify smoking marijuana. Still, with my background in Christianity, I played the role of a professor of Rastafari. I was going to tell it to the judge.

On the day of our hearing, the four of us got all dressed up and drove to the Franklin County Courthouse. At the courthouse, Morris, tall with short, dark, nicely combed hair and a trim Van Dyke beard, suit and tie, lawyer extraordinaire, related a conversation he had with the prosecutor and Ted, chief of the Wendell Police.

"Everyone wants to be your friends now. If you plead guilty to marijuana possession, the prosecutor will drop the distribution charges. Nobody wants the publicity of a big trial."

Smiling, I spoke up. "I want the publicity of a trial."

Lacy, five-months pregnant, looking a little uncomfortable, barked sharply, "Scott, be quiet."

Morris continued. "Ted is really sorry. If you plead guilty to possession, he agrees to be less confrontational. Let bygones be bygones. He promises from now on, if he has any questions about the farm and marijuana, he'll come and ask you." Then it got a little strange as Morris went on, "The Town of Wendell also wants to apologize for the inconvenience of the raid, arrest, and trial. Ted has agreed you can peacefully grow and smoke pot on the farm without interference from the town or the police, as long as you don't sell anything you grow. The town doesn't want the publicity of a jury trial. They would be grateful if you accepted a plea."

I asked, "Why don't they just drop the charges?"

Joe, having been through court before, looked as uncomfortable as Lacy. "Scott, the system is the system. You've got to give it its due. We got busted. The prosecution is ready to deal. We take the deal. I've been through this before. Pay a little money, kiss a little ass, and it all goes away."

The four of us huddled in the hallway. Lacy, Joe, and Bruce were eager to take the deal and go home. I wanted to defend my First Amendment rights, but I felt very alone, facing my three friends and Morris. Reluctantly, I agreed to accept the prosecution's offer, plead to possession, have the distribution charge dropped, and no jury trial.

We accepted a small fine and six months of probation. The judge's gavel came down and it was over. As I turned to walk out of the courtroom, Morris approached me.

"The judge wants to talk with you. I gave him the statement you wrote up, and he's interested in what you have to say. Would you talk with him?"

Intrigued, I said, "Sure, Morris, I'll talk with him."

We walked through a door beside the judge's bench, into a room whose walls were covered with large books. The judge, gray-haired with a pleasant smile, for a moment, dressed in his robe, reminded me of Reverend Boswell, the minister of my church when I was six. The judge was another man of power.

"Mr. Hunter, please sit down. Thank you for agreeing to talk with me. First, I'm happy you have cooperated with the prosecutor. Pleading guilty to possession has saved Wendell the embarrassment of a trial. Even the thought of a "volunteer training mission" by a local police force on American citizens is an affront to any legal search and seizure. Volunteer training mission? I would have thrown the case out of the court if it had reached my bench."

"Excuse me, sir, what did you just say? If the case had gone to trial, you would have thrown it out?"

The judge leaned forward and folded his hands on his desk. "The raid was totally against any concept of civil liberties. Actions like that might happen in totalitarian countries, but it is not just or proper in the United States of America."

My face tightened with a scowl. I glanced at Morris, who had a sheepish look on his face. I thought, *You motherfucker, you screwed us.*

The judge continued, "Scott, I'm interested in the paper you wrote, about your religious beliefs. My daughter smokes pot. I don't know what to do. It's illegal, but she's my daughter. Can you give a father some advice?"

My anger disappeared. I told him about the Rastafari religion, then explained, "Pot gives me this feeling that I am at one with the universe, like insight into the mystery of existence. There's no separation. You're one with the trees, the rocks, the air. The Rastafari call it 'overstanding' instead of understanding. It alters your perception."

His brow wrinkled. "But what should I do about my daughter?" He wasn't interested in the mysteries of existence and the universe. His mystery was his own child.

I tried to explain my perspective. "Rebellion is what young people do. What? I can't smoke pot? I'm going to smoke pot. There isn't much you can do. You have to love and accept your daughter."

I wish I could have told him that marijuana was insulating me from the demons bent on destroying me. I wish I could have explained to him that his daughter was probably going through feelings as a young adult she didn't understand, and that marijuana shielded her from those emotions.

I continued, "Marijuana isn't the problem. The criminalization of marijuana is. If you're worried your daughter is doing something illegal and it might jeopardize your position in society, well, that's not your daughter's concern. We live in a society that criminalizes a personal choice. If people can drink alcohol, they should be able to smoke pot. That makes sense to me. Your daughter loves you, and you have to love her back."

The judge stood and held out his hand. I stood, and we shook hands.

"I'm glad I met you today and we had this talk. I'm not sure I understand all that you told me, but I think I might understand my daughter a little better."

My anger at Morris for selling us out lessened as our relationship to the town changed. Friends saw us as heroes. Town officials were grateful that we'd accepted the plea deal. The publicity of a trial would have been an enormous embarrassment for them. If a volunteer training mission could happen at Jimmy's Popcorn Farm, it could happen at anyone's place.

Ted was asked to resign as chief of police. The following

spring, Dennis was the new chief of police. He came up to my teepee.

"So, this is the teepee I've heard about."

"Welcome to the woods, Dennis. Sit down. Want to smoke some pot?"

He laughed, put his hands on his hips, and feigned seriousness. "I'm in uniform. I'll pass on that offer. I'd hang out, but I've got a lot of things to do now that I'm chief. If you could show me around the farm and where you're planting your pot, I won't bother you again."

I showed him the farm, introduced him to Daisy, the milk cow, and the chickens. Everyone had gathered in the kitchen and I introduced him to them. Bruce came along with us to point out where he had planted marijuana in a wheat field, and I showed Dennis my plot in the woods. Back at the driveway, Dennis thanked us for the tour.

"You guys have to promise me one thing. Don't sell your pot. If you do and I find out, I'll be back."

That summer, a group of citizens placed a referendum to legalize marijuana on the town ballot. It passed in November. Though illegal throughout Massachusetts, we pretended it was legal in Wendell.

The spring of 1978 came to Jimmy's Popcorn. Though I planted a big garden, I really wasn't into farming any more. I spent most of my time at the teepee and in the forest away from everyone on the farm. The bust and hearing faded from my mind.

One morning, I met Meredith on the path down the hill from the teepee. She told me that Les was back and talking about getting back at the police. She said that everyone except Bruce, Joe, and Lacy avoided him. But those four, fueled with alcohol and Les' drug supply, sought revenge.

Les, Bruce, Joe, and Lacy cleared the lower acre pasture of stones and built a large stone pyramid in the center. They planted alternating pie-shaped wedges of wheat, barley, and rye around the pyramid. After the grain was planted, Les gathered everyone together and led a witching ceremony. Holding hands, they circled the pyramid and raised a prayer to the spiritual powers existing in the universe.

Les chanted, "Lords of the Darkness, hear us. We have been wronged. The raid upon Jimmy's Popcorn Farm has offended the universe. Since we, insignificant beings, do not have the power in this physical plane to retaliate against those who led this volunteer training mission upon us, we ask the Dark Lords to mete out the revenge that is due. Restore the balance. If we are not entitled to revenge, then let the revenge fall on us."

When I heard about the witching ceremony, I wondered what would happen. Over the next six months, Morris was in a car accident on Route 116 near Montague Road in Montague. His kidney was lacerated. He spent a few months in the hospital and several more being nursed back to health by his mother. Forced to resign as chief of police, Ted's financial health suffered, his wife divorced him, and he moved out of town. Lt. Johnson discovered his wife in their bedroom with another man. He shot and wounded his wife and killed her lover. He was convicted of murder and served a lengthy sentence in Cedar Junction State Prison.

The marijuana planted in the field around the stone pyramid didn't escape the invocation that afternoon. The pot plants produced three pounds of serious marijuana buds. Personally, I looked forward to smoking it all up over the winter, but Bruce had other ideas. He traded the three pounds of herb to an ex-Vietnam

War veteran who lived in Montague for an ornery three-year-old milk cow who was impossible to milk. The vet who bought the marijuana was so stoned from smoking our homegrown, he neglected to clean the chimney of his wood stove that autumn. The resulting chimney fire set the house ablaze. After escaping from the burning house with his wife, the vet realized the pot was still in the house. He reentered to retrieve it, and, overcome by the smoke and fire, died.

chapter 20

I avoided the farmhouse even more, spending little time in the garden. I spent most of my day at the teepee and wandering the state forest discovering hidden glens and rock cliffs. As peaceful as life was, I was lonely. One July morning, I was feeling especially down. On my way to the creek to fetch water for breakfast, noticing the Mascaras mushrooms were in bloom, I thought about picking some Caesareas, the non-poisonous Mascaras, for breakfast. A few Panterinas Mascara, described as possibly poisonous in books on mushrooms, called to me. *What the hell, I'm into research and development,* I joked with myself. *Let's eat some and see what happens.*

Drug and alcohol abuse are self-destructive, a slow and painful suicide. Suicide without total commitment. Whether it was sabotage by poisonous mushrooms, hits of LSD, constant pot use, failure at employment, anti-authoritarian behavior, or just plain loathing, I refused to allow myself to get my act together. I couldn't punish others for the way I felt, so I punished myself. I beat myself up and survived to prove how strong I was. It got to the place where I felt good losing, being down. At six, I knew I was a sinner. At twenty-eight, I was accomplished at suffering for those sins.

Picking out a nice-looking Panterina, I carried it back to the teepee, cut a few thin slices off the cap, just enough to see what might happen, and cooked up a three-egg mushroom omelet with some pan bread. Caesarea Mascara had a bland taste. The Panterina had a tangy, sharp, acidic taste. I waited around for a few hours and nothing happened. So much for poisonous mushrooms.

I ate the slices of mushroom around 6 a.m. Around 9, I remembered I had an Orange Food Co-operative membership work assignment painting the outside back wall. I still had a few connections to the outside world. I walked out to the main road and hitchhiked to the co-op. Around noon, I began to paint the southern wall.

It was always cool in the woods, and on the farm, the creek was never far away. At the co-op, the afternoon sun beat down on me. It was going to be a hot day. I took off my shirt and painted in cut-off jeans. By the end of the day, I felt like a lizard on the co-op wall, baking in the sun. When my skin began to burn, I figured I was going to have serious sunburn for the next couple of days. I finished painting the wall and returned to the farm.

During dinner at the farmhouse, everyone had a good laugh at how sunburned I was. In the evening, I noticed that my crotch and armpits were itching like crazy. Sunburn there? Then it dawned on me. I had eaten the Panterina Mascara about thirteen hours earlier. My skin glowed red. The itch was unbearable. Anywhere I had thin skin—my groin, armpits, behind my knees, ears, around my eyes, between my fingers—was on fire. Needing to cool down, I ran to the swimming hole and jumped in. The water was cold, and I relaxed a little. In the water, I didn't need to scratch. I ducked my head in the water as often as I could to stop the itching around my eyes and behind my ears.

Having lived through a few harrowing moments on psychedelics, I knew the longer I was alive, the better my chances of surviving. I stayed underwater with just my nose exposed. When I began to shiver uncontrollably, I draped myself over the large log we used to cross over the creek until the itching was too much, then back underwater. I was too busy to sleep.

By dawn the next morning, I was able to spend some time out of the water, lying down on the grass to rest until I itched too much, then getting back into the creek. The cold water was saving my life. I had a ton of energy. I needed to do something. It was going to be another hot day. My half-acre vegetable garden 300 yards up the hill needed water. I got a couple of five-gallon plastic buckets, filled them with water, and lugged them up the hill. While I walked the buckets up the hill, I couldn't scratch my skin. Running down the hill, then throwing the buckets into the creek, I would dive in and cool down. I watered the garden all day long and into the night.

The next afternoon, still wired to the max, itching like crazy, I called Mark Allen, a classmate from Amherst who was a doctor in Greenfield. I explained my situation to his receptionist and made an appointment for the next day. Mark returned my call a short time later.

"Scott, it's been a while. Are you living in the area? What about this mushroom poisoning?" He sounded concerned.

I was glad to hear from him. "Mark, I'm living in Wendell on a hippie farm. I ate some mushrooms yesterday. I think they were poisonous. My skin is bright red and I itch like crazy."

He didn't sound surprised. "You haven't changed. Always finding trouble. I know nothing about poisonous mushrooms. Did you eat any today?"

I answered his question and more. "No, I ate the mushrooms two days ago. I've been hanging out in the creek underwater. Cold is good. I have a lot of energy and I'm getting a lot done. I'm watering my garden by hand."

He responded clinically, "So, you are still alive and not ingesting anymore poison. The first twenty-four hours are the worst when you're poisoned. I know that much. You could come in and I could look at you, but if you continue to feel better, there isn't much else I can do."

I decided to stay and tend the garden. That night, between intervals in the cold water, I slept on the log. By morning, my skin was less red and didn't itch as much. I continued to water the vegetables for weeks throughout the hottest and driest part of the summer and harvested a bumper crop.

After I recovered from the mushrooms, news reached me: some students from UMass had bought the old Farley General Store. One afternoon in early August, I became curious and walked through the woods to the Farley House. It hadn't been a general store in a while, but the first floor still held the remains— shelves, a counter, and a pot-belly stove connected to a center brick chimney. The second floor was made up of eight small rooms off of a hallway; the stairs to the third floor led to four small rooms in the eaves. Rumor had it that the general store profited from the bordello on the second and third floors in the early 1900s.

There were five cars parked along the road in front of a large porch. Two guys and a woman sat on rockers drinking beer. I introduced myself. One of the guys reached into a cooler, grabbed a beer, and tossed it to me.

"Welcome to Farley House. Have a beer."

The two guys looked like twins with long brown hair and beards. I couldn't help but stare at the woman, her long blonde hair cascading down to near her waist, wearing bib overalls without a shirt.

I caught the beer, popped it, and took a swig.

"This is my first time here. You bought the place?"

One of the guys said, "Yep, closed last week. A couple of us are on the mortgage, but at least twelve of us live here and split the bills. Can't live much cheaper and have so much fun. Farley is a far cry from everywhere." We all laughed. "Go inside and meet everybody. There's a party going on."

I walked in. On either side of the potbelly stove, a group of people passed around a joint. Another group stood around the old counter of the store talking. Everyone had a beer. I walked up to the counter and was greeted by a short young woman in a sundress. She wore her hair in a pageboy. Her blue eyes sparkled.

"I'm Christine. And you are?"

I stuck out my hand. "I'm Scott. I live in the teepee over at Jimmy's Popcorn."

Christine reached up, put her hands around my neck, and gave me a big hug. I was a little shocked at her friendliness, but I enjoyed the hug. Parties at the farm were wild, but this felt like the farm on acid.

Christine snuggled up to me, then stood on her toes and whispered into my ear. "I'd introduce you to everyone here, but I don't know half of them." She giggled. "Let's go up to my room. It's quiet, and we can talk."

She took my hand, led me up the stairs to her room, and

flopped down on her bed. I stood there awkwardly.

"Come on Scott, sit here next to me."

As I sat down next to her, someone else appeared at the door.

Christine said, "Brenda, this is Scott from the farm in Wendell. He's the guy who lives in the teepee."

My eyes almost popped out of my head. Brenda had red hair down to her shoulders. She was tall and had an amazing figure. She wore a plaid shirt buttoned down the front and tied up at the bottom, exposing a flat stomach. She had shorts on that revealed a wonderful set of legs. She flopped down next to me, pushing me closer to Christine.

It was impossible to keep my hands off of them. They were a lot more relaxed about their bodies than I was about mine. I'd never been intimate with two women before. They were touching each other as they cuddled with me in the middle. I kept talking about the teepee, trying to create space so I could figure out what was going on.

Brenda, with her head on my shoulder, stroked my beard. "I really want to see what the teepee's like. I'm a city girl from Boston. This country life has me excited."

Christine said, "I haven't been to the farm yet. We should go up there and visit Scott."

Then she leaned over and kissed me on my lips and then kissed Brenda. With a big smile, she said, "Well, I have things to do. It was so nice talking with you, Scott." She got up and straightened her clothes. "Brenda, you take care of Scott for me. I have to start thinking about dinner."

Brenda sat up and stared at me. Her eyes were a bright green. "You have to take me to the teepee, Scott."

I stammered, "I'll show it to you sometime." I tried to figure out how to make a move on Brenda but couldn't. "You should come over tomorrow. We have a bonfire in the driveway every night."

Brenda must've felt my discomfort. She stood and took my hand. "Let's go downstairs, see what's happening, and help Christine with dinner."

I helped Christine and Brenda cook dinner, promising to bring vegetables from the garden next time I came over. After dinner, having lost track of my two new friends, I returned to the teepee and fantasized about the future.

The next day, I repaired fences so that Daisy the cow wouldn't eat all the vegetables before we could and picked tomatoes for canning and corn for dinner. Then I headed up the hill to check my secret field of pot. After a community dinner, everyone was standing by the bonfire smoking jays. I felt two arms wrap around my shoulders from behind me and a whisper in my ear: "Time to show me your teepee."

I turned, rubbing up against Brenda's body. Her arms were still around my neck and her face was inches from mine.

"Brenda, ah, it's so good to feel you, I mean, see you."

I couldn't believe I had made such a brazen joke.

Brenda nuzzled into my neck. Her arms slid around my waist and she pressed up against me. "Take me to your teepee."

I pointed behind her back. "It's up that way. There's a road next to the chicken coop."

Brenda whispered in my ear, "I'm afraid of the dark. Will you protect me?"

I was shaking like a leaf. "I'll keep you safe. Come with me."

We walked arm-in-arm to the cabin where the road turned into a path. The kisses we shared on the way made the years in the teepee worth it. At the top of the hill, our eyes had adjusted to the dark and we could make out the teepee's silhouette against the trees and the starry night sky. We crawled in and I started a fire. In the firelight, we took off each other's clothes. My lack of sophistication was balanced by Brenda's expertise. She guided me into her. It didn't take long until we lay in each other's arms, exhausted.

After a while, Brenda sat up and began looking for her clothes. "Scott, could you make the fire bright again? I need to find my clothes. Then you need to walk me down the hill. I should get back to the Farley House tonight."

Surprised and a little disappointed, I said, "You're not staying here? The sunrise in the morning is really cool."

Brenda was blunt. "Nope, I've got to get back. That was really fun, Scott. But I have to get home."

I was almost in love and Brenda was cutting it short. I relit the fire and we got dressed. I walked Brenda down the hill, and we kissed goodnight.

"Scott, why don't you come down to the Farley House tomorrow and bring some vegetables? I'm cooking. You can eat with us."

I was looking forward to tomorrow already.

The next day, I got all my chores done, gathered the best vegetables from the garden, bathed in the swimming hole, and drove the farm car over to the Farley House. Brenda and I kissed and cuddled as we prepared dinner. After dinner, everyone shared a slew of joints around the pot-belly stove. I helped wash dishes until someone turned on the record player. Brenda found me, and we danced to a few songs, then she took my hand and led me upstairs to her room. We settled down on her bed and began making out. I unbuttoned her shirt and played with her breasts. When she reached down and began unsnapping and unzipping my shorts, I reached into her pants to play with her.

Brenda whispered into my ear, "Be careful, Scott, I'm having my period."

I tensed up. "But we made love last night. Did you just get your period today?"

Unconcerned, Brenda replied, "No, I was having my period yesterday, too. That's why I needed to go home last night. I didn't have any tampons."

Still confused, I said, "But we made love last night."

Nonchalantly, she replied, "Sort of, Scott. Because I was having my period, I guided you into my ass. It's easier that way and not so messy. Anyway, I really like how it feels when someone fucks me in the ass. It gets me off."

"So, if we make love tonight, do you want me to…" I almost couldn't say the words, "fuck you in the ass?"

Enthusiastically, Brenda said, "Yeah, it's intense. I have huge orgasms."

I didn't say a word.

"Or, I could give you a blow job, or jerk you off. I don't mind as long as I have an orgasm too."

I was disoriented, but then Brenda began kissing me and I got back into it. We gave each other orgasms with our hands and cuddled for a while. I was feeling sick to my stomach and made an excuse to leave.

That night in the teepee I sat up alone, thinking. *I just fucked someone in the ass. How disgusting. I am a sinner, guilty, filthy. I'm on the road to hell.*

Brenda showed up at the farm often and we continued to have sex. Even though I was uneasy hanging out with her, it was hard for me to say no. Being intimate with her brought up painful but unnamed emotions. Then she convinced me to go to Boston and meet her family. After an uncomfortable dinner, Brenda took me upstairs to see her room.

She began taking off her clothes and said with a devilish laugh, "I want you to fuck me here. It would make my parents so mad to know I did something like that."

I watched Brenda take off the last of her clothes, lie down on her bed, and spread her legs. It was the first time I'd ever seen a vagina up close. I crumpled to the floor.

"Brenda, we can't do this." I grabbed my chest and lowered my head. I couldn't look up. "We have to go back downstairs. I want to go home." I started to sob.

Brenda's eyes widened. "Scott? Are you okay?"

I shielded my eyes. "It's okay. Let's just go back downstairs."

Brenda got up and put her clothes on. There was a distance between us as we headed home.

For the next few days, I spent my nights at the teepee upset and agitated. I couldn't understand my attraction to Brenda and the anguish and hopelessness I was feeling about who I was. I knew I wasn't evil, but I felt immoral. I was a bad person. About a week later, I woke up and noticed my penis itched. By afternoon, I had a rash on my genitals. My life was hopeless. I was condemned. When I calmed down enough to think rationally, I decided I probably had contracted a sexually transmitted disease. I needed to see a doctor.

Since I had talked with Mark Allen about the rash I'd gotten from the mushrooms, I got up the nerve to call him and make an appointment. His receptionist said he could see me in two days.

Two days later, when I headed over to Dr. Allen's office, the rash was gone. By that time, I had named my condition—herpes. Since I had made the appointment, I went just to talk with him.

"Mark, I think I got herpes. It was really bad for two days, then when I called you to make an appointment, it started to go away. This morning it was gone."

Stating the obvious, he said, "I can't diagnose it if I can't see it." Mark tapped his stethoscope on the examination table. "Disappearing like that doesn't sound like herpes. When it happens again, get over here as fast as you can. Are you still living on the farm? And the rash from the mushrooms went away?"

I nodded yes, and he let me go.

Over the next fifteen years, I struggled with physical contact with women. Whenever I thought about the possibility of intimacy or got nervous or extremely worried about anything, the rash would appear.

Resigned to a lonely life, I wandered the state forest and kept the fire going at night. I felt like I desired loneliness. It was now near the end of my fourth year on the farm, the third in my teepee. I hadn't found what I was looking for in the teepee.

One morning, I headed down to Les' new place. He had moved to a house trailer in a little hollow next to the stream where the farm road turned off. I knocked on his door. He invited me in.

"Just the man I was looking for." Les showed me a few sheets of blotter LSD, sixteen hits to a sheet. "I just got these last night, a new batch of acid from the 2001 community. No one's tried it yet. You'd be the first."

I was attracted to the danger. "Sure!"

The imprint on the blotter acid was a large American bald eagle with wings spread, an olive branch in one talon and arrows in the other, and thirteen stars in an ornate circle about the eagle's head. In the eagle's mouth was an E Pluribus Unum banner, the seal on the back of a dollar bill. All in black and white, the imprint was spread over four quarter-inch blotter squares. I was impressed. I tore off a hit, put it on my tongue, and let it dissolve.

I sat around Les' trailer for half an hour, waiting to take off. Nothing happened. Disappointed, I decided to head back up the hill to the farm and teepee. As I opened the trailer door and stepped into the world, I heard a loud buzzing in my head and saw a dull, almost black and white scene outside of the trailer turn bucolic—the trees growing, the stream flowing past, the Earth breathing and supporting it all. At one with the beautiful grove of trees and rushing stream, I was rooted in the prehistoric with the future spread out before me. There was light, time, brilliant color, and breath. Duality merged into oneness.

I went through the woods, splashing in and out of the stream. The sounds of the rushing water, the crunching of the leaves and sticks beneath my feet, and the warming morning sunshine delighted me. Emerging from the woods, I walked through the cornfield and heard the corn cracking as it grew. When I reached the garden, the squash plants swayed and grew, reaching for the sun right before my eyes. It was harvest time; abundance was everywhere.

Life was so overwhelming; I could hardly comprehend it all. My head was poking through the known universe into the gears working to propel existence forward to eternity. The words of *The Balance* by the Moody Blues, a song I'd listened to again and again when I was on the windowpane acid at McCormick Seminary, reverberated in my head. I thought I saw the balance. I thought I understood myself. I needed to tell the others on the farm what splendor there was out in the fields. I walked to the farmhouse, savoring every step. When I entered the kitchen, the atmosphere became magnetic. Everyone looked up and turned to me.

Frank asked cautiously, "How are you doing, Scott?"

I couldn't speak.

A portable radio was playing. It began to crackle, then stopped, and the line, "Trying to get off the L.A. Freeway without getting killed or caught," filtered through, then the crackling returned. I bowed, turned, and went outside.

I wandered all over the farm. Returning to the vegetable garden in the late afternoon, I planted my feet on the ground, and looked up into the sky. I grew, matured, aged. At last, I found myself staring into the side mirror of an old abandoned flatbed truck. I saw my face as four years on the farm flashed before my eyes. I was older, no longer the college student or the seminarian, now an old farmer, experienced beyond my years. Or just a fool?

That evening, I went down to the Farley House to party, smoke pot, dance, and stand by the stove. Brenda was gone. It was an excellent party. I had been away from my old friends on the farm and at the Farley House for a while. I didn't say much to anyone. They knew I was tripping. At that moment, I loved them. For them, there was anticipation in the air, a hunger for a taste, a glimpse of what I was experiencing.

When I returned home, I saw Joe standing in the middle of the driveway in front of the barn. He was transfixed, staring straight up at the sky. He stood there all night into the next day. He had done a full eagle, a four-way hit. He wasn't the same Joe when he returned to Earth. If you asked him a question, he would stare at you without answering, then smile and wander away. We began to call him Bongo Four Way.

scott hunter

chapter 21

Les had a way with women. He was always bringing them to the farm. A few days after I did Les' acid, he introduced me to Marsha, a raven-haired beauty. She wanted to be a feminist earth mother. At least, that's how she presented herself when, fresh off of a relationship with a jazz junkie, she moved to Jimmy's Popcorn.

Marsha was angry at her father, an abusive, tyrannical drunk. She took her anger out on men, seducing, then trashing and discarding them. I was desperate for companionship. It didn't take long for her to move into the teepee. Our common ground was the search for spirituality to ease our inner unrest. Drugs and alcohol were hindering my spiritual growth. Acting out her anger at her father crippled hers.

Our relationship, antagonistic during its better times and malevolent during the worst, was like trying to push the north and south poles of two magnets together. We would get close, then fight and separate. The makeup sex was great. Knowing nothing about relationships, submissive, uneasy with intimacy,

I was putty in her hands. She was in control. If our relationship had been a contest, she would've won.

Except for the makeup sex, our lovemaking was strained. I was anxious that I would get that rash again. Marsha wanted to have a baby. I didn't want children. My feelings about my childhood were too harsh to wish that on a child of mine. All this played out in the month of August.

By September, Marsha decided she wasn't going to spend winter in the tepee. She settled into my cubby hole in the attic above the kitchen for a week, then left for an out-of-state family reunion.

When she returned, she said, "At the airport for my flight, I saw a Krishna disciple give a book to someone who threw it into a trashcan. I picked it out of the trash and began to read it. I'm going to finish reading it here at the teepee. Krishna Consciousness is the way."

I spent the next four days working the farm. Marsha and I spent the evenings together. We didn't talk much. When I returned to the teepee on the fourth evening, she was standing next to the teepee with pursed lips, her arms crossed in front of her.

She proclaimed, "I've spent four consecutive days at the teepee. I've learned everything living in a teepee can teach me. I don't need to stay here any longer. I'm now Krishna conscious."

Only five feet tall, she gave me a 'What are you going to do now?' look. She turned her head when I tried to kiss her.

I said, "Four days and you didn't go down to the farm? Did you go up into the woods?"

Emphatically, almost yelling, she replied, "No!"

I sat down and leaned against the teepee. "Too bad. It's nice up there. I brought some turnips for dinner. Did you get water from the creek today?" I reached for my stash of pot, lit my pipe, laid back and looked at the clouds in the sky. "Now tell me about this Krishna Consciousness."

In a huff, she went into the teepee and returned with all her possessions in a cloth bag. "I didn't fetch water today. I didn't have time. I was too busy realizing I didn't need to stay here any longer."

Marsha's cat, Pussy, who'd come with her from Turner's Falls, appeared, climbed onto my chest, and purred. Marsha bent over, looked into my eyes, and seethed.

"Scott, you don't understand. I'm leaving. I understand it all now. Take my Krishna book, it's my present to you. I advise you to read it. Then you'll discover what I now understand. I'm leaving my cat. She loves it here. She's dying of cancer. There's no place for her where I'm going."

With all her possessions except the cat, Marsha walked down the hill. I never saw her again.

I fed Pussy pan bread and some cat food I found at the farmhouse for a few weeks. When she died, I buried her near the teepee.

I began reading the book Marsha left behind, the Hare Krishna version of the *Bhagavad Gita*. Not only was it a bad translation, but it was mostly commentary by His Divine Grace Srila Prabhupada. After fifty pages, I was as bored and confused as I'd been with the Moonie lectures. Essentially, the book promoted ISKCON, the International Order of Krishna Consciousness, the cult that venerated His Divine Grace, rather than Hinduism.

I went to the Sirius Bookstore and picked up a better translation of the *Bhagavad Gita*. It's an allegory, a discussion between Arjuna, the student-warrior, and Krishna, the teacher, on the attitudes, merits, and methods essential to the discovery of liberation. It is a cornerstone of Hinduism. Removing all the cultural and mythological trappings of Hinduism, its philosophy is similar to other Eastern ways of thinking. The four pillars of Hinduism are Proper Ethics, Proper Work, Proper Desires, and Proper Liberation. I began to chant:

> *Hare Krishna, Hare Krishna,*
> *Krishna Krishna, Hare Hare,*
> *Hare Rama, Hare Rama,*
> *Rama Rama, Hare Hare...*

I immersed myself in mantra meditation, chanting in the morning and evening. Except for a few tokes of pot in the morning and evening, my drug and alcohol use stopped.

I was trying to pull myself together, but a different scenario was playing out down the hill. The farm was out of control. It was cheaper for Joe, Bruce, Andy, and Allen to invite all the local drug addicts and alcoholics to the farm to party than to drink at the local bars. At one party, the four of them got into a fight to determine the farm's alpha male and destroyed one wall of the farmhouse. The proposed bay window that was supposed to replace it never appeared, and winter was fast approaching. Along with the other two Amherst College alumni who were the mortgage signees, Jason, who was living in Washington, D.C. painting portraits, began pursuing court-ordered eviction notices for everyone, including me.

Since I didn't want to be involved in the chaos, I continued to wander up the mountain, spending all day in the hidden glens of the forest. It was beautiful. There were times when the singing of the birds was symphonic. Other times, their silence spoke louder than words. I was Adam in Eden without Eve. I contemplated the secrets the apple on the Tree of Knowledge of Good and Evil held. I was happy.

The Hare Krishna mantra was pushing all other thoughts out of my mind. All I needed was my teepee, blankets for warmth, my skillet for cooking vegetables and pan bread, and my kettle for carrying water and popping popcorn. The brilliant colors of the autumn foliage were stunning. The stars and the fire at night were eternal wonders.

One day I awoke, fetched water, ate, and began my morning meditation. The Hari Krishna chant had a hypnotic cadence.

Hare Krishna, Hare Krishna,
Krishna Krishna, Hare Hare,
Hare Rama, Hare Rama,
Rama Rama, Hare Hare...

That morning, I realized I could turn the eight-phrased chant into a four-phrased chant if I started with the last phrase, *Hare Hare*, first:

Hare Hare Hare Krishna,
Hare Krishna Krishna Krishna,
Hare Hare Hare Rama,
Hare Rama Rama Rama...

I could chant the four phrases twice as fast as I could the eight-phrased chant. When I became comfortable with the new rhythm of the chant, I increased my chanting speed. My meditation became ferocious. Without restriction, I sped through the chant, again and again and again. My mind spiraled out of control. It imploded into nothingness.

Suddenly, I opened my eyes. I felt refreshed. I wondered how long I had been meditating. Twenty minutes perhaps, or half an hour?

As I gathered myself to spend the day, I noticed the daylight was not getting brighter. It was getting darker. I realized it was no longer morning, but evening. Had I been chanting for more than eight hours? Had I been chanting at all? I was confused. Should I go into the forest? Should I prepare dinner? I decided to sit and chant. I could not chant. *The Fool on the Hill* by The Beatles came into my head. I was the fool on the hill watching the world spin around, morning, afternoon, evening, night, morning. I had been roaming around the woods like a wild animal. There were days but no weeks, no months, the sky only getting lighter or darker, the weather getting warmer or colder. There were no Mondays or Tuesdays, no six o'clock or seven o'clock.

Standing next to the teepee as the evening light descended into darkness, the scene became vivid; the configuration of the trees, my teepee behind me, the blades of grass on either side of the gray dirt path worn to dust by my footsteps over three years. I realized my life at the teepee on top of this little hill was at an end. A strong yearning was pulling me down to the farmhouse. I hadn't been down to the farm for a while—three weeks, a month, more? Forty days?

It was getting dark. While I walked down the path, I remembered the evening when I became the hermit in the woods my mother had warned me to fear. Now, three and a half years later, I would be a wanderer, the next incarnation of the person I was told to fear. All I could see was the path ahead of me, although I could not see very far. It was easier that way, seeing no future, no past, only what was in the present.

The farm was dark and empty, eerily quiet. When I was last there, they'd had no electricity. As I walked into the living room, I saw a television next to the wood stove. I turned on a light. I turned on the television. It was 6:30 on November 18, 1978, and the evening news was breaking. A group of 900 people, the members of The People's Temple, led by Jim Jones, a cult leader from San Francisco, had relocated to Jonesville, Guyana to create a socialist utopia. They were a commune like the farm, only much bigger. They had committed mass suicide.

I was numb. The world I had returned to was suddenly strange. Electricity? Mass suicide? Were my experiences in the forest relevant to a world gone crazy? I heard cars coming down the road. The residents of the farm were returning from town.

"Scott's back from the woods. Here, Scott, have a beer."

I recognized them, but they were strangers. I no longer lived on the farm. I walked back up the hill to the teepee. My journey was headed to the open road.

After celebrating Thanksgiving at the farmhouse, I returned to the teepee to pack up. On Sunday evening, I left without a word. As I walked away from the teepee and Jimmy's Popcorn, I picked up the backpack I'd hidden in the woods with a clean set of clothes, a blanket, and a stash of marijuana. My life as a vagabond began.

chapter 22

There had been glimpses of stillness in Vipassana (mindfulness) and mantra (chanting) meditation. My meditation now became one of motion. I abandoned all semblance of normal life (if you could consider living in a teepee at all normal) and wandered the world without plan or future, hoping I might find a path that led to a deeper understanding of the conscious and unconscious mind. Maybe I could figure myself out. I'd read Ram Dass' *Miracles of Love*, on the life of Neem Karoli Baba, Maharaj-ji, a sadhu, an ascetic who devoted his life to an abstract god through reflection. He encouraged service to others as a form of unconditional love. The story in the book that impressed me began when Karoli got on a train in India without a ticket and sat in first class. The conductor kicked him off the train. Karoli sat down on the station platform and waited. The train wouldn't start until the conductor decided to let him back on the train. I wanted that power.

Karoli became the guru to famous people. I wanted that too. I looked back on my life and all I saw was failure. I had nothing except my small family inheritance, and I had no followers. I was nobody, lost. I hoped I could find myself somewhere on the road. I decided to use the Maharaj-ji's life as guide.

A bunch of students who lived in Williamstown gave me my first ride. I shared some pot and told them of life in the teepee. They invited me to spend the night on their couch. In the morning, we smoked a little marijuana before I left. They assured me I could sleep on their couch whenever I was in Williamstown. To borrow a term from the FBI, it was my first of many safehouses, places in various towns in western Massachusetts where I could go and hang out with friends, share a dinner, and sleep on the floor or couch. I was an apparition. No one knew where I was until I suddenly appeared. They didn't know where I was going when I hitchhiked away.

That morning, I hitchhiked back east on Route 2 to Greenfield, where I could head east to Wendell or south to Amherst. In Greenfield, I stopped by Les' new apartment. His place became a second safehouse. I bought some pot from him with my inheritance money. I used marijuana as currency, trading it for rides, meals, and couches.

I must have been an intriguing sight on the side of the road, long red dreadlocks, a red beard down to my chest, a multi-colored headband, and a small army knapsack on my back. I rarely waited long for a ride. Sharing pot and conversation with the drivers made vagabonding easy. I was full of energy and marvelous stories. Those who gave me rides found company for lonely drives. Those who passed me by probably saw someone homeless and on drugs.

Finding places to sleep at night wasn't a problem either. Many times, late afternoon rides would offer an evening meal and a place to sleep. When I left in the early morning, I made sure their home was in better condition than when I arrived. I swept the floor and did the dishes, chores neglected by many households that welcomed me. Usually, I would leave before anyone awoke. If I ever encountered them again, either through a ride or stopping by unannounced, I was welcomed back.

I became secure with insecurity. Whatever I needed—rides, evening meals, places to stay—would appear. There were times, after last call at whatever Amherst bar where I was drinking, no cars on the road, stranded, drunk, and stoned, I would simply walk. Many times, I walked the twenty-two miles from Amherst to Wendell, arriving at a safehouse in the early morning tired, but refreshed by the sunrise. I became good at accepting what was given to me. Still, the truth was I was traveling in circles, around and around, always in the same place, getting nowhere, stoned, just surviving. It kept my mind from dwelling on my suffering, the guilt, the self-loathing. I traveled light, not weighed down by past or future, or physical or emotional baggage.

I became aware of the mental and physical procedure I went through as I wandered on my path. I'd set out on the road walking. Breathing a few deep breaths, I'd accept the anxiety of not getting a ride and let go of the need to be somewhere. In my mind, I'd become part of a scene, a bearded man with a backpack hitching a ride. I was a still life, only existing in the eye of the beholder. Occasionally, I could see this scene from above. A car would stop and give me a ride. The day would evolve with chance meetings and spontaneous plans, meals shared, and evenings enjoyed. It was rare that a couch or floor was not available for a night's rest. In cold weather, people were accommodating. In warm weather, there was always a pond to sleep by.

I began to believe in a third eye in the center of my forehead, a lens projecting a picture from my mind. I was creating my reality on a blank screen. Whether something good or bad happened, it did not happen to me, but by or because of me. We all are the creators of our own universes; reality is a collection of individual universes.

My life as a vagabond was essentially homelessness. Without my small inheritance, pot connections, or other addicts as friends, I would have been homeless. Back then, I glamorized it as sadhu meditation, the ascetic life. In reality, I was a drug addict and alcoholic, a nobody, a sick puppy. My deep-seated emotional issues were enormous. The resourcefulness and the creativity needed to survive day to day on the road, drunk and drugged, was exhausting. Living was a constant struggle.

Three days before my thirty-fifth birthday, Saturday, June 14, my father died. He was thirty-five when I was born. That devastated me. We buried him on my birthday, June 17, 1980.

I'd been angry at him because he didn't get my hints for money that I wanted for a trip to Jamaica. In my mind, my anger had killed my father. I was guilty of his death.

But then, after his death, I saw that I was no longer my father's son. I was the heir apparent, the man of the family. A sense of triumphant relief flooded over me.

Then, sadness and loss overcame all my mixed emotions towards him. A cry welled up inside me. I wanted my father. It didn't matter that I was angry about all the petty things, Christmas presents I'd wanted and hadn't received, the one share of IBM stock when I was seven years old, the piccolo when I was fourteen. I wanted my father. It didn't matter that he never took me camping. I'd lived in a teepee for three years because of that anger. I wanted my father. It didn't matter that he wasn't there to support me in my relationship with my mother and mentor me into adulthood. I wanted my father.

I returned to New Kensington for the funeral. How outlandish I must have looked to my relatives and Dad's clean-cut friends, my long reddish-blond hair immaculately combed, my long full beard flowing over my suit coat. Only six months earlier, we'd been celebrating Christmas with Dad. Now, Mother, Marilyn, and I huddled in the front row pew of the church. When the casket was removed from the hearse at the cemetery, I stood aside as others assumed the role of pallbearers. One pallbearer stumbled, and I replaced him by my father's side. I was so thankful for that moment, carrying my father. At the church dinner after the funeral, everyone sang Happy Birthday to me. My anger consumed me. I was relieved my father was dead. I was sad, sad, sad. I was a thirty-five-year-old child who had lost his father. My love for him ran deep.

chapter 23

When I returned to Massachusetts from Dad's funeral, I found out that the 1980 Rainbow Gathering was coming to West Virginia, the first time it had been east of the Mississippi River. It had been eight years since I'd freaked out at the Gathering in Colorado. No longer the seminarian, I was a hippie farmer. I was going.

I shared a ride with a pretty brunette named Donna in a caravan led by Atlas Green, a self-proclaimed spiritual guru. When we reached the gathering in the Monongahela National Forest in the late afternoon, Donna and the rest of the caravan disappeared to set up a campsite. I wandered around introducing myself to everyone. No longer Chicago Red, clean-cut seminarian, I was a long-haired, bearded, teepee living, back-to-the-land farmer, a member of the Rainbow Family. I met the Shanti Sena, the peacekeepers, security for the Rainbow Gathering, who told me there had been some confrontations with the local rednecks at the campsite gate. The rednecks didn't appreciate the Rainbow Family, West Coast hippies invading their territory. I decided to head down to the gate to see if I could help and volunteer to direct traffic.

A bunch of trucks with West Virginia plates were parked along the dirt road. I watched as some local good old boys, beer-drinking, truck-driving young men, harassed the gatekeepers and bullied the frailer Shanti Sena. The locals were West Virginia farmers' sons. They'd grown up on hard physical labor, and their muscular physiques showed it. Some of them had beards, but none had the hippie look. The Shanti Sena looked like hungry vegetarian hippies, lean with no body fat—two of them might have outweighed one of the local boys. Though I was tall and lanky, working on the farm had put some muscle on my frame.

The years drinking and dealing with the locals in Wendell served me well. I had spent time at the family farm in western Pennsylvania with my redneck cousins. I wasn't going to be intimidated by a few West Virginians. One burly guy recognized my western Pennsylvania accent and asked me, "Where are you from? What are you doing with these West Coast hippies?"

I took him aside and said, "Hey, I was born in western Pennsylvania, moved to Massachusetts. I ain't no West Coast hippie, brother. See it from my side, these hippies have some excellent herb and women. California girls are friendly."

His eyes lit up as he smiled. He said to me, "I'm Bud. I like your straw hat."

"You like this hat? I'll trade you for your Ford baseball cap."

"Deal," he said.

I also traded him pot for a six-pack of beer, then took the beer to some Rainbow women and said, "You know, flirting with these locals might be fun. It might help. These guys aren't half bad and they're dying to meet you. They're shy and you're so beautiful."

We all laughed. Two of the women strolled over to the local

boys and struck up conversations. Everyone at the gate became one big happy family. I became the head gateman.

Later in the evening, a group of forest rangers showed up. My status with the Rainbow Gatherers at the gate skyrocketed when three of them, attracted by my Ford baseball cap, assumed that I was a local and approached me.

"These hippies giving you any trouble?"

I said, "We're having a fine old time, sir. No problems here, sir. If you want to check out what's going on, I'll walk you around the campsite in the morning. It's cool. I'll introduce you to security, explain Rainbow policy, answer your questions. We've done this before out west. We'll leave the national forest a better place than we found it."

Early the next morning, I took the rangers on a tour. They relaxed and realized we were harmless.

Mid-morning, a few of the Shanti Sena took me to a large teepee, the command and control center, and introduced me to Red Hawk, Fisherman, Raven, and Wavy Gravy, the organizers of the Gathering. Red Hawk looked like a young MBA intern from a Wall Street brokerage firm at an Outward Bound camp. His hair was cut short; he was wearing a white t-shirt, dark pants and sandals. One of his pant legs was rolled up, and Raven, a dark-haired beauty in Native American dress, was stuffing an infected hole in his ankle with iodine-soaked gauze. She looked up at me.

"He had a splinter in his ankle, and it got infected."

"It looks bad."

Fisherman, a tall, long-haired, blond surfer-type wearing a vest with fishing flies hooked to it, shorts, and no shirt, said, "You should have seen it a week ago."

I had heard about Wavy Gravy. He was the official clown

of the Grateful Dead and famous for his "Nobody for President. Because Nobody's Perfect" campaign. Wavy, dressed in his clown suit, orange wig, and face paint, mumbled something about going out to meet and greet the people and left. Red Hawk motioned for me to sit down.

"We heard about you. Sounds like you did a good job down at the gate."

Wanting to be helpful, I said, "I'm glad you brought the Rainbow Gathering east. Made it easy for me to get here. If there's anything I can do to help you out, let me know."

Raven addressed Red Hawk more than me. "They need help in Marlinton. The people at the welcome center directing new arrivals to the campsite are having some problems with the local residents and police."

Red Hawk turned to me. "Can you help out there? A couple of nights ago, some trucks drove by and people shot off guns. And the police are keeping a close watch on everything."

I agreed to go.

I got a ride to Marlinton and introduced myself to the folks working the welcome center, then walked across the street to the diner with all the trucks parked in front. The place was packed.

I interrupted the quiet conversations with a loud, "Morning, folks. Am I late for breakfast? Haven't had real food in a couple of days."

The waitress put an empty coffee cup in front of me and said, "Coffee? We serve breakfast all day. What's your pleasure, hon?"

I ordered a three-egg western omelet, sausage, and toast.

A heavy-set male customer sitting a couple of stools down from me leaned over the counter and asked, "You one of those hippies over in the park?"

I sensed more interest than antagonism in his voice. "Yes, sir. I'm a farmer from Massachusetts. Heard there was a party in West Virginia. Came down to check it out."

I was hit with a flood of questions: "How many are up there? How long are you going stay? I heard the forest service is booking overtime. You causin' any trouble?" From one of the booths, I heard, "You anti-war? Fucking un-American as shit."

The waitress raised her voice. "Stan, you shut up. This is West Virginia. We treat guests kindly. You may not like what they think or stand for. I don't like those protests either, but we respect everyone here."

I took a sip of my coffee and turned around. I explained the history of the Rainbow Gathering, fielded questions, and answered them as best I could. Everyone was just wondering what was going on.

I learned what the problem with the police was. Prior to the Gathering, two unsavory, disruptive, outspoken lesbian heroin addicts from New York City had been killed. The police were questioning some local suspects and the Rainbow Gatherers.

When I left the diner, I saw a parked police car, walked over to it, and introduced myself.

Before I could get into anything, he interrupted me.

"I don't recognize you, son. You're friendly with the hippies, then you head over to the diner. Where you from?"

He thought I was a local boy. My Ford baseball cap worked again.

After I explained who I was, I continued, "Sir, I heard about what happened to the two women. I don't think it was anyone headed to the national forest. There's a lot of peaceful people up there, I assure you. Nobody has guns. It's all love, if you get what I mean."

The well-fed chief of police chuckled, then opened the cruiser's door a crack and spit some tobacco juice onto the street. "Well, son, you just make sure you keep it all love and peace up there. I'll keep it love and peace down here."

He spat again, closed the door, and looked away. I was dismissed.

I went over to the town park and sat down on a bench. Two hippies came over and sat beside me. One was an older woman with gray streaks in her dark brown hair, in a full dress covered with designs I thought might be Navajo. The other was a young man, with long black hair in braids, who I thought might be Native American.

The woman spoke first. "Hi, I'm Lucky Fox. My friends call me Lucky. This is Talbert Morning Sun. We've been here at the welcome center for a few days now. I want to go back to the main camp. Your ride told us you wanted to help out. Talbert knows what's going on. He can fill you in."

With a nod, I stuck out my hand and agreed to take her place.

"You just talked with the cop, so I figure you know the problem about the murders that happened before we got here. The other problem is the guy in the house over there." Talbert pointed to a small wood cabin with a large front porch. The cabin's front yard was an extension of the town park. Both the cabin and town park had a great view down to the Greenbrier River. "He yells and screams obscenities all day and night. The cop won't do anything. No one knows what to do."

I replied, "Well, he's not around now and it's quiet, so let's wait until something happens and we'll try and figure out what to do."

Night came, and I needed some coffee to stay awake. The welcome center had run out of sugar. We had plenty of coffee though, so I took a couple of cans, walked over to the complaining neighbor's cabin, and knocked on the door.

"I got some cans of coffee here. The welcome center over at the park don't got no sugar. I was wondering if I could trade some coffee for sugar?"

A young guy came to the door, yelling, bitching and moaning about all the hippies over at the park. "It ain't quiet here no more. All that guitar playing late at night. How does anyone sleep?"

With two cans of coffee in my arms and a smile on my face, I joked, "If you can't sleep, you probably don't need coffee. But I need some sugar for mine. Maybe you should come and join us. I can't carry a tune, but I enjoy watching other people singing, having fun. Anyway, I'm Scott."

Reluctantly at first, he took the cans, went into the house, and returned with a half bag of sugar. "I'm Robbie. I live with my mother and father. They hate all this damn noise. They finally stopped complaining and fell asleep."

Sensing that I was getting somewhere, I said, "Listen. I'll take this sugar over to the welcome center and come back. We can talk."

When I returned, Robbie was sitting in a rough handmade rocking chair. He motioned to another one beside him. I sat down.

"I know who killed those girls. I met those lezzies in town a couple of days before they died. They were trouble. We got opinions here. Hard drugs and women in love with each other don't go over too well. Goddamn, they were flaunting it, kissing in the park, leaving needles around. Damn, you don't do that. This ain't where they come from. Hippies didn't kill 'em. Police chief over there should be looking for a '77 green Chevy C30 Silverado. Seen the guy talking to the ladies the night they were murdered."

That evening, a few townsfolk came to the park and sat around the fire with us. A country and folk sing-along began when guitars appeared. The next day, townsfolk showed up at the park with garden vegetables and home-baked goods. The next morning, I said goodbye to my friends in town and at the welcome center and returned to the campsite. Despite my sadness at my father's passing, I was feeling good about myself.

When I got back to the campsite gate, a woman stopped me: "Excuse me, someone wants to talk with you."

She grabbed my hand and led me to the ultimate psychedelic, multi-colored hippie bus. I climbed the steps into the bus, and there was Felipe.

I cried out, "Felipe Chavez! It's been a while. Hey, I guess I'm no longer Chicago Red. I live in Wendell, Massachusetts. With my red beard, I guess I'm Wendell Red now."

Felipe was dumbfounded. "I didn't realize it was you. I heard about the new guy at the gate and down in town, just wanted to thank him." He laughed.

"Yeah, you told me to go to the lost and found and get found, remember?" I asked.

We hugged each other for a long time. Felipe pushed me back and held me by my shoulders. "Eight years since Colorado. You're no longer a straight white guy in a button-down shirt."

I stroked the length of my beard. "I guess I've been found."

I told Felipe about my teepee and the farm, and he introduced me to his bus family. Bright Eyes, the woman who led me to the bus, was Felipe's current girlfriend, a wealthy young New Yorker who was financing the bus and its journey around the country. Chaco, a very funny jokester, seemed to control the marijuana stash. He was always coming up with another joint from somewhere to smoke. He was Felipe's sidekick. Chaco's wife or girlfriend, Christi, was a blonde California girl with two young ragamuffins, Skipper, a five-year-old boy, and Glory Bea, a three-year-old girl. Reuniting with Felipe had put me in a very good place.

The five of us shared a joint and Felipe asked, "What are you doing after the Gathering?"

I felt a cloud of sadness descend on me. "My father just died a couple of weeks ago. I'm headed home to stay with my mother in New Kensington, Pennsylvania. I want to make sure she's okay."

His joyfulness vanished. "I'm so sorry to hear that, Scott. Why don't you join us? We're going to the International Gathering for Peace in the Black Hills of South Dakota in a few weeks. It's Native American, a Lakota Sioux gathering. A lot of healing is going to happen there. Spend some time with your mother. We'll stop and pick you up in New Kensington. It'll be good for you."

I agreed to go with them.

The Black Hills Alliance Gathering was a peaceful protest against the proposed strip mining of uranium from the rolling hills and plains at the base of the Paha Sapa, the Black Hills area sacred to the Sioux. It was big sky country, undulating plains covered in dry brown grasses, sagebrush, and a few isolated bushes and trees. Our days began with a huge prayer circle to welcome the rising sun. Each person in the circle inhaled tobacco smoke from a peace pipe and said a few words. Days were filled with classes on ecology, protesting, Native American traditions, trips to swimming holes and into town for cheeseburgers and fries, and lazing around the bus enjoying the company that stopped by to talk and smoke weed. Evenings around the campfire soothed the sorrow of my father's passing.

Near the end of the week, after an afternoon swimming in Rapid Creek and lunch in Rapid City, I returned to the bus. Felipe was sitting on a cushioned platform in the front of the bus. He was bent over with his head in his hands.

"What's up, Felipe? You look sad."

Felipe looked up with tears streaming down his cheeks. "My father just died in California. There is no way I am going to be able to get to his funeral."

I sat down next to him, put my arm around him, and said, "Felipe, I'm so sorry. You need to go to his funeral."

He pushed away his tears at my words. "Scotty, I don't have the extra money. I've got to get the bus to Washington, D.C. for the end of the American Indian Movement's Walk Across America for Peace. That will take everything I got. I can't leave the bus with Bright Eyes, Chaco, and Christi. None of them can drive a stick shift."

I stood up and got my wallet out of my pocket. I had two $100 bills folded up in one of the slots, some of the emergency inheritance money I always had handy. "Felipe, let me take care of everything." I handed him one of the hundreds. "This will get you to California. I drove tractor-trailers. I have a class-one license. I'm headed to Chicago to see my aunt. I can drive the bus and teach Chaco and Bright Eyes how to shift gears with a stick until we get to St. Louis. Everyone should know how to drive the bus by then. We'll meet up again in Washington, D.C. in September."

Felipe headed west to the funeral, while Bright Eyes, Chaco,

Christi, and I prepared the bus to head east. They practiced with the clutch and stick shift while the bus was standing still. On the morning we left the Black Hills, a solitary cloud drifted east over the bus. As it passed over us, a small rainbow appeared within it. We smiled.

On back roads, Bright Eyes and Chaco practiced shifting gears while the bus was moving slowly. That night we headed out onto the interstate and practiced at full speed. The next day was smooth-running.

When we reached Interstate 55, I jumped off to hitchhike north to Chicago. No one stopped to pick me up for hours. I thought, *Maybe I should have stayed with the bus*. I noticed a t-shirt lying up the interstate about 100 feet away and got a strange feeling. After more waiting, I walked up to it and picked it up. On the front was a rainbow in brilliant colors and underneath it, the words 'Rainbow Inn.' As soon as I picked it up, I got a ride.

chapter 24

It had been eighteen months since I had decided to leave the teepee. I knew I could survive as a vagabond. My experience at the two gatherings gave me confidence that I could be beneficial to society. Dad's death gave me the incentive to become someone. Now I had to find my voice to tell people what I'd learned, though I wasn't quite sure what that was.

I'd always enjoyed the poems of Robert Frost. He was a New England farmer. I was a New England farmer. He'd held poetry seminars at Amherst College. I'd written poems while at Amherst and given them away. I hadn't kept copies for myself. Deep inside, I knew those poems were good.

Robert Frost wrote the poem, *The Road Not Taken*. I had traveled a road not taken by many people. His poem, *Stopping by Woods on a Snowy Evening*, spoke to me. I stopped by the woods for three years in my teepee. I had promises to keep and miles to go before I slept. I needed to find the meaning of life, somehow tell others about it, and discover why I was so troubled.

I made a decision that I hoped would change my life. I became a poet. Instead of trading pot and stories for rides, meals, and couches to sleep on, I began to write poems and print hundreds of copies to trade them for rides. I left them where I spent the night, thumb-tacked them on bulletin boards in dormitories and halls of the five local colleges, passed them out on buses, at concerts, anywhere, everywhere. Everyone would know my name and my poetry.

Inspired by the University Without Walls, a program for non-traditional students at UMass, I imagined my own program, the University Off the Wall, with a post-graduate degree, Out in Left Field. The requirements for my imaginary undergraduate degree were two poems per semester the first year, four poems each semester the second year, eight poems each semester the third year, and sixteen poems each semester the fourth year. For my imaginary post-graduate degree, I would publish my book of poetry. To other people, I may have sounded bonkers, but I thought I was on the cutting edge of creativity.

I asked myself, *What inspired other poets—a need to express their emotions?* My needs clashed. I needed to express my emotions, but I couldn't tell anyone what I was really feeling—guilt, pain, anger, and shame—so I cloaked them in secrecy. I hid behind drugs and appearing and disappearing like an elusive muse that no one knew anything about. I would dazzle the world with words that disguised and transformed my emotions into beauty.

Was I aware that I might be losing it? Asking that was like asking surfers staring down a seventy-five-foot wave if they thought they might be in danger. I understood my choices were dangerous and crazy, but to me, in those years, it was necessary.

I participated in two UMass student organizations. Since I was an ex-seminarian, I joined The United Christian Fellowship.

I was really not sure what their function was except to support Christian students. It didn't matter to me what they did, as long as they listened to me recite my poetry. I was radical, so I joined the Radical Student Union. They protested everything and scoured the campus for drugs. They liked me. I always had drugs. Everyone accepted me as an enrolled university student, even though I wasn't. No one guessed I was just a creative, stoned, crazy, couch-surfing hippie trying to get along in the world.

In November 1980, during my first self-declared semester, one of the Atlas Green gang, a rich vegetarian into whole foods and good diets, decided to open a bakery in Amherst. He rented a basement cubbyhole beneath the Silverscape Jewelry Store, installed a convection oven, and hired some attractive women to bake for him. Though afraid of intimacy, I was still attracted to the women, so I offered my services as a salesman. I supplied samosas and baked goods on consignment to the Blue Moon Co-op and the restaurants in town.

One afternoon, I volunteered to clerk late and close the store that evening. I invited a new friend, Sam, to meet me there. Sam was a top-tier drug dealer from Boston. He was getting pot right off the boat. His lifestyle was similar to mine—stoned, crazy, couch-surfing, and living out of his car. We'd become the best of friends. He showed up with a large loaf of hashish, and I bought a chunk of it. Instead of smoking it, I broke off a nugget and tucked it between my cheek and jaw. It dissolved slowly, and by the end of the evening, I was blasted. There were few customers at the bakery, so I daydreamed, imagining myself transported to a bakeshop in Paris in the 1790s. Outside, the communists were carrying banners, singing the *Internationale*. A poem poured out of me. I found a piece of paper and wrote the poem I called

Jeanne d'Arc.

The next day, I went to a protest in Holyoke, Massachusetts against the Salvadoran death squads. Some UMass students wanted to get arrested in front of the Holyoke police station, thinking they could inspire Hispanic residents to protest. A few activists from the Holyoke Hispanic community took part in the demonstration, but only UMass students were arrested. I watched from the sidelines, sucking on another piece of hash. In a few moments of inspiration, I wrote *Ahora, Wheel Along Unbroken Ground,* my second poem in two days. I typed up the poems, printed a couple hundred copies, and handed them out everywhere. Both *Jeanne d'Arc* and *Ahora* were published in *The Massachusetts Daily Collegian.* Even though my friends in the United Christian Fellowship and the Radical Student Union were impressed, I had no idea how to feel successful. Success wasn't in my DNA. I'd never been taught how to accept praise.

I never let anyone get close to me, wandering through campus for a few days, then disappearing. I'd command the attention of bus riders, recite my latest poem, and vanish at the next bus stop. There was a letter to the editor of the *Amherst Student,* wondering who the pushpin poet was. I never revealed myself. I was welcomed at informal discussions during lunch at the University Food Co-op and evening and weekend gatherings at the homes of friends, but I wouldn't let anyone know me. I had too many unexplored secrets to become intimate with anyone. I was angry and in a lot of pain. Only my pot-smoking friends understood me. They were addicts too.

That autumn, I made a deal with Mom. I'd cut my hair and

beard and appear presentable for Christmas. In exchange, I wanted the stock certificates that had been providing me with dividends for the past eight years. If I had the stocks, I could sell them. With that money, I'd create a sphere of influence in which I'd be a well-liked and respected leader.

When December came, I cut my hair and beard and looked like I did when I'd graduated from college. I was headed to Marilyn's place in California to spend the first Christmas with Mom, Marilyn, and her family, without Dad.

The day before I flew to Los Angeles, I stopped by Marco's apartment. Marco was an ex-Army Ranger I'd met through Les. He always had pot to sell and let me wash my clothes whenever I stopped by. Of my few friends, he was most enthusiastic about my poetry. "Scott, if you are going to be a great poet, you need to write an epic poem, like Coleridge, Longfellow, or Poe. Those guys were alcoholics, right? Do what they did."

I thought that was great advice.

Marco stopped at a liquor store and bought a pint of Chivas Regal. He said, "Drink this on the plane. When you get to L.A., write the epic poem."

That made perfect sense.

The next morning, Marco drove me to the airport and wished me luck. The temperature was around freezing. On the plane, the stewardess provided me with ice. I sipped the Chivas Regal for six hours across America. When I got off the plane in L.A., the temperature was in the low eighties and I was a blithering drunk. I cried all the way to my sister's house, a total basket case.

Mom and Marilyn kept repeating, "Scott, are you okay?"

I smelled like Chivas Regal. They must have known I was drunk, but they kept asking, "Why are you crying? Stop crying and tell us what's the matter."

Between sobs, I said, "I'm okay. I just miss Dad so much."

Marilyn had wisely sent her three kids, Ethan, Katie, and Nicholas, to hang out with Brian. She and Brian had separated because of Brian's drinking and gambling.

Mother was a rock. She kept her emotions well hidden. "Scott, we have to accept that your father is dead. We can't change that. We just have to go on living. Crying doesn't help. It just makes us all feel worse."

I was so drunk, only more alcohol would straighten me out.

Mother questioned me: "Scott, do you drink a lot?"

For the first time in my life, I was willing to be truthful about my drinking. "Yes, Mom, I drink a lot."

Bluntly, she said, "Scott, you just have to stop. Drinking is not good for you."

It wasn't that easy. Marilyn, like a good co-dependent, put another Black Russian in front of me; mixing another for herself, she offered a different view.

"We're grieving Dad's death. It's difficult for all of us. It's good you're crying. We need to express our emotions. If you don't, you'll go crazy."

Mom touched her mouth in surprise. She clearly didn't believe that was true.

Marilyn went on, "Scott, you remember Maria, my high school friend? She was staying with me for a while. She held her feelings in, went crazy, and is in the mental hospital. She can have visitors now. Do you want to go see her tonight?"

Mom was glad we weren't still talking about feelings. "Yes, poor Maria. You should go and visit her."

I was relieved not to talk about my drinking and possibly

admit to drug use, too. I agreed to visit her.

That evening, Marilyn and I left Mom at the house and went to visit Maria. She had checked herself into the Municipal State Hospital. As Marilyn and I walked in, we saw the initials MSH (Municipal State Hospital) carved into the large stone blocks above the main entrance. My father's name was Matthew Scott Hunter. Marilyn and I looked at each other, thinking *Dad's watching us.* We were not entirely sure he liked what he was seeing, but we felt his presence. We took a long moment to hug each other, unsure what lay ahead.

We found Maria in her hospital room, disheveled with a blank look in her eyes. She barely recognized us and was not interested in conversing, so we didn't stay long. We were concerned, but had our own grief to deal with. We rode back home in silence.

The next morning, hungover but sober, I wanted something to do. The shed behind Marilyn's house needed to be cleaned and straightened up. The first thing I picked up was a milk crate full of Maria's stuff. A small, half-empty vial of white powder was on top. I remembered I had received a call from her in late November, asking me if I could get her some drugs. One of Marco's friends had some white powder. He didn't know what it was, but he said it was good. I had sent Maria the vial. *Had it put her in the hospital? Was it still any good?*

Despite the warning from the Yao silversmith, I didn't care what happened if I took some. I just wanted to shut off my emotions and escape. I unscrewed the black cap, dumped a small pile on my palm, and licked it off. An hour later, I realized how exciting the white powder was. It wasn't coke. My mind was ablaze like it had been back in Plainville, Pennsylvania eight years before on my aborted trip west. Over the next seven days, I consumed what was left in the vial and wrote the trilogy *The Meeting of the Traveler and the Magus*, a fifty-six-stanza poem, an allegory of my life and feelings.

The first third of the trilogy, *The Tale of the Magus,* set out my hopes and dreams of becoming wise and knowing the mysteries of the universe. The second third, *The Tale of the Traveler,* told the story of a young man who was kidnapped and enslaved. He escaped to travel the world and reach enlightenment. The last third, *The Meeting of the Traveler and the Magus,* melds both their spirits to carry on the wisdom of the ancients. My soul went into that poem.

I was amazed that a drug could let me sit day after day and type the words pouring from my mind. It bubbled up from somewhere in a consistent cadence that became the poem's meter. I began to wonder about the origins of Samuel Taylor Coleridge's *Kubla Khan; or, A Vision in a Dream: A Fragment* and some of Robert Blake's poems. *Did my drug experience aid my poetry as Coleridge's opiate addiction aided his? Were Robert Blake's neurology and his poetry affected by the chemicals he encountered working in etching factories as a child and young man?* I wondered if a poem's meter was a result of the chemical configuration of the drug the writer was using. Whatever the drug was, I didn't suffer any withdrawal when I finished it.

Before leaving L.A., I called Marco: "I wrote the epic poem. Can you pick me up at the airport?"

He feigned distraction. "No, I'm busy. Stop at the apartment in Holyoke on the way north. I should be home by then."

I was a little annoyed he couldn't pick me up, but that was Marco. I hitchhiked from the airport. Much to my surprise, on the last bridge in Connecticut over Interstate 91, before the interstate crossed into Massachusetts, Marco and his friend had painted "Welcome, Homer" on the overpass. When I reached Marco's apartment, I gave him a hug.

"Marco, that bridge was so cool. Thank you so much."

Hugs were too much for Marco. He pushed me away. With a little twinkle in his eye, he said, "I don't know what you're talking about."

I replied, "Come on, Marco. I know you did it."

He picked up his duffle bag and headed for the door. He was playing with me. "'Welcome, Homer.' Who would do that?"

chapter 25

In the middle of January, Mother sent me the stock certificates in the mail. I picked them up at the Wendell Depot post office and tore open the envelope. I had no confidence that anything I could do or any idea I had was worth anything. My plan was to sell the stock and invest in projects other people had. I would be a philanthropist, creating a village of my own in Western Massachusetts. All my friends would love me because I helped them.

Turning the stock certificates into cash was easy. I found a stock broker who was delighted to help me. He got a commission for each stock I sold. He was astonished that I was giving the money away. I thought he was greedy.

I said, "I have a plan. I'll be the leader of a community and no one will own anything. Like in the Bible, where Paul says that all things should be held in common."

His eager reply was, "If you have any money left over, you could buy me a car. I had one client who was so grateful, he gave me his father's car."

I began my search for my village in Wrentham, Massachusetts, where Atlas Green lived.

"Atlas, you have to come out to Wendell and see the barn that's for sale. The house in front of it burnt down, but what is left is the barn made out of chestnut beams. It's beautiful. We can buy it and build a house out of it."

Atlas, a graduate of Bowdoin College, star of the basketball team, was a fitness nut, all muscle, no fat. He was a self-proclaimed spiritual guru and expert carpenter. His Italian father was a jack of all trades and had taught Atlas well. Like me, Atlas liked physical labor and the outdoors. When he came to Wendell and saw the barn, he was excited.

"Scott, I can turn the barn into a home, but I have no money."

I explained my plan to him. "I have the money, Atlas, but I am a member of the Pioneer Tax Resister Movement Against Nuclear Proliferation. If I own property, the U.S. government might take it. Betty, the woman who told me about Jimmy's Popcorn, said that the government took her house. I'll put up the money, but my name can't be on the deed."

Atlas saw the opportunity. "I'll put my name on the deed."

I gave him $12,000 to buy the property.

Over the next six years, Atlas turned the barn into a beautiful four-story home that became the meeting place for all the pot smokers in Wendell. I was welcome at the barn when Atlas needed money. He would sweet talk me into paying for a project, then bully me away. It was a confidence game; Atlas, the master manipulator, and I, the willing contributor. We both got what we wanted. He got a house for free and I proved to myself I was worthless.

Instead of purchasing the barn and property free and clear,

Atlas took out a mortgage on the property and used most of the money for construction, drugs, and travel. When the property neared foreclosure from neglected mortgage payments, I provided more money to cover the delinquent payments. Some of that money was used to bail out David, one of the Atlas gang, who had been arrested for lighting up a joint in the New York subway. I never allowed myself to be aware of what was happening. It didn't matter.

I had met another group at the Rainbow Gathering, the Nowatama Community from Centerville, New Hampshire, led by Old Wisdom, a Wampanoag Indian storyteller, and his wife, Joan Moonglow. They helped Jack Peace Arrow set up a satellite community across the Wendell Common from the barn. Jack planned to buy an old school bus, fix it up, and drive it to the next Rainbow Gathering in Washington State. After the Washington Rainbow Gathering, he planned to use the bus to start a low-cost transportation business. A cross-country trip to the next Gathering seemed like a great idea to me, so I supplied the money to purchase and renovate the bus. Before long, we were on our way across the country.

Something on the trip to Washington was not right. I felt like there were a bunch of people having fun, but I was an unhappy loner. My money wasn't working to make friends. I couldn't connect with anyone. My sadness turned to anger when Helen, a well-respected woman in the Nowatama community, penciled annotations throughout my prized possession, the *I Ching*, or *Book of Changes*. I challenged her in front of Old Wisdom and Joan Moonglow.

"How could you be so inconsiderate to write in my book?"

Her arrogant response was, "I thought you might enjoy my

comments."

Moonglow refused to support me. "You shouldn't be so concerned about material possessions, Scott. Friendship is more important."

Friendship? I began to realize these people weren't my friends.

Back home in Wendell, the feelings of alienation from the Nowatoma Community continued. Only Jack Peace Arrow was friendly. He wanted me to buy another bus, so he could start a bus company to take people on long trips to Mexico and beyond. When I refused, he ignored me, too. I was no longer a member or even a friend of the community. After a Saturday night gathering where no one would even look at me, I thought, *So this is what being shunned must feel like.*

My dreams of a community in Wendell were falling apart. It didn't matter. There were other people I could give my money to and hope for better outcomes. Fred, the younger brother of a marijuana connection, was looking for investors in a butane-powered nail gun. I put up the money for the patent process and to furnish a shop where Fred could build the prototype. Fred built the shop in the barn of a guy whose name was the same as my closest childhood friend. That serendipity and the appearance of an eagle overhead when Fred and I signed the loan agreement convinced me this investment was going to pay off.

When a Japanese power tool company contacted Fred and made him an offer, $200 grand up front and a paid position to develop the prototype, everyone was excited. Allen, the other major investor in the enterprise, and I encouraged Fred to take the offer. Fred could pay us back with a small profit, keep the rest of the money, and work for a legitimate company.

There was one problem. The Japanese company would retain

all rights to the patents and products. Fred refused the offer.

The Japanese company made a few modifications to Fred's design and obtained international patents on butane-powered jackhammers and nail guns. Fred was out of business. Allen and I have become close friends over the years and we still share laughter over our foolish investment.

The purchase of a CDC 6600, the flagship mainframe computer of the '80s, manufactured by the Control Data Corporation, was an investment I made with Joshua, an old white-haired hippie who had spent the '70s on a bus traveling the country with his wife and kids, and Danny, a savant in the UMass computer department who had red hair and a beard longer than mine. Danny smelt like a wood fire from his primitive cabin in the woods. He reminded me of my teepee days. They needed a computer to start a software company. I saw an opportunity to combine my money and Danny's expertise to make millions. In exchange for the money, I was promised a computer education and a place to crash at Joshua's whenever I was in Amherst.

The day our CDC 6600 was delivered to Joshua's house and set up in his basement, I was excited.

"Alright guys, who's going to give me my first lesson on the computer?"

Joshua and Danny looked at each other. Danny reached in his bag and pulled out a book.

"Here is a manual on coding and program language."

So much for the promised instruction. I was on my own. Late one evening when I arrived at Joshua's home to sleep, I found a greasy car axle wrapped inside of my sleeping bag.

My search for community and friendship was a pipe dream. My need for drugs and alcohol was my only reality. Grief at my father's passing and the desire to rid myself of the investments that I wrongly imagined Dad had loved more than he'd loved me left me an easy mark.

I didn't lose hope that I might find community and invest in a way that would turn my sadness and anger into success and happiness. My next investment was The Greenfield Spa. Jacob, my dentist, was building it with John, a Connecticut man, who owned a plot of land at the beginning of the Mohawk Trail section of Route 2. The Spa promised six Jacuzzis, an alcohol and juice bar, and women just sitting around, ready to jump into a Jacuzzi with a guy. During the building phase, all the construction costs were to be split equally. John had complete control until The Spa was completed. When it was completed, Jacob would be CEO of the business and run the place.

Jacob never became the CEO. John spared no expense during construction, adding a state-of-the-art sound system, a superb lounge area, an outdoor porch, and additional Jacuzzis. As the building costs escalated, Jacob borrowed money from me to stay in the game. John squeezed Jacob dry, until he had to drop out. Then the business and property were all John's. John found more dupes to buy the business. Each purchase of the business was a windfall profit for John. When the businesses failed, John retained ownership of The Spa.

I also gave away money thinking my spiritual life would benefit. The Rowe Camp and Conference Center, a Unitarian Universalist retreat center west of Greenfield, needed a new cafeteria roof when snow crashed through during a January snowstorm. I provided the money to repair it. I even joined the Amherst UU church when Mom visited me for my thirty-ninth birthday, signing my name in the book of members in front of her. That made her very happy, even though she had to stay at the Lord Jeffery Inn during the visit because I had no obvious place to live. In exchange for my investment, the co-directors of the conference center invited me to spend weekend retreats there free of charge.

Ram Dass, the new age guru, author of *Be Here Now*, and ex-cohort of Timothy Leary, was the guest at the first retreat I attended. At the Friday afternoon reception, I explained how I was using his book, *Miracles of Love*, as a guide to spiritual enlightenment. Ram Dass seemed amused with my stories. During the Friday and Saturday group gatherings, as I annotated Dass' stories with ones of my own, the conversation became a tête-à-tête between us. By Saturday evening, I imagined I was as important as Ram Dass.

Sunday morning, Ram Dass took me aside. "Scott, I thoroughly enjoyed our conversation this weekend. I hope you find a way to guide people to the devotion to the spiritual path that you are walking now. I commend you on your spirit."

I bowed to him. "Ram Dass, it has been a pleasure talking with you this weekend. Maybe we'll meet again."

Full of myself, I left that weekend thinking I might actually be a spiritual guide.

The next month, I attended a weekend led by a spiritual guide who channeled past lives. I found myself monopolizing the conversation and thinking, *Wow, maybe I could be a weekend leader.* The co-directors of Rowe thought not. The next time I asked to attend a weekend retreat, the co-directors discouraged me. That hurt.

In the fall at the annual UU member retreat weekend, I couldn't connect with anyone. Ignored at the Saturday afternoon reception, I drank the alcoholic punch and got wasted. After dinner, I sat on the kitchen floor alone. I was a drug addict and alcoholic. I couldn't admit it, but I did see the writing on the wall. No one wanted me around.

My last investment was with Vicky, the owner and one of the cooks at the Green River Café in Greenfield. The cafe was the meeting place of the whole foods crowd, vegetarians, and the lesbian community. She also cooked at the Rowe Camp and Conference Center. While I was eating lunch there one day, she sat down with me.

"You did a real good thing up at Rowe, when you donated the money for the dining hall roof."

My heartbeat quickened. Maybe she liked me.

"Yeah, the food you cooked for the retreat this summer was great."

Then she made her pitch: "Scott, do you think you could loan the restaurant two thousand dollars? Running a restaurant is difficult. We're trying to make a go of it, but sometimes expenses get ahead of income. It would get us through some hard times."

I was so happy she asked me. "Vicky, certainly, I'll give you two grand to keep the restaurant opened."

I left the restaurant walking on air. Maybe she liked me more than she liked her girlfriend. Maybe we were more than just friends. It was a crazy hope, but who said I was a sane man?

chapter 26

With my first two poems in print and the reception of other poems on the street, I imagined myself another Pablo Neruda. I would be the poet at the vanguard of the American socialist utopian revolution. Left-wing books like Marx's *Das Kapital, The Communist Manifesto,* and Engels' *Anti-Duhring* inspired me. Like Engels, my family had money, and I tried to shed my religious past and embraced left-wing politics. Jesus said, "Love one another, do unto others," and Paul said, "Hold everything in common," but communists said, "Organize the masses!"

I decided to learn to organize. At protest rallies, I met the people who were distributing *The Daily Worker,* the voice of the Communist Party USA, and *The People's Tribune,* the newspaper of the Communist Labor Party. After donating some money to the CLP, I received fifteen copies of the paper monthly. Fulfilling a boyhood dream of being a paperboy, now I was delivering *The Tribune* to righteous university lefties. On one hand, it was very cool. On the other, it was sort of a drag. The lefties couldn't come up with the quarter to buy the paper, so I gave it away. What the heck; charging money for a communist paper sounded like capitalism to me.

In the early spring of 1982, I met Nelson Perry, the chairman of the CLP. He was a black man, short in stature and with boundless energy. He visited me after a speaking engagement in Boston, stopping in Amherst on his way back to Chicago. I was enthusiastic about establishing a communist cell in Amherst, even though I was the only communist I knew. Nelson gave me advice and encouragement. "Scott, invite J. L. Chestnut to Amherst. He's a prominent civil rights attorney in Selma, Alabama working on voter registration. He was Martin Luther King's sidekick during the 1960s civil rights marches in Selma. Chestnut has a speaking engagement about voter rights fraud in Boston next month. He might enjoy speaking at the university."

I contacted Chestnut, and he agreed to come to Amherst. I was on the right track to organize Amherst.

Charles, chairman of the Black Student Association whose office in the UMass Student Union was near the Radical Student Union and the United Christian Fellowship, was a friend of mine. I stopped by to tell him the news. He was standing, squeezed behind his desk, looking through some papers when I walked in.

"Hey, I got this guy, Chestnut, a civil rights lawyer from Selma, who wants to speak about voter fraud in Alabama here in Amherst. Is there a place at UMass where he can speak?"

Charles, who was always immaculately dressed, looked up in disbelief. "J.L. Chestnut? How do you know him?"

"I contacted him after Nelson Perry suggested it."

Shocked, he said, "And you know Nelson Perry, too? You amaze me, Scott." Charles smiled and nodded. "Sure, the Black Student Association can find a place for him to speak. We'll take care of everything—getting the student union ballroom for the speech, printing flyers, distributing them. Wow, this is going to be big."

A week before Chestnut's speech, I hadn't seen any publicity. I saw Charles in the student union.

"Charles, where is all the publicity? I haven't seen any flyers."

He frowned and tried to hide his unhappiness. "Scott, when John Blakley, the chairman of the Black Studies Department, found out Chestnut was going to speak at the university, he stepped in and changed the plans. He said the student union ballroom and lots of publicity wasn't the way to go, suggesting a more intimate setting for such a prominent lawyer—the faculty lounge at Smith College. We're going to invite members of the Western Massachusetts progressive community to meet Chestnut. It will be nice and quiet. A real social thing."

I was stunned. My blood boiled, and I raised my voice. "Charles, how could John change our plans so drastically? This is for the students to learn about the sixties! Chestnut walked right next to King. He could be right here on stage, telling it like it is. Charles, students here need to know about the suppression of voter rights in Alabama!"

Charles winced and shrugged, helpless. "Scott, John stepped in. I had no choice. He said UMass was not ready for a big speech about voter rights. Chestnut's a communist."

My heart went cold. "Oh, I get it. Chestnut's a communist. Too radical for John. What a bitch."

I had no recourse except to show up to the soirée at Smith College. All the liberal politicos were there, fawning over Chestnut. Grabbing some crackers and cheese, I watched the afternoon unfold. I couldn't believe how much fear these progressives had.

I didn't understand how much they had to lose if they were associated with communism. They had jobs in a capitalistic society. I didn't.

Near the end of the gathering, I found a moment to approach Chestnut. He was a distinguished-looking man, dressed in a well-tailored suit, white shirt, and silk tie. I introduced myself. Chestnut's face brightened and with a big smile, he reached out for my hand.

"Mr. Hunter, yes, we talked on the phone. You set this meeting up. I really appreciate all your work."

His firm grip on my hand and his smile sent a shock through me. A famous man appreciated me.

"Sir, I'm sorry, we had a big speech planned in front of the student body. It's a five-college area. Everyone was going to come, then a professor stepped in. All of a sudden it was 'Oh, Chestnut's a communist. We can't have that. Let's have this guy over for tea.'"

With a laugh, he explained, "This has happened to me before. My political persuasion is an affront to some. Martin Luther King always chided me for being so far left. He wanted to cultivate the middle. The liberals were fighters once, but now they don't want their power threatened. Communist is a bad word. Still, I am so happy you invited me."

From 1978 to 1983, after five years of vagabonding, I told everyone I was a *fakir*, a wandering ascetic (excuse me, homeless person), investor (excuse me, giving away money), poet, political organizer. My life was drugs, drugs, drugs. I was numb, down, and out.

In January of 1983, I decided to go big and challenge John

Kerry, recently elected lieutenant governor of Massachusetts, to a literary tête-à-tête. I showed up at his 'meet and greet' in Greenfield with a hundred copies of my poem, *North Vietnam Lament 1968-1973*. John was a Vietnam vet. My poem was about the sadness of war. John and I would bond. We were brothers. It was going to be great.

After presenting each person in the room a copy of the poem, including John Kerry, I stood and waited for a reaction. No one looked at me, approached me, or spoke to me. *What? Was Kerry afraid of me? Did he think I was a long haired, red-bearded North Vietnamese sympathizer? Did people warn him? Tell him to avoid me?* It never occurred to me to go up and speak to him.

I felt myself filling up with anger, about to explode. If someone had actually acknowledged me, I would have exploded. I left the meeting and went home, finished with politics.

I was finished with giving away money, too. Some of the people whose projects I supported were successful, but once my money was not forthcoming, I was left out in the cold. I had no one else to blame. I wanted to be a failure and needed to be alone.

Though I hid my emotions behind drugs and alcohol, drugs, alcohol, and my imagination were keeping me alive. I had sold so much of my inheritance that the dividends I lived on were dwindling. My friends at my safehouses were less welcoming. Walking all day, only hitchhiking when I needed to be somewhere, I would head to the woods and spend my time alone. I knew all the back paths. At night, I would unroll my blanket next to a babbling brook or a pond, sleep undisturbed, and rise in the morning to bathe in fresh water. Nature was my friend in the spring, summer, and fall, but winters were hard. I imposed on the few friends I had left when it got too cold.

I did have my poetry, twenty-nine poems, enough for a book, which I decided to publish myself. I titled it *Sledgehammer Poetry*. The cover was a drawing by Jack Peace Arrow's wife. Robert, a graphic artist from Northampton, had seen *The Meeting of the Traveler and the Magus* poems back in 1980 and asked if he could draw some illustrations. I commissioned nineteen drawings and was going to self-publish *The Illustrated Meeting of the Traveler and the Magus*, but then Robert disappeared. I never got the illustrations.

I still had a good connection for marijuana, but the quality of acid from my West Coast connection was not what it used to be. I was going down.

One day, I decided to have breakfast at a restaurant in North Amherst where I had thumbtacked my poetry. One of the waitresses introduced me to Solomon, a jolly black guy full of energy.

Solomon wasted no time. "Scott, I publish an entertainment calendar for the Amherst/Northampton area. I graduated from Oberlin College, president of my senior class, big man on campus. I've read your poetry on the bulletin boards in town. Good stuff. If you need a publisher, I'm your man. For a price, of course."

I sat down, ate, and Solomon paid the bill. That was the last check he ever picked up, but he did supply me with drugs.

When breakfast was finished, I tried to get away. "Well, Solomon, good to meet you. I'm learning the publishing trade, so if I need some help, I'll look you up."

He did not relent. "No need, Scott, I can help you right now. I'm headed over to Hamilton Newell, my printer. I can introduce you. And I have some very good herb. We can smoke a joint on the way."

I couldn't pass up the joint, and I couldn't pass up the cocaine that Solomon always had on him. I began to use coke. Tired of living this way, always needing my next drug or drink, I couldn't see a way out.

On a Friday morning in February of 1983, I got a call from the guitar player from Loose Caboose, the reggae band in Wendell that I supplied with herb at gigs.

"Hey, Scotty, it's Johnny from the Caboose. I got a problem. Right before we left for a gig out of town this weekend, the toilet wouldn't flush. Could you head over to the house and get the wood stove cooking, open the doors to the basement and garage and unfreeze the pipes?"

I had a place to stay for the weekend.

"Sure, Johnny, I'll head over there right now. I'll take care of everything. When are you coming back?"

Much to my delight, he said, "Be back Sunday night. The band will really appreciate your help."

I unfroze the pipes and cleaned up the basement, creating a small space to sleep. I spent the weekend there. At night, I laid on the cement floor, surrounded by cement. It was like a tomb. I felt close to my father, both of us underground in a confined space.

On Sunday afternoon, alone in the house, I happened upon a Joan Armatrading album. When I heard the song *Down to Zero*, I realized how much I loved my father. The rhythm, the beat of the song, and the tone of Joan's voice broke me and slammed me to the ground. Sadness welled up from deep inside me and I cried, sobbing like I had never cried before. When I was finished crying, I stood up. I'd released a lot of sadness and anger.

Life didn't suddenly get better, but on Monday, I sensed a light at the end of a deep dark tunnel. I had a long way to go. I spent more and more weekends sleeping in my cement basement tomb when the band was out of town. I was spending my nights with Dad. When spring came in late March, I began digging up the backyard at the house and planting a garden. I transplanted a few birch tree clumps into the front yard. Dad was in my thoughts all day. I felt closer to him than I had when he was alive.

Over a pipe full of herb on a weekday afternoon, I told the band's long blond-haired, skinny, rot-toothed bongo player, Brooksie, about the Armatrading song.

"Brooksie, I just cried and cried. And when I stopped, I felt okay. It was like I wasn't sad anymore. Sleeping in the cement basement was like sharing my life with my father. I've gotten really close to him. Now when I'm working in the garden, it's like he's with me. I'm having fun."

The next week, Brooksie shared a spliff with me. "Scotty, it's time for you to move out of here."

Stunned, I asked, "Why?"

"You're living in our cold cement basement storage room. You got nothing. You're taking over the garden, planting trees. You're spending more time here than we are. You're happier than any of us. We can't stand it anymore. We appreciate the herb you share with us, but we don't want you living here."

I packed up my bed roll and headed out on the road again.

chapter 27

Living at the Loose Caboose house had gotten me through the winter. By May, I was back in the woods, walking all day, using the little cash I had for an occasional breakfast at the restaurant in North Amherst, eating nuts and dried fruit for lunch, and stopping by friends' houses, hoping to be invited to dinner. I ran into Sam frequently and replenished my supply of herb to sell and share. I regularly stopped by Solomon's place, looking for a few snorts of cocaine and help getting Hamilton Newell to agree to print *Sledgehammer Poetry*. Once in a while, I heard that small voice in my head scream, "You're addicted to drugs, Scott." I knew it. Everyone I knew used drugs. I still couldn't see a way out.

In the spring of 1983, the Vietnam War was long gone; the protest du jour was nuclear weapons. I heard about the Nuclear Moratorium Vigil, patterned after the anti-Vietnam protests of the 1960s, held every Sunday morning at eleven on the Amherst town common. I joined the group, usually ten or fifteen people, standing silently for an hour. I got to know some straight people. My Sunday mornings were drug free. It was a beginning.

On June 4, a bright, sunny Sunday morning, two monks in yellow robes joined us. Kato from Japan and Sister Claire from Boston belonged to the Nipponzan Order of Nichiren Buddhism, begun by Nichidatsu Fujii, who dedicated his life to nuclear disarmament. They believed chanting their mantra, Namu Myōhō Renge Kyō, was a vehicle to enlightenment.

I introduced myself to Kato and Claire. "I spent time in Thailand. I studied Buddhism."

Kato's white and yellow robes and hairless head radiated light. He bowed slowly from his waist. "So, you understand Buddha. We're marching to the Women's Peace Encampment. The women there are protesting nuclear weapons. We, too, don't agree with nuclear weapons. Will you join us?"

I felt like I was in a force field of good. I bowed to Kato. "I walk all the time. You're walking all the way to New York? Sounds like fun."

Sister Claire, hairless in her white and yellow robes, radiated light, too. "Scott, it would be wonderful if you could join us."

I felt a connection. Their energy reminded me of Phra Sohm's.

The next Sunday, twenty people finishing a week-long walk from Boston showed up at the vigil and stood with us. Afterwards, Kato and Sister Claire invited everyone to walk eight miles to Northampton with them. The Walk for Peace would leave Northampton on Tuesday for a three-week journey through Massachusetts and upstate New York to The Women's Peace Encampment in Romulus, New York, the home of the Seneca Army Depot, where nuclear weapons were allegedly stored. I followed the monks and their Namu Myōhō Renge Kyō banner out of Amherst. I thought that a few weeks on the walk would get me away from Solomon and his coke stash and cut down on my pot use.

Walking out of Amherst, I found myself talking with Jake, the owner of a Greek pizza shop in New Hampshire, who said he was visiting a friend when he'd encountered the walkers. He, too, decided to tag along.

I asked him, "Jake, do you wonder what Namu Myōhō Renge Kyō means?"

Jake thought a second. "Probably something in Japanese."

Before I laughed out loud, I said, "Did you figure that out yourself?"

With a straight face, he said, "No, one of the walkers told me." When we stopped laughing, we chanted down the road. The chant was made up of four slow syllables, 'namu myoho,' and three rapid syllables, 'ren ge kyo.' Accompanying the seven syllables, the monks and walkers beat four slow taps and three rapid taps on paddle-like drumheads, tap tap tap tap taptaptap.

I asked a few of the veteran walkers, "What's the chant mean?"

Only one came up with an answer: "Oh, it means we're walking for peace."

I pressed further. "No, can you translate the words into English?"

He answered blankly, "We don't understand Japanese. We just chant it, like Kato and Sister Claire."

I found Kato and Sister Claire. "I can't chant Namu Myōhō Renge Kyō unless I know what it means in English. It must mean something, right?"

They looked at each other. Kato finally said, "It's untranslatable. We just chant it."

Though I liked Kato and Sister Claire, their refusal to explain the chant seemed arrogant to me. I walked back to Jake.

"I think those monks just brushed me off. They said there is no translation to the chant. I'm not going to chant it all the way to Northampton, let alone upstate New York, if I don't know what it means."

Jake suggested, "Scott, maybe you should just let it go. Let's chant the Greek word, '*laska*'—it means 'let go.' Then '*milenka*.' *Milenka* means 'asshole.'"

He and I continued the walk, laughing, and chanting '*Laska Milenka*,'—'Let go, asshole.'

During a rest stop on the common in Hadley, I realized I could not continue on the walk until I figured out the chant's meaning. My dilemma led me to an old monk smoking a Camel cigarette and folding paper cranes. I bowed to him and explained my situation. He asked to see my notebook and opened it to a blank page. Borrowing a piece of charcoal from an artist who was sketching next to him, he wrote, *Give reverence to the essence of the Lotus Sutra.* He closed the notebook and vigorously rubbed the front and back cover. When he opened the notebook, he pointed to the mirror image.

"This is what it means."

The depth of the old monk's answer resonated somewhere with me. It wasn't the words, themselves, that had meaning, it was the spiritual meaning behind the words that should be the focus. That was all I needed. I was going to walk with the monks to New York.

When the Walk for Peace set out from Northampton headed to Cummington, twenty miles away, I found a place at the end of the line of walkers. The Nichiren banner led the parade. The monks in gold and white came next, drumming and chanting. The lay drummers and chanters followed. I talked with Pete and Diane, a Vietnam veteran and his girlfriend, street people who joined the walk in Northampton. I recited my poem *Jeanne d'Arc* to them. They were excited.

"Wow, Scott, that's a great poem. You're a good poet."

Street people, my kind of people, liked my poem. I hadn't smoked pot or drunk alcohol in two days. My self-esteem blossomed.

I picked up discarded cans along the side of the road, which I could return for five cents. Pete found a large potato sack, gave it to me, and I began filling it. The walk stopped for a rest at a parking area near a stream, and a few of us scrambled down to the stream and jumped in for a quick swim. As I climbed back to the road, I noticed some wooden branches that beavers had chewed into beautifully carved staffs. Picking a nice staff, I tied my half-full potato sack to it. I saw myself as the first card of the Major Arcana in the Tarot deck, the Fool, the bearded vagabond, willing to step off a cliff into an unknown future. I found a crow feather and put it in my headband.

The walk was similar to a family with intense sibling rivalries. There were few dull moments. Everyone was vying for position, seeking attention. Without drugs and alcohol for a few days, my head was clear. I was seeking attention too.

We crossed the border into New York, and I began to see the Walk for Peace as a dragon inching along the road. The Nichiren banner was the head and neck of the dragon. The walkers were the body. The chanting and drumming were its roar. I was the tail of the dragon, spreading peace flyers to onlookers we passed, introducing them to our purpose. At times, the universe seemed to be in tune with the walk. On hot afternoons, the skies would fill with dark clouds and thunder would echo the drums. Nature was taking notice.

After another week of countryside and rural towns, the walk

reached Syracuse, New York, cement city. We couldn't wait to get back into the country. Our next stop was the Onondaga Nation Indian Reservation, where we were going to spend the night. The asphalt roads we'd been walking turned to dirt, and the houses along the road turned into trees. Strolling through the peaceful forest, a full-sized Ford Thunderbird pulled alongside of us and stopped. I recognized the passenger in the car immediately. It was Dennis Banks, the founder of the American Indian Movement and a fugitive wanted by the United States government for his role in protests at Wounded Knee in South Dakota. Onondaga was his sanctuary.

The driver of the car, a tall elderly man with gray braided hair, got out and spoke to us: "I'm Oren Lyons, Faithkeeper of the Turtle Clan of the Seneca Nations. I welcome you to my home. We'll see you again at the schoolhouse ahead, our tribal meeting place."

He got back into the car and sped off.

When we reached the schoolhouse, the Thunderbird was parked outside. Inside, Lyons gave another short welcome. His dignity commanded respect. Kato and Sister Claire responded with short speeches, then there was an awkward silence. Feeling the urge to speak well up within me, I stepped forward and bowed.

"Thank you, Faithkeeper Lyons, for your hospitality. We feel more welcome here than any other place on our journey." Without thinking, I took my potato sack off my staff and presented the staff to the chief. "The spirit of the earth gave me this staff carved by beavers. I'd like to give it to you as a symbol of our gratitude."

Lyons' eyes lit up and he smiled as he accepted the staff. The Native Americans present and the walkers, now twenty-five of us, applauded.

As the meeting broke up, everyone engaged in animated

conversations. I stood spellbound by the energy flowing through me, shaking without moving. A Native American woman asked if I needed a massage. She brushed my back with her hand in a way that produced a bunch of loud cracks. Suddenly, I was completely relaxed.

The walk left the reservation on Saturday, July 2, traveling twenty-six miles to Cortland, then twenty-one miles to Ithaca on Sunday. We rested on Monday, the Fourth of July, celebrating the holiday at Taughannock Falls, the highest waterfall east of the Mississippi, and at Buttermilk Falls, where early Tarzan movies were filmed, facts I knew from summer vacations visiting my grandparents in Troy.

The next morning, we climbed a long hill out of Ithaca on Route 89. At the top, we had wonderful views of Cayuga Lake.

Suddenly, a colorfully dressed hippie with a long, bright red beard and matching hair bounded out of one of the small houses alongside of the road. "Aieeee!!!"

Running, jumping, and yelping like crazy, he could have been a leprechaun. He was carrying a large staff, similar to the one I'd given Oren Lyons. It was a third longer and twice the diameter.

He ran up to me, hugged me, kissed me, handed me the staff, and said, "You gonna need this where you're going!" He produced a large belly laugh and ran back into the house.

The commotion had stopped the walkers. They all were watching me. I turned to my compatriots and raised the bigger and better staff over my head. I pounded it on the ground, producing a solid sound.

One of the walkers let out a "Whooppee!!! Scott has his staff back."

I felt the energy from meeting Faithkeeper Lyons coursing

through me again. I moved to the front of the dragon. I began slamming the staff on the pavement in time with the drumming. When we reached Trumansburg, New York, we danced through a section of town with NASCAR signs in every front yard. With me, the Fool in the lead, the foreign banner, the yellow and white robed monks, and a long line of followers all drumming and chanting, the onlookers' faces told me we were a mystifying sight.

I awoke the next morning on the lawn of a farmhouse overlooking Cayuga Lake. There were miles of patchwork fields between the lake and where I stood. The view looked like an eighteenth-century folk-art painting of upstate New York. A huge fireball of sun peeked over the horizon. Everything was red, gold, and shades of green. The smell of lavender from the nearby garden was soothing. The last day of the walk was here.

We walked through the small towns of Interlaken and Ovid, conservative upstate New York. We were met with glares and insults from patriots with American flags. Behind the walk's banner, we felt invincible. At the main gate of the Army depot, we drummed and chanted across from soldiers lined up with guns ready for action. When we finished drumming and chanting, we headed to the farmhouse across town that was the Women's Peace Encampment. We drummed and chanted there.

The next day, the Walk for Peace was disbanded. Kato and Sister Claire were headed back to Boston to begin their search for land to build a temple. I had my poetry to publish. I felt good that I'd been without drugs and alcohol for three weeks, but the summer's fantasy was over. I looked forward to smoking some pot and having a beer.

chapter 28

Before I'd left Amherst in June, I'd contracted with Hamilton Newell Printing to print 500 copies of *Sledgehammer Poetry* for $1,500. Since returning from the walk, I'd started smoking pot again and doing coke with Solomon. I wasn't paying attention to how long Hamilton Newell was taking to get the books printed. July turned into September. Because Hamilton Newell mainly did posters and flyers, they weren't paying attention to *Sledgehammer Poetry* either. In September, I finally caused a scene at the shop.

"Where's my book?"

To calm me down, I was introduced to Sarah, who was assigned to typeset the book. After meeting with her, I realized Sarah was an alcoholic, maybe on drugs. She couldn't do her job. I confronted the owner and demanded he fire Sarah, or at least get me someone who could publish my books.

The next day, I was introduced to the guy who was going to get on my book, finish setting it up, and get it printed. To my great surprise, it was Henry, the resident from Belchertown State School I'd weaned from Thorazine. I was excited to see him again.

When Belchertown closed, community-living houses were established in the surrounding areas. Henry had moved into one of the houses and gotten a job at Hamilton Newell. I gave him a hug. He didn't know how to react. I guess not many people were giving him hugs.

I said, "Henry, you look great. And you got a job."

Henry said, "Yes, Scott. I...have a...a job. I...I am taking over from...Sarah." Each time he struggled with a word, he jerked his head down and he got the word out. "...Sarah did not do a ...good job. I will...fix the problem for you, Scott. You will have your...book very...soon. I will do a good job." He looked up at me and smiled.

Within two weeks, I had 500 copies of *Sledgehammer Poetry*. I gave signed books to all my friends and left more copies at all the bookstores on consignment. I met a doctoral student at UMass who'd been a teaching assistant for Allen Ginsberg. He suggested I send a copy to City Lights, Ginsberg's bookstore in San Francisco. The reactions from my close friends were positive, but I didn't get much acclaim from the people I'd hoped would be impressed, the local left-wingers with influence. I sold two or three books at the local bookstores. I began to do more drugs to keep my spirits up. That was as effective as cutting off my legs to grow taller.

One day, while I was in Northampton distributing *Sledgehammer Poetry*, I ran into Robert, who was supposed to have illustrated *The Meeting of the Traveler and the Magus* two years before. I was shocked to see him and angry that I'd never gotten the drawings I paid for.

"Robert, where have you been?"

Before I could ask about the illustrations, he gave me a big hug. I was getting angrier because he had this big grin on his face.

"Great to see you. How've you been? I never heard back from you about the illustrations. How'd you like them?"

"Illustrations? You never gave me any illustrations."

Robert's mouth opened wide. "I left them on the bulletin board in the kitchen of my old house in Northampton. My house-mates never gave them to you? I left town right after I finished them. I just got back. It's been two years, but my housemates still live there. Let's go see if the illustrations are still in the kitchen."

We hightailed it over to his old apartment. There they were, thumb-tacked to the bulletin board. They were fabulous. I mocked up forty-two pages, took them over to Hamilton Newell, and showed them to Henry first. He flipped through the pages and studied each one.

"These...pictures are real...good, Scott. Do you want me to... make a...book out of them, too? It won't...take long."

I grabbed Henry by his shoulder. "Henry, I want you to help me with this book, too. You're the best printer in the world." I was so proud of him.

I arranged with Hamilton Newell to print 500 copies of *The Meeting of the Traveler and the Magus* for another $1,500. Henry had them printed up in three weeks. That buoyed my spirits for the next few months, but without sales or enthusiasm from a wider audience than my friends, I sank back into drugs and alcohol. I struggled through the winter and into summer of 1984.

One night in August 1984, I dropped a hit of acid and walked the back roads to the Rusty Nail, where Gil Scott Heron, the famous jazz poet and author of *The Revolution Will Not Be Tele-*

vised was playing. I shared a joint with the doorman and got in for free. As soon as I sat down at the bar, my old friend Rick, the manager, came up to me.

"Listen, I read your Joan of Arc thing and I loved it. I want to introduce you to Gil Scott Heron. You've got to meet him. You've got to tell him your poem. He'll love it."

I laughed. "Meet Gil Scott Heron? Recite *Jeanne d'Arc* to him? You've got to be kidding me."

Rick dragged me upstairs into the green room where Heron and his band were drinking Courvoisier.

"Gil, this is Scott. He's a local poet. You've got to hear this poem he wrote."

Gil looked like the pictures on his albums: short, tight afro, trimmed beard, thin but muscular. He reached out to shake my hand. "Good to meet you. Call me Gil. Here. Take a swig of this." He handed me the bottle. "Drink up, my friend."

I looked at Rick. He was nodding his head, yes. I took a hit of cognac. *Pow*, it exploded in my head. The acid was kicking in. Gil motioned me to take another drink. I did.

He took the bottle, tipped his head back, and drank. "Time to recite your poem, brother."

With all the passion I could muster, I recited *Jeanne d'Arc.* By the time I finished the poem, Rick had rolled and lit some joints. We passed them around.

Gil took a long draw on a joint and said, "That's a good poem. Recite it again."

Into it now, I yelled it out. I had the attention of Gil and his band. Some of the band members chimed in: "Stop the killing. Stop the killing. Peace is love. Peace is love."

When I was finished, Gil turned to his band. "You guys liked that? Cool."

The band members replied, "Cool, man. Right on. Peace is love. Stop the killing. He knows it, Gil."

Gil turned to me. "Scott, I don't have an opening act. Go on stage and recite that poem, man."

I was shocked. "Gil, I can't do that."

"You gotta, brother. I'm not goin' on stage 'til ya do." He looked at his watch. "It's twelve o'clock already. You're my opening act. Get on stage and recite that poem. No poem, no music, no Gil Scott Heron. Right, guys?"

One of the band members said, "Opening act, brother. You're it. We gotta go on sometime."

Rick took my arm and walked me downstairs, then backstage. It was wicked late. The crowd was restless.

Rick looked at me: "No poem, no music and no Gil Scott Heron." He pushed me onstage.

I walked up to the microphone, introduced myself, and recited *Jeanne d'Arc.* I bowed to scattered applause. I walked off the stage. Gil appeared to thunderous applause.

High as a kite, I saw Vicky, the woman from the Green River Cafe. I'd opened for Gil Scott Heron. Maybe she would love me now. I walked up to her. Talk about awkward moments. The acid and the Courvoisier didn't help. Hopeless and humiliated, I retreated to the bar and traded more joints for drinks. I waited for people to come up and congratulate me.

No one did. *What happened? I opened for Gil Scott Heron. Where were my fans? Was this stardom?* More like loneliness. My books were printed, and no one was buying them. My only fans were Rick, Gil Scott, and his band. Despite my love for acid highs, I couldn't get much lower.

When Rick closed the bar, I wandered into the deserted parking lot. It was a cold, clear night. The band's bus sat in the back corner of the lot. The door was open. It beckoned to me. I walked over to the door and stood there. I could walk into the bus and become part of the band. I could leave Amherst and travel around the country, writing poems and songs for Gil Scott Heron. I would become famous. Then everyone at the Rusty Nail would know who I was.

I felt like Alice standing at the rabbit hole. If I walked through the door, I would enter another universe. I hesitated. I was afraid. Deep, deep, deep in the recesses of my mind, there was something that kept me from taking that step forward. Maybe it was the summer on the walk to the encampment. I had a taste of life without drugs and alcohol. Maybe it was the voice of the Yao silversmith. Gil Scott Heron was a heroin addict. I didn't need to hang out with him. Yeah, I was alone and depressed, but I was alive. As strong as the pull into the bus was, I turned and walked away. Halfway across the parking lot, I heard the bus engine start. As I exited the parking lot and turned towards my current home, a house on nearby Juggler Meadow Lane, the bus slowly passed me by. Once again, I was a nobody.

One afternoon a few days later, Marco showed up in his tricked-out van.

"You want to go out tonight and pick up women? I'm going to a concert in Hartford."

Marco was a parachutist, an Army Ranger veteran, a loner, a player not into intimacy. He was handsome. He had a seething anger that attracted co-dependent women. I'd seen women come up to Marco, give him their phone numbers, and beg him to call. There were always women around him. He dated women and trashed them. *Going out with him to pick up girls? Maybe I had a chance to meet someone.*

"I'm ready. Let's go."

I was too eager, and Marco sensed it. "Ok, put on a t-shirt, some shorts, and your tennis shoes," he said, playing with me. "If you can run a mile with me, we'll go out tonight."

I found some clothes and shoes and returned outside. Marco was stretching, warming up. He pointed across Route 63.

"I figure we'll run down that dirt road, back along the edge of that field, through those woods to here. That's a mile. You ready?"

I shrugged.

Marco was off. I followed, struggling to keep up. Marco picked up his pace on a little grade at about three-quarters of a mile, disappearing around a corner onto Juggler Meadow. I had nothing left by the last quarter-mile.

When I turned the corner, I noticed Marco was sitting in the driver's seat of his van. I walked over to the passenger side.

Through the open window, Marco sneered, "When you can run a mile with me, you can come party with me."

He started the van and drove off without me.

As I watched Marco's van disappear, I thought, *Marco, you are such an asshole. You just wanted me to feel bad, so you wouldn't be the only one who felt bad. But, hey, you did come over to see me. You're probably the only friend I have.*

Suddenly, I saw a clear picture of who I was: an out-of-shape slob, overweight, smoking cigarettes, drinking, and doing drugs. I was in no shape to go out with Marco to pick up women. What good would it do me, anyway? I didn't know how to connect with people in any meaningful way. I never ended up with a girl. No girl would want me. I had no idea what I needed to do.

Giving up drugs and alcohol was the furthest thing from my mind. They were keeping my secrets hidden from the world and from me. They were keeping the guilt and anger in check. Without drugs and alcohol, the guilt would've killed me. I couldn't have faced my anger. I blamed the world, too, transferring my anger toward anyone I could. Without drugs and alcohol, my anger would've killed me or someone else. I couldn't have been more depressed.

Then, from deep inside of me, I realized, perhaps for the first time, I was the problem. I could continue to be depressed, angry, and guilty for the rest of my life. My mind screamed, *NO!!! DO SOMETHING ABOUT IT!!!*

I thought, *Damn it, I'll show Marco.* I had stuck with him for the first three-quarters of a mile. Running like that made me feel good. I could sit on a couch for the rest of my life and bemoan my fate, or I could begin to do something. *Screw being nobody. I'll become a runner, like Marco.*

The next morning, I ran four miles. I ran slowly. Okay, I jogged slowly. I attacked those four miles with the same determination I'd had when I sewed my teepee together ten years earlier.

A mile into the run, I passed the cemetery. *At least I'm not dead.*

It was a warm, beautiful, sunny day. I felt good for the first time in a long time. My mind was clear for a few seconds. Taking a deep breath, I found the energy to run over the railroad tracks up the hill, right onto another country road deeper into the woods. I imagined the trees watching me. I was exhaling carbon dioxide for them to breathe, while they were exhaling oxygen for me. I was at one with the world and I hadn't done any acid. On the gradual ups and downs through the woods back to the house, I picked up my pace. I was going to finish strong. After four miles, back at the house, bent over catching my breath, I was overwhelmed with positive energy. I had accomplished what I set out to do. It didn't matter what anyone else thought. I loved myself just a little bit.

Over the next six months, I became a runner, four miles, three or four times a week. I gradually increased my mileage to six, ten, sixteen-mile loops. I was creating space in my head, positive energy, endorphins, sweating out old and useless thoughts. After each run, I loved myself a little more.

I continued to fight my depression. Throughout the fall of 1984 and spring and summer of 1985, I would run in the afternoon and feel good, then go out at night and drink and drug myself silly. I would wake up in the middle of the night and run for hours, alone, happy with myself. Then, during the day, people would irritate me. They wouldn't do what I wanted them to do: pay attention to me, care for me, help me understand why I was so fucked up. I was blaming them for my loneliness. My guilt and anger were forcing them away. I couldn't accept my emotions, so I had to use more drugs and alcohol.

I camped at the Juggler Meadow house through the winter, then moved out in the spring to return to living the life of a vagabond. When I was alone, life was tolerable. I enjoyed quiet evenings and glorious early mornings, but my need for drugs and alcohol was ever-present. I had to connect with people when I bought and sold drugs to stay afloat, but when I was with them, life was unbearable.

On a warm afternoon in late November, smoking pot and reciting poems on the UMass Campus Center patio, I noticed a very good-looking blonde, blue-eyed coed listening nearby. Our eyes met a couple of times. She approached me when the crowd thinned.

"My name is Caroline. I love your poetry."

I didn't fall head over heels in love with her, having come to the realization that I was incapable of loving. When asked by people why I didn't have a girlfriend, I would reply: "I'm in love with Mary Jane, marijuana, and Lucy in the Sky, LSD." I would laugh while my heart broke inside. I looked at Caroline without feeling anything. I saw myself standing in front of this beautiful woman: empty, going nowhere, very sad.

Caroline continued coming on to me. "I live in an apartment above Bart's Ice Cream Shop in Northampton with two other women. You can stay with us whenever you want."

Her invitation felt like a come-on, but I was too numb to respond to her advances. "Thanks, but I can't right now. Maybe some other time."

I did stop by her apartment the next time I was in Northampton. After meeting her apartment mates, Jackie and Maryann, sharing some pot and wine with them, they asked me to move in. Their apartment was a two-story loft with exposed rafters, an open kitchen/dining room/living room area with three small bedrooms on one side. A four-by-eight piece of plywood in the rafters with a mattress on it became my space. I supplied the herb and they supplied the wine. I should have been thrilled, living with three women, but I never slept with any of them. We partied every evening until we all left for the Christmas holidays.

Back at my childhood home in New Kensington around Mother, Marilyn, and her kids, I feigned optimism. I didn't want to let them down. It had been six years since the drunk and drug-fueled L.A. Christmas, and I pretended I was on top of the world.

"Mom, Marilyn, my books are published. How about that? I'm a well-known poet in Massachusetts."

I was oblivious to the looks they were giving me.

No longer clean-shaven, I had five years of beard forming two dreadlocks hanging down to my chest. My matted hair was down to the middle of my back. They made comments about shaving and cutting my hair. I caught them staring at me. I put up a happy front as best I could, but I was devastated inside. I was letting my mother down.

I returned to Northampton. My roommates wouldn't come back home for a few days. I bought an ounce of mushrooms to share with friends on New Year's Eve. Around seven o'clock, ready to party, I took the mushrooms out of the refrigerator. An immense pain welled up from somewhere inside of me. The mushrooms were mine. I couldn't share them. I needed them to stop the pain. I ate all the mushroom caps and left the stems for later. Sitting in the apartment alone, I waited for enlightenment.

Instead, a darkness descended upon me. Thoughts began to spill out of my head. The first half of the 1980s had been filled with the tragic deaths of large numbers of innocent people, airplane crashes, terrorist attacks, natural disasters, and wars. On December 27, 1985, terrorists had killed 17 and injured 116 people in two attacks at airports in Rome and Vienna. The television news media continuously replayed the attack in Rome, focusing on the death of Natasha Simpson, the eleven-year-old daughter of an American journalist. I couldn't get those images out of my mind. Feeling sad for all the innocents dying in the world, I started writing what became a four-page poem, *Elegy to a World Graveyard - 1985*.

I felt that *Elegy* was my *Howl.* Unlike Ginsberg's poem, a big orgasm of madness, spirituality, drugs, conventional society and outsiders, mine was one of mourning. Death was all around me. The year was dying. I was dying.

The next morning, exhausted, still stoned on the mushrooms, I felt a lightness of being. I had released a lot of emotion, anger, sadness, compassion, but I was still very much in the pit of hell.

A few days after writing *Elegy*, my roommates returned. Living with three women above Bart's should've been a slice of heaven. I had excellent marijuana and we drank bottles of wine each evening. The potential for lovemaking was epic, though it didn't happen. In reality, life was a horror show. Instead of cultivating affectionate relationships, I was getting into arguments that turned into shouting matches late at night. The wine was unleashing some deep-seated anger from within me, and I feared the arguments would turn into physical violence. I knew something was very wrong with me. I could neither identify what exactly was wrong nor how to fix it.

All my relationships were crumbling. I'd had a blowout with Sam, my best friend and marijuana supplier, the previous winter, when he arrived screaming drunk at the cabin where I was staying. We'd gotten into a fight and I'd called the cops. He disappeared into the woods. That was the end of that friendship.

Les and Marco were still my friends, but I was getting tired of them bullying me, always putting me down. They were going to Jamaica for two weeks in January and asked if I wanted to tag along. Les would buy my plane ticket if I told his lawyer that the drug money the police had confiscated from him in a November drug bust was money I'd lent him to buy a car. His lawyer and the court bought the story. Despite the prospects of extraordinary marijuana, bikini-clad women, and fun in the sun, I decided I didn't want to go to Jamaica with them. I was almost out of money anyway. Most of the stock certificates I'd inherited and the dividends they produced were gone. Sam had disappeared, so I had no more pot to sell. I'd asked Les for money instead of the plane ticket, needing to buy Christmas presents for Mom, Marilyn and the kids, the only people who I knew deep down really cared about me.

So, instead of heading to Jamaica in mid-January, I was hanging out with my roommates at the apartment, drinking, smoking, and arguing. The argument on January 14, 1986 was really out of control. It was all yelling and screaming. I couldn't stop drinking wine. I wanted to smash something, somebody. On the edge of violence, I knew it would be dangerous to be around my roommates for one more night. I went to bed.

I awoke early the next morning and quietly packed my belongings into the car I'd gotten in September, a belated birthday present from Mom. I ate the mushroom stems left over from New Year's Eve, bought a pack of cigarettes, and smoked them. I was broke and broken.

I went to Amherst and searched for people to talk to, friends at the United Christian Fellowship and the Radical Student Union offices at UMass. I sought out the Unitarian Universalist minister at the UU church. No one wanted to talk to me. Around 11 a.m., I smoked my last cigarette—twenty in four hours. I was stoned and had nowhere to go.

I was sitting on the wall in front of the Unitarian Church when a car horn beeped. There was Sam stopped at the light. I hadn't seen him since the fight at the cabin. He had a big smile on his face.

"I'm back in town. Get in the car before the light changes."

I ran over to the car and jumped in. I was sure glad to see him.

"Sam, I can't believe it. I did some mushrooms this morning and you show up. It's like magic."

Calm and focused, Sam asked, "How are you doing, Scott?"

The magic of the mushrooms suddenly wore off and I was back in reality.

"Not good, Sam. I was living with three women and we were fighting all the time. Last night, I was so angry I wanted to hit them. I had to leave. All I can do is smoke cigarettes. I need some pot. Something."

Sam had a big smile on his face now. He knew something I didn't know. "How about some food? You want to eat? I'll take you to lunch. How about that?"

His calmness was rubbing off on me. I took a deep breath. "Lunch, sure. I just need someone to talk to. I haven't seen you in ages. How are you doing?"

Still smiling broadly, Sam explained. "I've been at the Cape, living at my parents'. Life is getting better. I need to stop at the bank and get some money. I got to go to a meeting before lunch. Do you want to go to a meeting? It's only an hour, and then we can eat and talk."

I had no idea what meeting he was talking about, but I needed desperately to talk. "Sounds good to me. I got nothin' else. I just need someone to talk to."

I felt safe as I relaxed in the passenger seat and let the haze of the mushrooms wash over me.

A half an hour later, we went through the side door of the

Unitarian Universalist church in Northampton, down the stairs into the basement where tables and chairs were set up in a large square. I looked around and recognized about six people, old druggy friends of mine. They came over and greeted me. Sam hadn't told me the meeting was the Nooner, the noon meeting of Alcoholics Anonymous. He'd been in AA for nine months, beginning shortly after our fight.

The meeting began with a man telling his story of alcoholism and recovery. As the discussion part of the meeting inched its way around the tables toward me, I was flooded with emotions.

When it was my turn to speak, I barely got out, "My name is Scott. I'm an alcoholic and drug addict."

I broke into tears. The discussion continued past me, and I cried. I was forty years old. I haven't had a drink or a drug since that meeting.

chapter 29

After the meeting, Sam gathered a group of recovering alcoholics and took me to lunch.

I couldn't remember the last time I sat around a table with five or six other people and just talked. Everyone was very happy. We laughed. Mike, a landscaper, was there. He was five years sober. I met a thirteen-year-old girl, Sarah, who was at her first AA meeting with her mother, Jane, and her mother's girlfriend, Diane. Jane and Diane were newly sober. For the next nine years, we all attended AA meetings regularly and became close friends.

After lunch, Sam suggested we go to another meeting. I couldn't think of a reason not to. At the 3:30 afternoon meeting at the Franklin Medical Center Detoxification Unit in Greenfield, I met Big Rich and Frank. They were paid by the hospital to manage the detox unit and lead the afternoon meeting. As I listened to them, the saying I had heard in Thailand, "When the student is ready, the teacher appears," came to mind. I spent many afternoons over the next six months listening to wisdom and common sense from them.

After dinner, Sam and I went to the 7:30 Two-Wheels to Recovery meeting sponsored by the local sober motorcycle club—"Live to Ride and Ride to Live Drug Free." I felt right at home with my beard and hair and stories of my Triumph Bonneville 650. I met Dr. B, an ex-con Hell's Angel from California.

When the meeting was over, he came up to me. "Welcome to AA, Scott. Remember, it's one day at a time. Don't worry about anything else, just staying sober today."

He was shorter than I was. His light brown curly hair stood up on his head. The sides and back were completely shaved. His stocky build was all muscle.

I began to tell him about my motorcycle. "I had a 650cc Triumph Bonneville…"

Dr. B. cut me off. "Fuck your motorcycle. Did you hear what I said?" Emphatically, he said, "Don't drink, one day at a time."

I smiled sheepishly. "Okay, I get it. Don't drink, one day at a time."

He laughed. "Hey, guys, I think we got a winner here. He's figured out you don't drink one day at a time."

I heard a chorus from the guys: "Don't drink. Keep coming back," and a bunch of laughter.

Dr. B. looked up at me. "Listen, Scott. I was fucked. I had a ten-year bid in federal prison. It could have been worse. I was lucky. I got sober in prison. Got out early because I behaved. I got a G.E.D, then community college, then San Diego State. Now, I'm here at UMass, getting my doctorate in Public Health. If this can happen to me because I'm sober, just think what can happen to you. Here's my phone number. Give me a call when you need to."

Gratefully, I said, "Thank you, Dr. B. I will."

After that meeting, Sam and I walked over to the Congregational Church in Amherst for the 8:30 evening discussion meeting. All the people I met at the Northampton Noon meeting and ate lunch with were there, plus another thirty recovering alcoholics. It was at this meeting that I first noticed "The Twelve Steps, The Road to Recovery" posted on the wall. I got an *AA Big Book* and a daily meditation book. By 10 p.m., I had sixteen hours of sobriety.

Sam asked me, "Where do you live, Scott? I got to drive you home."

I spread my arms with my hands palm up. "I don't live anywhere."

Sam's eyes lit up. "You can sleep in my room on Green Street in Northampton. That'll give me an excuse to stay with Cathy, my girlfriend. I'll pick you up at 7:00 for the morning meeting where the Nooner was, then we can eat breakfast."

Sam dropped me off. I read a little of the *AA Big Book* and went to sleep.

The next day, we went to the morning meeting, ate breakfast, went to the Nooner, lunched again with the gang, and hit the Greenfield detox meeting.

As we left that meeting, Sam asked, "What're you going to do for the weekend?"

I had no clue.

"Do you have any money?"

I knew there were no dividend checks at the post office. "Nope."

"Do you know where you can get some?"

We were in Greenfield. "I know someone who owes me money—Vicky. She runs a restaurant. She paid me back most of a loan, but still owes me 200 dollars."

Sam ordered, "Call her up."

I hesitated. "I haven't seen her in months."

A little louder, Sam said, "Call her up."

I did, and she agreed to pay off the loan. She gave me her address, and Sam and I went to pick up the money. I was no longer in love with her. I was focused on me.

Sam and I headed to a Narcotics Anonymous meeting and met more friends in recovery. NA meetings became my home, since AA meetings had some alcohol purists who frowned on talking about drug use. To them, cocaine was a little scary—LSD was really scary. NA meetings were no-holds-barred. LSD was just another addictive drug.

After the NA meeting, a group went to McManus's at the mall, talked, and ate ice cream. I had two days of sobriety.

Sam drove me back to Green Street. "You're coming to the Cape with me this weekend. If you're on your own, you'll use again. I'll pick you up at 6:30, we're going to the morning meeting at the UU church."

After the morning meeting, Sam and I hung around until the Nooner, then headed down to Cape Cod for the three-day MLK Day weekend. On the Cape, we went to AA meetings, ate, and slept. We headed back to Amherst on Tuesday, arriving late in the morning.

Sam looked at me and sighed. "Scott, six days is all I can handle. You're so needy. Get out of the car. You're on your own."

Eternally grateful for those six days with Sam, standing in front of the Jones Library on Amity Street, I was at a crossroads. The only alternative I had that didn't lead back to my old life with drugs and alcohol was Dr. B's telephone number. I called him.

"Dr. B., it's Scott from the Two-Wheels to Recovery meeting a week ago. I have six days of sobriety. All I've been doing is going to meetings. I burnt Sam out. He let me off in Amherst. You gave me your number. I thought I'd call and tell you how inspirational you were. I'm going to take a deep breath and see if I can stay sober and straight on my own. I'll try and get to the Wednesday meeting."

Dr. B's voice had some urgency to it. "Before you do anything, Scott, do you have a car?"

"Yeah."

"Okay, do you know where Atkins Reservoir is?"

That was easy. I'd slept there many times. "Yeah, in North Amherst, off Market Hill Road."

"Drive out here right now. I live in the first house on the right after you pass the reservoir. I'm waiting for you."

Dr. B. welcomed me into his house. We talked recovery. His wife cooked us a delicious meal. He and I went to the Tuesday night meeting in Sunderland. I slept in a real bed in a real house that night. I met Sam at the morning meeting in Northampton. He was happy I'd made it through the night. I went to the Nooner, the detox meeting, and met up with Dr. B. at the Two-Wheels to Recovery meeting. I stayed at Dr. B.'s the next two nights.

On Friday morning, he informed me, "Scott, like the old saying goes—guests and fish begin to stink after three days. You're on your own."

I understood, thanked him and his wife, and set out, again on my own.

I went to the morning meeting and the Nooner by myself. Mike, Sarah, and her parents were there. Sarah's sister, Joselyn, newly sober, ate lunch with us. I headed up to Greenfield for the detox meeting.

I stopped by to see Jacob, my dentist, whom I hadn't seen

since The Spa failed.

"Jacob, I'm clean and sober for eight days, one day at a time."

"Congratulations, Scott, it's about time. I'm chairing the Greenfield Friday Night NA meeting. Would you like to come with me? I need a speaker. You want to speak tonight?"

"Don't I need at least ninety days to be a speaker?"

"Who cares? You're sober, right? If it keeps you sober, you should speak."

Then, it dawned on me. "Wait a second, you're chairing an NA meeting?"

With a Cheshire cat smile, Jacob said, "Scott, I've been in the program for a year. Couldn't stay away from prescription drugs. Almost lost my license. You haven't stopped by since The Spa went bust. You don't love me anymore?"

I was amazed that now two of my best drugging buddies, Sam and Jacob, were straight. "I love you, Jacob. I was just so fucked up. I guess I forgot where you lived."

Jacob's nurse came over and gave Jacob a scowl. He had patients waiting.

"We're better now. Let's take it one day at a time. Come to the house around five and we'll go to dinner and talk. Then we can go to the meeting and you can tell everyone what it's like to be clean and sober for a week, okay?"

Jacob and I ate dinner at his favorite Chinese restaurant and went to the NA meeting.

I was nervous before I spoke, but after I introduced myself, I said, "I am an alcoholic and drug addict," and I got into my story.

I didn't have much recovery yet, so I spoke about my first acid trip, my Yao silversmith friend, and how happy I was to be straight and sober for a week. Some of the recovering addicts were upset that I was asked to speak with such short sobriety, but speaking at that meeting was good for me. It became one foundation stone in my sobriety. I admitted I was an addict. There was no going back.

The next morning, Jacob told me, "Get a place to live, Scott. It's time to get serious and grow up. You can't sleep on people's couches forever."

Here I was, forty years old with nothing to show for it. Jacob was right. It was time I got my act together and made something of myself. I remembered once sitting in his dentist chair. I was whining about how terrible my life was. Jacob slapped my cheek a couple of times.

"Scott, you graduated from Amherst College. If you wanted to be a millionaire, you could be a millionaire."

I remembered my friend Beth. With her inheritance, she'd purchased a house on Alden Street in Greenfield. She called it The Pond, where tadpoles became frogs, a place that fostered growth in human potential. I left Jacob's house and drove over there. A room was for rent for $120 a month. When my potential housemates found out that I was a good friend of Beth's, they said I could move in. I drove up to the Wendell Depot post office and one of my last dividend checks was there. It covered my rent. I was happy I hadn't sold all my stocks. For the first time since I had moved to Massachusetts in 1972, fourteen years earlier, I was going to live in a house where alcohol and drugs were not a factor.

Beth was right. The Pond House was where tadpoles became frogs. My first giant step in adulthood was admitting that I was addicted to alcohol and drugs. At the Pond House, I took another step. During my years of addiction, I'd avoided people more and more. Though I could be outspoken about public issues, when it came to more personal issues, I was intimidated. Standing up for myself was too dangerous. Someone might learn my undiscovered secrets. Flight was more comfortable than fighting for my interests.

I shared the Pond House with six other residents. There were two single guys about my age, Ben and Jack, who were working and enjoying their single lives. There was a recently married couple, Margaret and Terry, who were searching for a place of their own. Then there was another married couple, Joan and Frank, who had lived in The Pond from its beginnings. They were a bit odd. I was scared of them. Their anxiety made me anxious. At first, I adjusted my behavior to ease the tension. So much of my personal life was a reaction to what others felt. I wanted others to like me, to be my friend, but I always pushed them away.

I had a new life. I couldn't run away anymore. Instead of giving in and adjusting to others, I had to look at things analytically, to watch what was happening. I needed to figure out how to live with people.

One morning, I came down to the kitchen for breakfast. Joan and Frank were eating at the kitchen table. I could feel the tension in the room.

Joan looked up, obviously annoyed, and asked, "Scott, was it your turn to do the dishes last night?" I looked at the dishes I had stacked on the drying rack and pleasantly replied, "Yeah, I did a pretty good job, don't you think?" Joan got up and went over to the kitchen cupboards, opened two adjoining doors, and snapped angrily. "You put some of the dishes in the cupboard without letting them dry in the drying rack."

A chill went through my body. I could feel the tension in the room wash over me. I remained pleasant.

"Yes, Joan, as you can see, the drying rack is full of plates. I took the glasses that were partially dry and turned them upside down so that they would dry in the cupboard. I put some paper towels underneath the glasses to catch any water that drained off of them."

Frank stood up and like a professor who was impressing the importance of the law to his students, leaned on the table, and made his point. "In this house, Scott, we put all the dishes in the drying rack. If the drying rack is full, we spread the dishes on a dish towel to dry." His voice rose a pitch as he finished. I'd been reprimanded.

Joan added loudly, self-satisfied, "You're newly sober. You need to learn to do things right."

Instead of cowering and apologizing, I reached up and closed the two cupboard doors and leaned against the kitchen counter. "Joan, Frank, what's interesting to me is that whenever there is tension in your relationship, I do something wrong. I walked in here this morning and could feel the tension between you two."

Joan and Frank scowled at each other, then glared at me.

Ben, Margaret, and Terry walked into the kitchen.

Margaret asked, "Hey, what's up? Joan, you and Frank yelling about something again?"

Ben looked at me, smiling, and asked, "What did you do wrong?"

I looked at Joan and Frank. "Yeah, Ben's right. When you claim I do something wrong, I get tense. You relax. It's like you're transferring your tension to me."

Joan was angry. She ignored Ben, Margaret, and Terry, and confronted me. "You're new here. The rules are the rules. If you can't follow them, maybe you need to find another place to live."

Terry cut Joan off before she said anything else. "Joan, Scott's right. You and Frank transfer your tension and anger to someone else. It's funny how everyone else here stopped doing things wrong when Scott moved in. He's your scapegoat now."

Margaret put her hand on my shoulder. "Don't let them get under your skin. We've all been through it. I'm making pancakes. Who wants breakfast?"

Joan's face turned pale. She looked at Frank and then left the kitchen. Frank huffed and followed her out.

Jack appeared at the door and said, "Pancakes? Maple syrup? I'm in."

We talked about what we were going to do that day. No one mentioned Joan or Frank.

The dynamics of the Pond House changed after that breakfast conversation. Joan and Frank spent more time by themselves and less time in the common rooms. Ben announced he was in a relationship with a woman he had recently met and was moving in with her, and Jack decided to move out of Greenfield to a more rural setting. Margaret and Terry found a house they decided to buy. They were moving too. Joan and Frank began looking for more housemates. It hadn't taken me long to grow from a tadpole to a frog. I was ready to move out of The Pond.

In mid-February, I ran into Marco while I was picking up my mail in Wendell Depot. He saw my car at the post office and stopped.

With the bravado he always displayed, he said, "Hello, Scotty, you missed a good time in J.A., mon. I smuggled some righteous herb into the U.S. You want to smoke some weed, mon?"

"Marco, I don't need to smoke weed anymore. While you and Les were in Jamaica, I got into Alcoholics and Narcotics Anonymous. I have almost thirty days without a drug or drink. Marco, I'm happy. I don't need drugs or alcohol."

"Come on, mon, this is good herb, the kind, ya know. Just smoke a little with me."

I couldn't back down. "I have the twelve-step program now. I am powerless over drugs and alcohol, so I can't drink or drug. Do you understand, Marco?"

His reply began as intimidation: "I smuggled this shit into the country in a toothpaste tube so you could taste what you missed in J.A., Scotty." Then it turned into a plea: "I did it for you."

I stood up to him. "You can't manipulate me anymore, Marco."

Miffed, he said, "If you don't want to smoke herb, I'm out of here." He jumped into his van and drove off.

A few days later, Marco called and asked me to take him to a meeting. I met him at the Thursday evening Narcotics Anonymous meeting in the basement of the Lutheran Church in Amherst. He stopped drinking and drugging that evening. We went to meetings and ran together. Suddenly, I was the strong one in our relationship. When I decided to move out of the Pond House, Marco offered to rent me a room at his third-floor apartment in South Hadley.

Life at Marco's apartment was not bad. He demanded his way, but I was beyond manipulation. The apartment's common space was still Marco's, but I had my own room. Our relationship wasn't one between equals, but it was better than living alone. In the eleven months I lived in South Hadley, I grew emotionally, absorbing the twelve-step program. Realizing I was powerless over substances, I turned my life and will over to a higher power. Making amends to others when I could, I began to take a moral inventory of my life. I didn't drink alcohol or use drugs. I went to meetings. The program suggests ninety meetings in the first ninety days. I went to 270.

The state of bliss I experienced during those first months of sobriety was like an extended acid trip. I was high on life. The joy I felt each morning and the gratefulness I felt after another day in recovery was immense. The acid that had saturated my brain for so many years was slowly melting. At times, it felt like acid was seeping out through the pores of my skin. There were days I took three showers to cleanse and relax.

At the end of 1986, during the holidays, an emotional time for everyone, my relationship with Marco changed again. I returned from the Nooner in Northampton one afternoon and Marco was standing in the kitchen, filled with anger.

"Scott, why didn't you sweep the floor this morning before you left?"

Having learned to say calm and strong dealing with Joan and Frank, I folded my arms in front of me and replied pleasantly, "Was I supposed to sweep the floor this morning?"

Marco could never admit that he had a lot of anger and had no idea how to deal with it. He bellowed, "You're living off of me, Scott. You never do chores. You're never around. You're always going to meetings. If you're going to live here, you have to take responsibility."

I moved toward him, raised my voice, and spoke pointedly. "Marco, I'm taking responsibility. I'm going to meetings. You're a dry drunk. You're not going to meetings, working on your recovery. You're here all day by yourself, not talking with people, isolating. You've got to process your feelings. Marco, you're angry. I'm not responsible for your anger, you are. Let's go to a meeting tonight and we'll talk about it."

Marco backed up into the stove. A plastic cup fell to the floor and bounced at his feet. He lashed out, "I don't need meetings. You go to your meetings. I need to live by myself. Scott, you have to move out."

I shook my head sadly. "Marco, I love you. I'm sorry you're angry at me. I understand. I should move out. It's been a good year. That's long enough. I'll start looking for a place to live. If you can give me a month to find a place, I'll be gone by February."

I searched the housemate ads in *The Valley Advocate*, the local alternative newspaper, and found a group of tenants seeking people who were interested in community-building. It was the perfect place for me to relate to people as an equal and develop my social skills.

I embraced recovery from drug and alcohol addiction completely. When I wasn't going to meetings, I was holding court in front of the Unitarian Church (the same church where I had blatantly smoked pot when I was using and where I'd met Sam on my first day of sobriety). Talking about recovery lessened the chance I'd pick up a drug or a drink again.

I made a new friend in front of the UU church. I'd never noticed the sidewalk stand of Sue, the Wandering Ewe, until I got straight and sober. She sold colorful hats and scarves she knitted from wool she gathered, carded, and wove from her own sheep. I bought a multicolored hat she made from scratch and wore it religiously. She also sold clothing and blankets she gathered on trips to Central America. One day, she asked if I'd like to work for her, minding the stand while she did other chores.

I blossomed as part of the sidewalk scene in Amherst. Sitting at the stand, selling beautiful clothing and making people happy made me happy, gave me purpose and a positive role to play. No longer an outcast, I was motivated not only to help Sue, but to share my happiness with the customers. I experienced the sensation of Not Me. I saw myself from above, part of the scenery, the meditating monk in the reality of other people.

When I wasn't working for Sue, I visited the Sophia Bookshop (Sirius Books' new incarnation) to get out of the cold and look at books. I knew Sandy, the owner, but had never really talked with her. Now that I was sober, we became friends. I shared my joy with her, talking about my wild and crazy life and how empowering sobriety was. One afternoon, she asked if I'd like to clerk in the bookstore part-time and help with the inventory.

Sophia Bookshop became my spiritual home. I was surrounded by a collection of Eastern and Mideastern books, Islamic, Sufi, Hindu, Buddhist, and Zen. The year-end inventory introduced me to all of them. Before computers, we did the inventory with pencil and Rolodex cards. Each card recorded a book title and the number of copies in the store. Every time a book was sold, I found its card and lowered the number of books remaining. If someone came into the store and asked for a book and we had it, I could walk to the shelf where it was, pick it out, and hand it to them.

With the advent of computers, my relationship with the books changed. Each book was an ISBN number on the computer. Since I didn't want to lose touch with the books, when there were no customers, I would browse through each and every book in the store. Occasionally, I would put a book aside and buy it later, at a discount, of course.

One slow afternoon, as I was browsing the bookshelves, I noticed a few books sticking out. I attempted to push them back in line, but couldn't. Removing the protruding books, I found one wedged behind them. It was a small, thin, dusty volume that looked like it had been there a long time. The price on the back cover was $1.95. In the mid-'80s, soft-cover books were $10.95 to $12.95. Sometimes, you could find a book on the shelf for $7.95 or $8.95, but those were becoming a thing of the past. A chill ran through me. Finding this book at this time in my life was a bit mystical, as was the name of the book, *The Supreme Sign*. I checked for the title in the inventory. It wasn't there. I felt blessed with such a gift, certainly a supreme sign. I bought it.

I have vivid memories of reading about the author, Bediüz-zaman Said Nursi, an Arabian student who felt an urge to write a book, but wasn't sure if he was able. I read that he went to his spiritual teacher and asked, "Should I write this book?"

The teacher replied, "Of course, you should write the book."

I remember that the author occasionally questioned the reader, "Why are you reading this book? Why are you not outside looking at nature?"

After reading thirty pages, having been urged to go outside and observe nature numerous times, I put the book down and went outside and looked at nature. I didn't pick up the book again.

Funny thing is, I have spent the majority of the last thirty-three years outside—landscaping, gardening, running trails, walking with my partner, Kate—just being outside. Recently, I discovered *The Supreme Sign* in my stored belongings. I read the first thirty pages of the book again. It seemed to be total gibberish. There's nothing in the book about the author talking to his teacher or advising the reader to go outside into nature. How did I ever get the idea this book commanded me to pursue the outdoors? What tricks did my conscious and unconscious mind play on me? I still have the book. Every once in a while, I think about reading it. Most of the time, I go outside.

Three months into recovery, I noticed I was smoking a lot of cigarettes. I'd buy a pack of cigarettes in the early evening before meetings and by the next morning, the pack would be close to empty. Whenever I began to feel emotional, I'd light a cigarette, concentrate on smoking, and forget about my feelings. There was something about meetings, listening to speakers, talking about recovery, the companionship, the freedom to feel, that triggered emotions, and the need to smoke a cigarette any chance I got. Before and after meetings and during breaks, I'd stand outside, puffing on cigarettes with a lot of recovering addicts in the same boat.

When I mentioned this at a meeting, someone said, "You're smoking your feelings."

Nicotine was a substitute for alcohol and drugs. As time went on, I was smoking stronger and stronger cigarettes. At the Tuesday night meeting in Sunderland, just before the Easter weekend, I noticed I was ripping the filters off Salem menthols and chewing on the tobacco so I could get more nicotine into my system.

I got it. Cigarettes were blocking my feelings and the nicotine was killing me. I decided to stop smoking.

Two days later, I was going to visit with my mother and sister in Baltimore, where Marilyn now lived. Marilyn and I had shared joints together, but I had never smoked cigarettes around them. If I stopped smoking Tuesday night, didn't smoke on Wednesday, and didn't smoke in Baltimore, one day at a time, I would have a week without cigarettes by the next Tuesday's Sunderland meeting.

It was the first time my mother, Marilyn, and I were together since I'd begun my recovery. Mother was now seventy-seven. She was overjoyed by my happiness and enthusiasm. At the end of the four-day visit, she took me aside.

"Scott, I haven't seen you this happy since you were a little boy playing in the yard with your toys. I never knew you drank so much."

I wondered how she couldn't have known I was an addict. I'd smoked pot in the house after Mom and Dad went to bed. She must have smelled the alcohol when I came in late and she and Dad were waiting up for me. She was being kind.

I apologized as best I could. "Mom, I'm sorry for all the worry and heartache I caused you. I was addicted to drugs and alcohol. Now I'm learning to live life straight and sober." I choked up a bit and tears welled in my eyes. "I wish Dad was here to see me."

Mom gave me a big hug. "Your father would be proud of you. He was always proud of you. You were his son." She wiped a tear from her cheek. "And here's an early birthday present. I'm proud of you, too." She slipped a check folded twice into my hand. "This will help. I don't want you to worry about anything except this AA program that has made you so happy."

Marilyn was a little more skeptical, and rightly so. I'd always showed up with the best drugs and put on the front that everything was okay.

"So, now you aren't drinking and drugging. You and I smoked a lot of good pot last Christmas in New Kensington. Then you stopped? What really happened?"

I explained drinking wine with Caroline and her housemates

and the fear that my anger could turn into violence. I explained about Sam: "He took me to my first AA meeting, and I had a spiritual awakening."

Marilyn's focus on life was all political. She had always been skeptical about my association with religion.

"A spiritual awakening? Like you had at the teepee? I'm sorry, you're my little brother and I love you, but you have to admit you're crazy."

I laughed. "Marilyn, it was the drugs that made me crazy. I'm getting my life together now."

She shook her head and hit her hand on the side of her forehead. "I still remember the Christmas in L.A. after Dad died and you wrote that long poem. I thought we were going to have to put you in the hospital with Maria."

I told her about the vial of speed I'd sent Maria. "Marilyn, it's probably my fault that Maria went crazy. I'm sorry for that, but the drugs made me crazy, too."

Marilyn stared at me. She looked angry, but said, "Well, I've done my share of drugs, so..." She paused. "Maria was a bit crazy anyway." She paused again, then turned her head and looked at me out of the corner of her eye. "And you haven't had any alcohol or drugs in ninety days?"

I stood up straight. "Eighty-seven days without a drug or a drink. I'm no longer a kid doing drugs. For the first time in my life, I feel like an adult. I'm going to take responsibility for my life."

I left my *AA Big Book* with her and told her to read it if she got the chance. When I returned to Amherst, she called and told me she was going to stop smoking pot.

A few months after stopping cigarettes, I noticed that I was drinking a lot of coffee. At a Thursday NA meeting, I found myself drinking my third cup of coffee before the preamble was finished. Thinking back through the day, I realized I'd had eighteen cups of coffee since morning. Now caffeine was blocking my emotions. The phrase "addictive personality" kept popping up at meetings. The problem wasn't the addictive substances, it was the need to block emotions with substances. I stopped drinking coffee after that night's meeting. That summer in recovery, I learned that I was not unique, not the center of the universe. I saw myself as just another addict trying to be happy and survive one day at a time.

In the fall of 1986, I had around seven months in recovery. I was feeling pretty good.

After one Nooner meeting in Northampton, Mike, the landscaper, asked me, "Want to earn some money? I'll pay you five bucks to load my '51 Ford dump truck with two cords of wood. It'll take you about an hour, hour and a half. It'll be good exercise."

Getting paid for exercise? Work, five dollars, purpose, worth.

"Sure, I'll work."

Once or twice a week, I would go up to his property at the top of Gulf Road and toss cordwood into the Ford. The view of The Mt. Holyoke Range from his place was breathtaking. It took me about an hour and a half to load the truck, so I was earning less than five dollars an hour, but I was getting exercise outside.

On a brilliant New England morning in October, I went up to the top of the hill to load the Ford. The leaves on the trees were at peak color. I was feeling very successful, not having had a drug or a drink during eight months of one day at a time. Physically, I was strong and enjoying every breath I took. There I was, a forty-one-year old Amherst College graduate with a master's of divinity from

McCormick Seminary, throwing wood onto a beautiful '51 Ford dump truck in the clear morning air, with all the leaves turning a brilliant rainbow of colors, earning less than five bucks an hour (not the typical salary of an Amherst alumnus).

Suddenly, a thought entered my mind—the Zen koan. I hadn't thought of that koan for fifteen years:

When the monkey lets go of the branch
and falls into the pool of water,
the whole world will shine with dazzling brilliance.

The meaning became clear to me:

When the person lets go of the ego
and falls into reality,
reality shines with dazzling brilliance.

My mind exploded. Tears came to my eyes. I wept. Pure joy overpowered me. If ever there was a moment of Samadhi, enlightenment, that was it.

After a short time, I returned to my reality. I was alive, sober, straight. There were still things that bothered me, that nagging guilt from childhood that I couldn't shake. I knew something had happened that kept me from healthy relationships with women, but I couldn't figure it out.

Most people don't know where emotional revelations come from, and I'm no different. Sometimes, they're sudden; sometimes, it takes years to come to some kind of understanding about yourself. I'd spent twenty-four years using drugs and alcohol to avoid understanding who I was and why I felt the way I did. A couple of years into recovery, without drugs and alcohol to block my emotions, the horrible truth of my childhood started demanding attention.

One evening, after the Monday Night Beginner's Meeting and Speaker Meeting at the Episcopal Church in Amherst, Mike and I were sitting in his truck talking. I'd been working with him, landscaping and mowing lawns. As we worked, Mike and I spent a lot of time processing our thoughts and feelings, so we had a great rapport. This evening, I struggled to work through all the intense emotions that were bubbling up inside me: sadness, anger, fear, loss, emptiness.

Finally, I leaned forward and put my head in my hands. "Mike, I don't know where all these emotions are coming from, but I understand why people in recovery drink. I'm feeling so bad right now that if I had one drink, I'd have another and another. I wouldn't stop until I passed out. All this sadness is welling up from inside me."

It hurt like a physical pain, like I couldn't breathe. I was gasping in his truck, scaring him. I could sense him leaning away from me as I went on.

"I don't know where it is coming from. I don't know how to deal with it."

He held his hands up like a shield. "Whoa, Scott, you're so upset, you're making me emotional. You need a therapist. Talk to Cliff. He's some kind of a minister counselor and in the program. He understands. You're making me nervous." He glanced at his hands. "Scott, look my hands are shaking. You gotta do something besides talking to me."

I caught my breath. "Yeah, Mike, I've gotta talk with someone who knows more about this than just you and me. Thanks for listening. I've gotta go. Pick me up tomorrow at the coffee shop. Nine-thirty, I'll be ready to work."

I saw Cliff at the next AA meeting. "Cliff, I'm going crazy. I'm feeling all these emotions and don't know where they are coming from. I've got two years of one days at a time. I'm not going to drink, but the sadness I feel, it's not good. Do you have room for another client?"

Cliff nodded his head like he understood. He pushed up his glasses and said, "Scott, sounds like you need a safe space to explore some emotions. I could look on my schedule and see if I can squeeze you in. I charge twenty-five bucks an hour."

"Money's not a problem, Cliff. I need to deal with the way I feel."

He patted me on the back. "You know where I live. My office is in the basement of the house. Come see me Friday morning at eight o'clock."

I spent an hour with Cliff every Friday morning at eight o'clock for the next two and a half years. We dug away, uncovering memories and emotions. Then, four years into recovery and two years into therapy, I had the recurring dream I'd had all through my adolescence. In this dream, I'd wake up and need to use the bathroom. I'd walk down the hall to the bathroom. The shower curtain next to the toilet was pulled closed. As I stood in front of the toilet and tried to pee, I sensed that there was something behind the shower curtain. I'd try to be brave and pull back the curtain, but there was always someone or something holding it closed. I always woke up very frightened. This time, the dream had a different ending. I pulled back the shower curtain.

I awoke before I was able to see what was behind it, but as I lay awake, I knew something terrible had happened when I was young that destroyed my trust in everything. *Was it while someone was giving me a bath? That sounded right.* I felt nauseated, sick to my stomach at the truth of what I had faced. I'd been terrified, out of control, frightened, vulnerable.

Flashes of my childhood raced through my mind. Why had a babysitter scolded me one time for suggesting a touching game I had played with my cousin? And another game, playing Roy Rogers and Dale Evans with my sister and her friend. They were Roy Rogers and Dale Evans. I was Boy, their son without a name. I'd felt humiliated. And another time, I was sitting in a tent in the backyard during a kid's summer carnival, dressed in my sister's bathing suit stuffed with rags with something fuzzy glued to my face. I was the fat bearded lady. I was so embarrassed when my mother came into the tent and began laughing hysterically. Somehow, it was my fault. It was my mother's finger wagging at me when I reached puberty: "It's your fault if you get a girl in trouble."

Your fault. Your fault. Your fault.

When I got out of bed that morning, I still didn't know for certain what had happened behind that shower curtain, but I knew it wasn't my fault. I wasn't guilty. My childhood wasn't my fault. Whatever had happened to me then, I wasn't in control. Those experiences happened to me. I had responded, and I'd been a participant in them, but I hadn't understood what I was doing. I dared to think it for the first time: *I was a victim.*

I rushed to my therapy appointment after breakfast. "Something happened to me when I was a kid. It's not my fault. I'm not guilty."

Feeling lighter than air, I was afloat with relief. *Not guilty.* I was exuberant. The hour of therapy flew by.

Later that morning at the Newman Center AA meeting, I waited for the discussion to begin. I raised my hand. When I was called on, I told everyone of my discovery. Then I said, "Drugs and alcohol are just the tip of the iceberg. There was a reason why I drank and drugged. Something happened."

One evening about a year later, after a Tuesday Night Speaker Discussion AA meeting in Sunderland, a guy named Ahmed was recounting a recent visit to a timeshare lecture in the Berkshires. It was boring, but he got a free vacation to the Bahamas for three.

"We fly to Fort Lauderdale, spend Saturday and Sunday there, take the ferry to the Bahamas, spend three nights there, and fly back from Lauderdale on Thursday. We just have to pay $200 for the round-trip airfare and forty dollars for the ferry. The rest is free. David said he's going. I need a third person."

Without hesitation I piped up, "I'll go."

Ahmed said, "You're on, let's go."

I was psyched. A real vacation? I'd never had one. Five days in Florida and the Bahamas? I would have rather been traveling with women, now that I was discovering that my sins of childhood were not sins at all, but I still had that rash that popped up occasionally. What was I going to do, avoid life? A vacation was a vacation. I was going to enjoy myself.

On the Thursday before we left for Florida, it occurred to me that Jen, my cousin who babysat me as a child, lived in Palm Beach, just north of Fort Lauderdale. I could spend Saturday evening and most of Sunday with her and her two kids, then return to the hotel in Fort Lauderdale Sunday evening and catch the boat to the Bahamas on Monday morning.

I got her telephone number from Mom and called her. She was as excited about my visit as I was. We arranged to meet at the Fort Lauderdale hotel Saturday afternoon and return there Sunday afternoon. As I was talking to Jen on the telephone, my crotch began to itch. *Oh, no.* I thought. *Herpes.* When I finished the phone call with Jen, the rash was in full bloom, the worst it had ever been.

It got even worse on Friday. My cousin, in her sixties, a retired school principal, gray-haired, her face covered with age wrinkles, was a far cry from that fifteen-year-old babysitter I had been so fond of. She picked me up in Fort Lauderdale Saturday afternoon.

I was a nervous wreck and my genitals were covered in rash. I agonized, *Why now? I'm going on a vacation. I'm not allowed to enjoy myself? I'm nervous and tense with my cousin and her family. This doesn't make sense.*

When we reached Jen's house and I was introduced to her kids, I felt guilty. *Guilty of what? I was going on vacation. I should be enjoying myself.* I took a deep breath. *I have to accept myself. So, the vacation is going to be a disaster. I am a horrible person, cursed for the rest of my life. But I have to go on living, despite my guilt and failure as a human being. Damn it, I'm going to enjoy the weekend and the three days in the Bahamas as best as I can.*

I suffered through my visit with Jen and her two kids, Susan and Phil. Susan was in her late twenties, teaching in a local elementary school. She'd just gotten engaged to a Kentucky horse owner and was planning the wedding and a move to Kentucky. Phil was four years younger, unemployed, and living at Jen's with a male friend who was out of town on business. Jen's husband, an airplane pilot, drank himself to death years back. I wondered what their life had been like.

On Sunday afternoon, Jen suggested, "Scott, it's time to take you back to the hotel. We'll take the long way back along the ocean. I'll show you the schools where I taught and the homes where we lived. It'll be a nice drive."

As we started back to Fort Lauderdale, I noticed my genitals itched less. After an hour and a half of touring and saying good-byes to Jen and the kids, I walked into the hotel. The rash was gone. I sat on the hotel bed and finally put it all together: I didn't have herpes simplex, I had hives.

I was no stranger to hives. I'd had them at age seven, when I had an allergic reaction to penicillin. An injection of an anti-histamine got rid of them. The Amanita Pantherina mushrooms, red itchy blotches all over my body, especially on tender areas, hives. After being stung by a swarm of bees, hives. My body was reacting to Jen the same way. She was causing stress. My reaction was hives, an inflammatory immune response.

Jen was my first babysitter. Did she sexually abuse me?

The next day in the Bahamas, Ahmed and David spent all day playing beach volleyball with the bikini-clad beauties at the Holiday Inn next to our hotel. I walked the streets of Freeport and biked the back roads of the island. I couldn't recall specific mem-ories of those early years, but I did remember another babysitter to whom I was attracted. I asked her to play some games with me. She was shocked. She told me they weren't games. They were very bad things. She asked me where I had learned them. I'd learned those games from Jen. I thought about the dream of trying to pull back the shower curtain. Cousin Jen gave me baths. I thought about my disgust when Brenda told me she directed my penis away from her vagina and into her ass. Did Cousin Jen penetrate me in the bathtub? Was that the pain I couldn't face behind the shower curtain? It became clear to me that my substance abuse had roots in my relationship with Jen when she was my babysitter.

Those three days were the last time I ever had hives.

My relationship with women began to change. My first attempts at dating were with women in the AA and NA programs. I was attracted to the most troubled ones. A few breakfast dates with an anorexic and bulimic woman didn't get very far. A relationship with another sexual abuse victim like me ended when our intimacy intensified. She crashed, burned, and vanished. I actually had a two-month relationship with a non-program woman. The relationship ended abruptly when she departed for the Midwest. Those three relationships taught me I could survive breaking up.

Analyzing my failed relationships, I realized I was not going to stumble into a healthy one. I had to learn how to interact with women. Just as I'd returned to the civilized world from the teepee and began my journey into poetry by creating classes at the University Off the Wall, I decided I could create classes in social relations.

My first course was Dating 101: Talking to Women on the Telephone. *The Valley Advocate* had a section for Women Seeking Men. I answered a few ads with a creative little message and phone number: "Hey, I read your ad. We have things in common. I like the outdoors. I belong to a health club. I love physical activity. Here's my phone number. Give me a call."

Karen called. "Hello, is this Scott?"

I was puzzled to hear a woman's voice. "Yeah, this is Scott. Who is this?"

"I'm Karen. You answered my ad in the *Advocate*."

"Oh, hi, Karen. I'm Scott. Er, I guess you know that already, since you called me. How are you?"

She was silent, then said, "I'm fine. How are you?"

I gathered myself a bit and said, "I'm fine. Do you want to get together?"

My conversation was so inept that Karen cut the phone call short. "Well, Scott, I'm pretty busy. Let me call you back when I have more time."

I stumbled through conversations like that and became more confident with each attempt. It took me a while, but eventually, I was able to carry on a conversation for more than a few sentences. After the introductions and the "I love the outdoors and exercise" routine, I would show my interest in their lives: "Enough about me. Tell me a little about yourself."

I even placed an ad myself and received calls from women who were interested in me. I learned to be glib, urbane, even sincere when I wanted to be. It took me three months to complete the course. I gave myself an A.

For a more advanced course, I created Dating 102: Going Out to Dinner. When a woman sounded interesting on the phone, I'd ask her out to dinner. Again, on the first few dinner dates, I was tongue-tied and clumsy. They weren't pleasant experiences. Eventually, I could comfortably converse through dinner and a short evening walk. Though hesitant, actually frightened, to suggest second dates with women I was attracted to, I did have some short relationships. I gave myself another A.

The third course was Independent Studies: Spending the Night. I had affairs with two women. The relationships were short, but I spent some nights with each of them. I'm sure I was awkward, but I was delighted to be conscious during casual sex. It was a huge step up from the fumbling drunken encounters in my previous life. I gave myself a very high grade in the course. I am sure it was higher than the grade the women gave me.

Those three courses taught me a lot. I knew they would pay dividends when I met the right woman. My fourth class was a graduate course, Get Involved in Situations Where I Could Meet Women. I became a member of the local health club. I got involved with the running community, participating in organized races. I joined Sugarloaf Mountain Athletic Club and got on the board of directors. Eventually, I became director of the 5K Summit Run, sponsored by the Friends of The Mt. Holyoke Range, and I also got on the Friend's board of directors. That's where I met Kate.

Ginnie, the ranger at the state park, prided herself on being a matchmaker. She'd met Kate on a hike she was leading and invited her to the September board meeting at the Summit House on top of Mt. Holyoke.

Before the meeting, Ginnie introduced us: "Scott, this is Kate. Kate, this is Scott. You both like hiking."

Kate and I talked for a while. She was cheerful, positive and vivacious. Something about her energy made me happy. I tried not to stare at her during the meeting. Driving home after, I thought, *Now, there is someone I could get interested in.*

A couple of weeks later, I directed the Summit Run. Ginnie suggested that since Kate was good on the computer, she could help me enter the results. I called Kate and asked. She invited me over to her place. When she answered my knock and opened the door, I began to fall in love with her short, dark hair, and the few freckles across the bridge of her nose. When she said, with a big smile, "Would you like some tea?" I was hooked. There was no turning back. She was the woman I wanted to wake up next to every morning, share breakfast and my day with.

After our third date, I told her I was in love with her and

wanted to spend the rest of my life with her. We settled into a wonderful routine—crossword puzzles with breakfast, evenings together, excellent vacations, and lots of fun. We have been friends and partners ever since.

I'm sure that if I hadn't created my educational courses, I would've been clueless when I met her and would never have been able to establish such a deep and meaningful relationship. I don't regret all the years I spent alone, because they make my relationship with Kate all the more valuable.

chapter 30

Five years straight and sober was a milestone for me. There was no way I was going to drink or drug again. I worked the program, attending a least one AA or NA meeting a day. I spoke at meetings whenever I was asked and traveled on commitments to other meetings with my home group to talk about recovery. When someone new to the program asked me to be a sponsor, I sponsored them. I ate a lot of ice cream at McManus's in the mall with friends after evening meetings.

Meetings took care of the urge to drink or use drugs. Therapy took care of deeper emotional issues. I wanted to do more, learn as much as I could about addiction—not only substance abuse, but the roots of all addictions, gambling, anorexia, bulimia, overeating. My undergraduate degree was in psychology. I had an inside look at substance abuse, twenty-four years' worth of education. Sam was studying for a master's in rehabilitation counseling with a concentration in drug and alcohol addiction at Springfield College. I applied for the same degree and was accepted.

I decided that school would be a test of my abilities. I was drunk throughout my undergraduate education and stoned throughout my seminary experience. I would find out what I could do straight and sober. I wasted no time completing the two-year program and writing my thesis, *Recidivism Rate in DUI Offenses Between Alcohol Users and Marijuana Users*, doing so in eighteen months with a 4.96 grade point average. The Springfield program was geared to a career in a general rehabilitation setting, with courses in assessment, appraisal, and referral in counseling, counseling techniques, organization and administration, developmental disability counselling, employment assistance, and career development. But there were courses in alcohol and the family, treatment of the alcoholic, and medical survey that provided insight into my childhood development and my physical and emotional dependency on addictive substances. With the discovery of my childhood sexual abuse and an intellectual and cognitive understanding of my addiction, I felt I was safe from ever using addictive substances again. At my graduation, with Mother and Marilyn watching me accept my diploma, my confidence and self-esteem was greater than it had ever been.

For three months, one semester of field work, I interned at the Veteran's Administration Hospital in Leeds, Massachusetts, working with Vietnam veterans with substance abuse issues. I quickly realized that as a conscientious objector to the Vietnam War, I was not the person to counsel war veterans. For my second semester of field work at the Detoxification and Counseling Centers of Springfield, I spent six weeks in an inpatient hospital detoxification setting and six weeks as an outpatient one-on-one counselor.

The perfect job opened up soon after I graduated: The Western Massachusetts Correctional Alcohol Center in Springfield, known as Howard Street, was looking for a director of their educational program. Howard Street was a rehabilitation program run by the Detoxification and Counseling Centers of Springfield for the Hampden County Sheriff's Department. Anyone convicted of three or more drug or alcohol related offenses in the four counties in western Massachusetts was eligible to serve their time at Howard Street instead of one of the county jails. There were seventy-two residents in the program.

As education director, I taught an orientation class for new residents and two daily classes, five days a week. There were four counselors who had caseloads of eighteen residents. There was a supervisor of the program, Stephanie, who oversaw the education program and the counselors. The counseling staff dressed casually. I was a teacher and wanted to impress everyone, so I wore a coat and tie. There was also a correction staff of twenty officers per shift. The correctional staff wore uniforms.

The retiring education director, Joan Fredricks, an elderly gray-haired woman who had taught classes at Howard Street for the eighteen years since the beginning of the program, ran it based on Alcoholics Anonymous. She taught Orientation, Recovery Based on the Twelve-Step Program, and a life skills course, How to Find Employment When You Get Out of Howard Street. When I looked over her teaching notes, I had no idea how she filled two hour-and-a-half classes per day, five days a week.

While Joan spent her last week teaching her final classes, I created a class schedule that included everything I'd learned in recovery and much of what I'd learned at Springfield College. My orientation class began with: "You were arrested three times or more for alcohol or drug related offenses. That's why you're here. Arrested three times. Jailed three times. Arraigned in court three times. More court dates three times. You paid some lawyer good money. And here you sit. It seems to me it would be easier to stop drinking and drugging than to go through all that three times. If you listen in my classes, you might discover why you go through all that trauma instead of digging deep and discovering why you drink and drug."

My general population classes were held in a large room that was part-auditorium with a stage and part-basketball court. The residents sat restlessly on uncomfortable metal folding chairs. They didn't want to be there, but they were a captive audience. Some of them sat up and listened when I told them they didn't have to drink or drug again.

The classes began with a short presentation and ended with a resident-oriented discussion. The Disease Concept of Alcoholism and Substance Abuse class focused on the emotional and social characteristics of addiction. The class discussion that followed usually avoided emotions and centered on social drinking, bars and parties, and drinking in the family. The Chemistry of Addictive Substances in Your Brain class described the chemical reaction when you put drugs and alcohol into your system. They produce tetrahydroisoqulnoline (THIQ). THIQ creates false endorphins in the brain that make you happy. When your brain uses up all the false endorphins that THIQ produces, you need more alcohol and drugs to produce more THIQ. Addiction is the endless need to create THIQ to stay happy, despite the emotions the drugs and alcohol are suppressing. The discussion focused on other ways to make you happy besides drugging and drinking. Kissing and making love were always the preferred alternative to substance abuse.

Most of my other classes were the same class with different titles. Relationships, Stress, and Anxiety classes discussed how they affected your emotions. Talking and Trusting was about trusting others enough to talk about your emotions with them. Group Therapy was about talking about your emotions. Relapse was about not talking about your emotions with others and resorting to substances to block your emotions. In my Emotional Process class, I would explain emotions and how we block them with substance abuse. I would then try to get the residents to talk about their emotions. By the end of their three months, many of the residents were ready to talk.

I'd end all my classes with this: "Substance abuse is the symptom of an emotional disease. Get it? Dis-ease. You're blocking emotions with drugs and alcohol. When you figure out your emotions, you have a chance to stop drinking and drugging."

Some of the residents were brave enough to come to me to talk about why they drank and drugged. "My father physically abused me. Once he kicked me when I was milking the cow and broke my arm. Instead of taking me to the doctor, he gave me whiskey for the pain. I never told anyone. I drink all the time." Another, "I was sent to Florida to live with my aunt and uncle when I was seven. My uncle started having sex with me when I was thirteen until I ran away at sixteen." Still another, "We never had anything to eat in the house, so we drank the alcohol and beer dad stashed in his workshop in the garage. I used to go into neighbors' houses and look for food. My childhood sucked."

I listened and then told them, "I'm so glad that what I say in class has given you the strength to come and talk to me about your emotions, but I'm not your counselor. I'm just the teacher who teaches your classes. You have a counselor. You need to talk with him or her. That's what they're here for."

I was pleased with my success at getting the residents to think about their emotions, but I was concerned about sending them to their counselors. The counselors were all recovering alcoholics well-versed in the twelve-step program of Alcoholics Anonymous. None of them had any practical experience with Narcotics Anonymous. The amount the job paid did not attract highly qualified counselors. They were all good people, but I wondered if they could counsel residents who were exploring ideas about why they were drug addicts.

The first thing I noticed when I met the counselors was that they all smoked cigarettes. When I'd realized I was addicted to cigarettes and my feelings were going up in smoke, I quit smoking. I wondered if the counselors, like me seven years ago, were stuffing their emotions with cigarette use. Unaware of their own emotions, would they be able to deal with the residents' emotional and psychological issues?

The counselors complained to Stephanie, the supervisor of the treatment program. They said I was causing problems by telling the inmates to express their feelings. Now, they were all talking to their counselors about emotional issues, childhood issues, and stories about abuse. The counselors complained that Howard Street was a drug and alcohol treatment center, not a mental hospital.

"We don't know what to tell them. Scott has to stop what he's doing."

Stephanie called me into her office. She was in her late thirties, probably ten years younger than I was. She had shoulder-length curly light brown hair and wore cat-eye glasses that ended in points by the temple pieces. She dressed in frilly dresses and lacy blouses and full skirts. Today she'd be a little geeky, but for me, to be called into her office was intoxicating. She looked up when I came in.

"The counselors are saying that the inmates are making up all kind of stories. They all have emotional issues now. What's going on?"

I explained my thoughts behind why the residents had to suppress their feelings and why I'd sent them to their counselors.

Stephanie wasn't happy. With a sour look on her face, she said, "It sounds like you're oversharing with the residents. The main focus here is to get the residents to realize that drinking and drugging is only getting them in trouble. We're counseling them to attend AA and NA meetings when they are released. I don't think Howard Street is the appropriate place to discuss emotional issues."

Even though Stephanie was a licensed psychologist, she needed to support her counselors. She was probably underpaid. I was underpaid too, but I was used to living without much money. I left Stephanie's office happy the residents were listening to me and thinking about why they were in Howard Street, but sad the counselors weren't able to help them.

I returned to my office and sat at my desk. I leaned back and put my arms up and locked my hands behind my head. I'd been working here for almost six months. Winter had turned to spring and it was almost June. I wondered if I was cut out for working in a big organization, sitting behind a desk. I wanted to be outside, getting exercise, working with my hands, doing more meditative, contemplative work. Helping people was great, but dealing with coworkers wasn't worth it.

Two days later, around twenty minutes to four on a Friday, as

I was preparing to go home for the weekend, Rick, a correctional officer who'd always had something nice to say to me, came into my office.

"Stephanie wants to talk with you."

Now he was officious, ushering me through the building to her office without a word. When we walked in and Rick knocked on the door frame, Stephanie stopped her paperwork, looked up, and met my eyes. She placed her hands on her desk palms down, as if to brace herself.

"Scott, the administration here at Howard Street has decided to terminate your employment. The officer here will escort you to your office, then out of the building. You must gather your possessions and leave."

I was stunned and began to protest, but she raised her voice and cut me off, "Scott, you have fifteen minutes to leave the building. You must leave now. The officer will escort you."

With a hand on my arm, Rick began to pull me out of Stephanie's office. "We gotta go, Scott."

I was fuming, about ready to boil over. Rick hurried me through the building and up the stairs to my office. He watched me and said nothing as I gathered my papers and the keyboard to my computer.

"What about your computer? That's yours, not Howard Street's."

I snapped at him. "My hands are full. I'll take this stuff to my car and come back for my computer."

He looked at his watch. "Can't do that. You gotta leave. Here, I'll carry the computer." He unplugged the computer and, carrying it, walked me out of the building and to my car.

When all my possessions were in the car, Rick apologized:

"Scott, I'm sorry for the way they treated you. Some of us know you were doing a good job. We noticed changes in some of the residents. You're a good man. The counseling staff had it out for you."

I leaned back against my car with a quizzical look on my face. "What do you mean?"

"There's been talk about getting you fired for weeks." A sheepish smile appeared on Rick's face and his friendly attitude returned. "You were a pain in their asses, Scott. The counselors got together and had you fired."

I shook my head. "I've been through this before, Rick. I'm used to it. I'm going back to landscaping. No one bothers me there."

Then, Rick dropped a bombshell. "I'm sorry I had to hurry you out before four o'clock. If you were in the building at four, you would've had six months of employment. You would've been in the union. You would've had union representation. They couldn't have fired you without cause." He looked me in the eyes. "You just got screwed."

He shook my hand, turned, and returned inside.

I was beyond angry as I drove through Springfield onto the entrance ramp to Interstate 91. At the top of the ramp, I intended to return to Howard Street, spend a few moments in the building, and demand union representation, but as each exit passed, turning around was too much trouble. I was angry at the traffic on 91 until the three lanes turned into two and the majority of the cars turned off into Holyoke. I was headed home to the country. I cheered up. Screw driving to Springfield on Monday morning or ever again. I thought of a plan on the way home.

On Monday, I drove to the Detoxification and Counseling

Centers of Springfield instead of Howard Street. They were the organization that hired me. Having interned there, I had a good relationship with the director. I walked straight to his office and knocked on his door.

He said, "Door's open. Come in."

"You heard I got fired at Howard Street Friday?"

He responded calmly, "Yep, I'm the director. I heard about it."

"No one talked to me. I had no warning. I wasn't treated fairly. I'm angry."

He folded his hands on his desk. "Yes, I can understand why you feel that way."

His calmness melted my anger. "I don't want to cause trouble. I understand there were some problems with me. I tried my best."

"You did the best you could. Howard Street might have not been the best place for your expertise." He motioned toward a seat in front of his desk and I sat down. "I'm sure there is a place in this organization for you, Scott. We could wait for another position to open up and you could apply for it. Would that work for you?"

Open to the possibility, I said, "Would you consider laying me off instead of firing me? I could collect unemployment while I look for a job."

The director smiled. "We could do that, Scott. I'm sorry you got laid off. We'll fill out the paperwork. If you hear of another job, I'd gladly give you a recommendation."

I left the director's office feeling confident. With years of sobriety and a support group in recovery meetings, I no longer saw myself as a failure. When I got fired from Belchertown State School and from the Blue Moon Co-op, when I left Llama, Toucan, & Crow and Jimmy's Popcorn Farm, when I realized my investments in other people's projects were not investments at all, when I was disappointed with the public reception of *Sledge-hammer Poetry* and *The Meeting of the Traveler and the Magus,* even after successful experiences during the Walk for Peace, I'd felt shame and embarrassment. It was *Poor me. I am no good, still a sinner deserving what I got.* Now, I knew I'd done my best. I was overqualified. It wasn't my fault. I had a master's degree in substance abuse counseling. I had a positive attitude. I was a good person. Nothing was going to stop me from becoming who I wanted to become.

chapter 31

At the next Monday Night AA Beginners and Discussion meetings, I ran into Mike, my old landscaping buddy.

"Mike, I got fired and I'm looking for a job again."

He smiled and said, "The guy who took over your job when you quit is quitting in a couple of weeks. Want your job back?"

Of course, I said yes.

Then I ran into Jim, a brick mason in the AA program. When I told him I had been fired and was going back to work with Mike in two weeks, he said, "I've got a two-week job re-grouting the junior high swimming pool. You want to help?"

I didn't miss a step. When the two-week grouting job was done, I started landscaping again. I continued working for Jim early in the morning, hauling brick and mortar up two stories of scaffolding on a large masonry job. I was still the Saturday clerk at the Sophia Bookshop. Since I had wasted twenty-four years of my life drinking and drugging, I decided to make the most of what was left. It was 1992. I was forty-seven years old. I worked my butt off for nine years already. I'd work the next thirteen years, save and invest, then enjoy my old age and retirement.

I was up at six, worked two hours with Jim, then met Mike and worked six hours with him. I was so enthusiastic about work that people began asking me if I could do some landscaping and gardening for them. Since Mike stopped work at 3:30, I would work my own jobs from four to seven, charging my customers twice as much as I was making from Mike.

When winter came, I would get up at four, go into Amherst, and shovel downtown sidewalks for Mike, who had contracts with local businesses. One snowy day, Barney, who owned a bunch of commercial properties in downtown Amherst, approached me.

"Want to shovel all my sidewalks? I got twenty of them."

I was interested, but said, "I'd love to, but I'm working for Mike. I need to talk with him first."

I called Mike: "We can make more money if we do Barney's walks."

He agreed and doubled my pay.

Soon after, I decided it was time to start my own business. Mike let me go and hired his son.

At a friend's birthday party, I sat next to Dan, a real estate developer. I told him I'd quit my job: "I've been working for a landscaper for nine years and now I'm starting my own business."

Dan asked, "How much you charge?"

I took a leap. "Twenty bucks an hour."

Without hesitation, he said, "When can you start putting in lawns for me at a couple of houses I just built?"

Even though I had no idea how to put in lawns, I said, "Give me two weeks."

I bought a shovel, a pickax, hard and soft rakes, hedge clippers, hand clippers, a wheelbarrow, and a '74 Chevy truck with a flat bed. I named the truck Walter. Well-equipped, I started putting in lawns for Dan.

All the big equipment guys thought I was crazy, raking the ground, removing the stones, seeding the lawn, and spreading straw all by hand. It took me a bit longer, but through sweat equity and minimal overhead, I put in lawns at a lower cost than the landscapers with expensive equipment.

I needed a name for my business. One of the Sufi books at the Sophia Bookstore described the human mind as a philosophical garden. I named my business Philosophical Gardening. I placed an ad in the local paper: "Philosophical Gardening. No job too mundane." In new age Northampton and Amherst, the ad was a hook. Homeowners would call wondering about a landscaper using the words 'mundane' and 'philosophical' in an ad. Telling them that I graduated from Amherst College closed the deal.

On off days, I wandered through the local nurseries, studying all the plants they had for sale. I'd read the description of each plant—when it bloomed, the amount of sunlight and moisture it needed, and what kind of soil it liked best. Clients referred me to their friends and neighbors. I traded a couple of hours of work for a used twenty-one-inch mower and began mowing lawns the rider mower guys didn't want to mow: too small, on hillsides, and inside fences.

I bought a thirty-five-dollar electric leaf blower and an extension cord and began fall clean ups. I had one big yard where I blew all the leaves down to the road and asked a friend who had a leaf sucker and truck to take the leaves away. He charged me eighty dollars. I thought about that expense and realized it was a lot of money to move the leaves from the edge of the road into the truck and dump them. I could make that money if I loaded my truck and took the leaves away myself. The next year, I bought two four-by-eight pieces of plywood. By flipping them up as sides, I created an open box truck, loaded the leaves onto the truck with a tarp, tied the tarp over the leaves, and dumped them at a nearby farm. When I didn't need the sides, I would flop the plywood down into the bed of the truck.

My second year began with spring cleanups in May and a couple of lawns for Dan in June. I had so much business from my ad, I taught one of Dan's workers how to put in lawns and quit working for Dan. One day, I got a call from a woman in Northampton who wanted a small garden cut out of her yard. I knew I'd spend more time driving to and from Northampton than it would take me to do the job, but I decided to do it anyway. I charged her seventeen dollars and fifty cents. She told everyone what a wonderful job I did, and I ended up with sixteen new clients in Northampton and a few in Amherst.

By my third year, I was overwhelmed with clients. I decided to increase my hourly rate from twenty dollars to twenty-five dollars, taking the chance of losing clients. Each time my workload become too heavy, I raised my prices by five dollars. I never lost any clients, and the price increases always renewed my enthusiasm.

I worked by myself for five years until I learned the business, then I teamed up with a Jamaican guy whose work ethic complemented mine. I always kidded him that we were brothers. We worked together for twelve years. Philosophical Gardening became a boutique gardening business—immaculate weeding, no job too small.

I wasn't going to garden forever. I knew I needed money for retirement. I remembered my father sitting at the dining room table making entries in a notebook when I was a child. The notebook was his stock portfolio. I'd look over his shoulder and wonder what he was doing. I'd ask him to explain it all to me, but he was very private about his business. Much of my anger towards him was a result of his not teaching me about investments. One day, it came to me: why be angry? I was smart enough to figure it out myself.

Since my father had invested in stocks, I decided that I'd learn about mutual funds. I spent my free time at the library reading *Morningstar* mutual fund reports, *Money* magazine articles, and any comparisons of different mutual funds that I could find. After digesting as much information about mutual funds and investment strategies as I could, I decided on three companies: Strong Investments (strong), Scudder Investments (Boston-based), and Janus Funds (I'm a Gemini). I diversified my holdings in those three companies by investing $1,500 in ten different mutual funds: three with Strong, three with Scudder, and four with Janus. One of the funds folded and I got my money back with a little interest. The rest grew and grew. Fifteen years later, the mutual funds totaled $45,000. It was time to divest.

A short time later, I was in the office of my insurance agent and met a well-dressed man from Longmeadow, Massachusetts. He was wearing a Pittsburgh Penguins baseball hat.

"Are you from Pittsburgh?" I asked.

"No, a high school classmate of mine plays for the Penguins. He got me tickets to the final game of the Stanley Cup in Detroit. The Penguins won, and I held the cup over my head. What a rush!"

"What are you doing in town?"

He went into his sales pitch. "I'm a representative from American Capital Real Estate Trust, a limited partnership that invests in small box commercial buildings and leases them to reliable companies like Pittsburgh National Bank, FedEx, Walgreens, CVS, and well-known restaurants."

It sounded like every shopping district I had ever driven through on the East Coast. The terms seemed good, a nine-percent monthly dividend. If I reinvested the dividend, I would receive an extra half-percent. The serendipity of that Pittsburgh Penguins baseball cap was too much.

Then, I heard my mother's voice in my head. Dad had given her money to invest. She'd bought stocks in Proctor & Gamble because she used Crest toothpaste, and Browning-Ferris Waste Disposal because everyone had garbage, and Pepsi, because we always had Pepsi and popcorn on Friday nights as kids. Marilyn and I always said she was a better investor than Dad. Mother's voice was saying *Invest.* I decided to invest my windfall mutual funds.

Over the years, my holdings in American Capital slowly increased. American Capital was eventually sold to Real Income Corp and I could no longer reinvest the dividends, so I began receiving monthly dividend checks. I was accustomed to risk from my drugging days, so I wasn't averse to risk investing. Since I was too obsessive and too old to invest in growth stocks and wait for them to increase in value over time, I decided to look for higher risk stocks that produced high dividends.

The stock market is a casino. The investor makes bets on a stock's future performance. Sometimes, if a stock goes up, an investor can make a lot of money if he sells at the right time. I couldn't take the pressure of that game. I liked dividends. I told my investor friends, "I'm a slow horse in a fast horse race."

chapter 32

I had all the building blocks of recovery in place, gainful employment, my retirement planned, a solid relationship with Kate, and I had the AA and NA programs. For many years, I averaged a meeting a day. It was group therapy. I listened to others and learned. I talked out my problems and shared my emotions during meetings with other addicts. Individual therapy had led me to the discovery of childhood sexual abuse and my mother's wagging finger, the roots of my addictive behavior. I had a rational mind that understood the mental, physical, emotional, and medical principles that explained why I abused alcohol and drugs.

I continued running in recovery. It became my next meditation, mindfulness in motion. After a day of landscaping, getting paid for exercise outdoors, I ran. Landscaping was contemplative and so was running. Whatever stress and anxiety I had, I'd find a back road or trails in the woods. With a gentle pace and a good breathing rhythm, I'd run the tension out of my system. After a nice shower and hot tub at the health club, I'd be ready to sleep soundly.

While I was living with Marco in South Hadley, he'd brought

home a flyer announcing The Calvin Coolidge "I Do Not Choose to Run" Run, a 10k race in Northampton. Coolidge, an Amherst College alumnus and lawyer in Northampton before he became president, famously said, "I do not choose to run" for a second term. What a crazy name for a race.

I ran it and got hooked on competitive running. I trained every other day and entered road races every weekend. The endorphins at six miles fed me focus and happiness. I learned there were endorphin rushes every six or seven miles. I entered half marathons and marathons. I was a drug addict who learned I could produce my own drugs naturally.

When I was training for my first marathon, a friend suggested I run the Savoy 20-Mile Trail Run. I quickly weaned myself off running on the road. The forest and hills were where awareness lived for me. Running on soft dirt instead of pavement was easy on my feet and legs. The oxygen in the woods was pure, no car exhaust there. The scenery, trees and rocks and streams, and the solitude were luxurious. I was home in the woods.

A friend of mine mentioned that she'd run fifty miles. That was beyond my understanding, but if she could do it, I could, too. I went out and ran my first fifty miler in just under ten hours. It was what runners called an LSD trip, Long Slow Distance. I was addicted to the endorphins, a positive addiction. The difference between positive and negative addictions was this: I was always excited before I drank or did a drug and felt terrible after the experience. Before I went on a long training run, I was hesitant. I knew it would be tough. There was a possibility I could get hurt. I would use up a lot of energy. I would definitely be tired when I finished. But I knew, when I finished thirty, thirty-five-mile training runs, I would be full of bliss.

And then, I discovered one-hundred-mile endurance runs. If I paced myself for fifty miles, ran within my breathing and ability, and ate and drank every chance I got, I'd begin to produce pain-numbing drugs. I tapped into energy. There's a saying, "At fifty miles you see god, at seventy miles you talk to him, and at 100 miles, he answers back." It's the LSD experience. At fifty miles, halfway through, it was all downhill from there. By then, I had sweat all the toxins out of my system. I was pure energy, at one with the universe. Time slowed down. I noticed every tree, every leaf, every stone on the ground. They were my friends. They encompassed me.

When I finished 100 miles, I had confidence, a faith. If I could do that, I could do anything. I lived for that feeling. I trained; thousands of crunches to strengthen my abdominal muscles to take the pressure off my back, hundreds of repetitions of weights for arm and leg strength, cross-training, swimming, and just plain long hours of physical exercise. I got so good at long slow distance that in 2000, at the age of fifty-five, I finished the Grand Slam of Ultrarunning: the Western States 100 Mile Endurance Race in the Sierra Nevada Mountains in California at the end of June, the Vermont 100 Mile Endurance Race on the back roads and hills of Vermont in July, Leadville 100 Mile Endurance Race above 10,000 feet in the Colorado Rocky Mountains in August, and the Wasatch Front 100 Mile Endurance Race in Utah, again above 10,000 feet, in early September. Four 100 milers in ten weeks. I was the 138th person to achieve that feat.

Like Vipassana meditation with Phra Sohm, mantra meditation in the teepee, Sadhu meditation of the homeless ascetic, like the twelve-step program in AA and NA, running was another meditation, a way to focus until I found awareness.

The River Disappears

How hard it is
Once the river's crossed
To turn around and ferry others here.

It's not the ferry part,
But catching their attention
That is so difficult.

I remember my attention to the mundane things.
The golden glitter, the illusion that was so real.
Each and every want that caused my suffering.

And now I see for what it is.
Hollowness that props up emptiness.
Coarseness hiding ethereal.

I laugh and stare. Reality shimmering,
Holey, like Swiss cheese, before my eyes.
Sparks of eternity shining through it.

I wonder how to tell them
The world illusory; the mundane nothing gained.
Their eyes so naturally turned from what is pure.

I laugh and smile and spark and glow.
I am the hole within the cheese.
The river disappears.

acknowledgments

This book was not written alone. Kate, my partner, spent many hours at three a.m. in conversation with me, helping me work through my difficult personal issues and keeping me alive. We had a ton of laughs, too.

My friend, Susan, read the first draft and pointed me in the right direction. Charles Coe assessed the second serious draft (the fourth or fifth rewrite), and gave me good advice as well as the confidence to carry on. Multiple drafts later, I finally got up the nerve to let Marilyn, my sister and harshest and most respected critic, read it. She suggested I show it to Julie Shiroishi, who put me on to Julie Chibbaro.

Julie C. demanded much from me and I responded. She saw what I had and made me go get it. We turned it into a memoir.

A quick shout out to Robin, too. He did a quick copy edit that he traded for some landscaping. I have made friends everywhere.

A ton of gratitude to my nephew, Ethan McQuerrey, for the cover illustrations.

I'd like to thank NPR for interviewing one of the authors of *JFK: The Last Speech*. As luck would have it, for the first time in ages, I turned on the radio while going home for dinner. Mascot Books was mentioned, and I added them to my list of independent presses. Seeing the potential, they introduced me to Lauren Kanne. We turned the memoir into a book.

I can't thank these people enough.